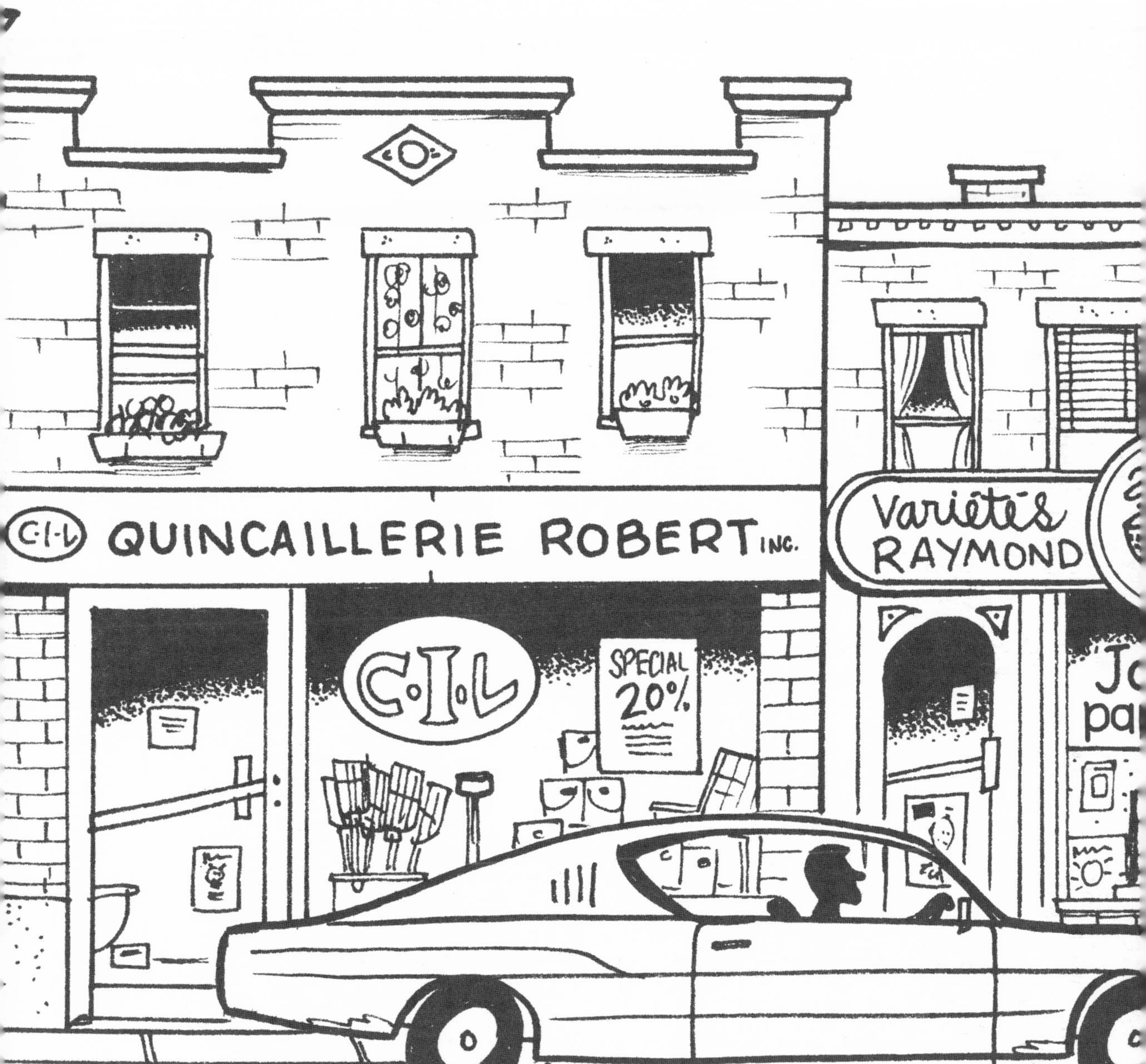
C-I-L
QUINCAILLERIE ROBERT INC.
Variétés
RAYMOND
C-I-L
SPECIAL
20%

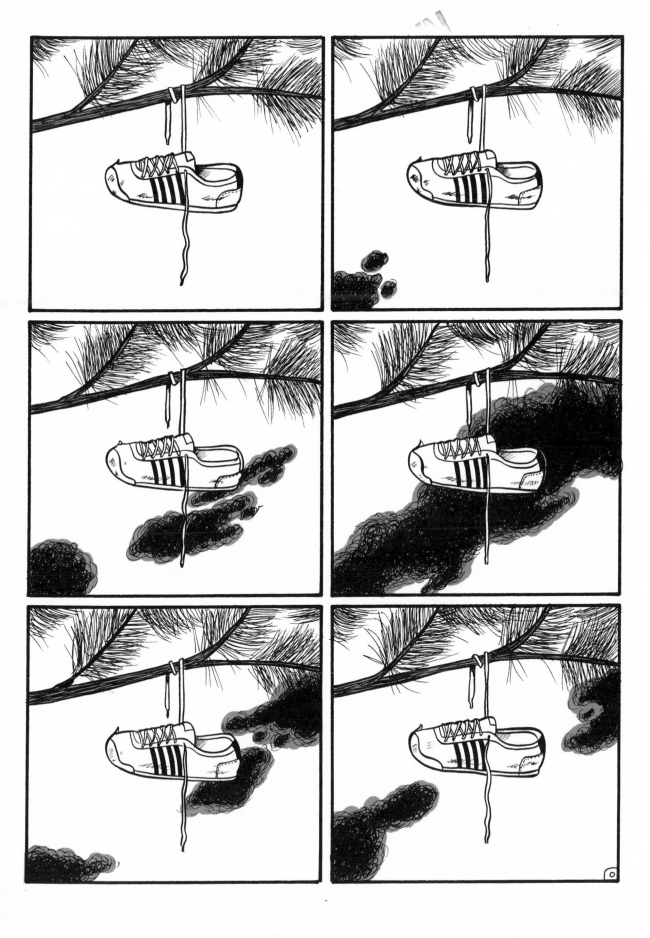

"Try to leave this world a little better than you found it and, when your turn comes to die, you can die happy in feeling that at any rate you have not wasted your time but have done your best."

— Robert Stephenson Baden-Powell

Michel Rabagliati

Paul Joins the Scouts

Conundrum

Originally published as *Paul au Parc* by Les Éditions de la Pastèque, © 2011

Translation by Helge Dascher
with special thanks to Kate Battle, Dag Dascher, Mark Lang and Dean Post

Editorial assistance by Rupert Bottenberg
BDANG logo by Billy Mavreas
BDANG Imprint edited by Andy Brown

Library and Archives Canada Cataloguing in Publication

Rabagliati, Michel
Paul joins the scouts / Michel Rabagliati ; translation by Helge Dascher.

Translation of: Paul au parc.
ISBN 978-1-894994-69-9

1. Graphic novels. I. Dascher, Helge, 1965- II. Title.

PN6734.P38624R3213 2013 741.5'971 C2013-900367-3

BDANG 12

First English Edition
Printed by Gauvin Press in Gatineau, Quebec, Canada

Conundrum Press
Greenwich, NS, Canada
www.conundrumpress.com

Conundrum Press acknowledges the financial support of the Canada Council for the Arts and the Government of Canada through the Canada Book Fund toward its publishing activities.

We acknowledge the financial support of the Government of Canada, through the National Translation Program for Book Publishing, for our translation activities.

Canada Council for the Arts Conseil des Arts du Canada

Canada

Paul Joins the Scouts

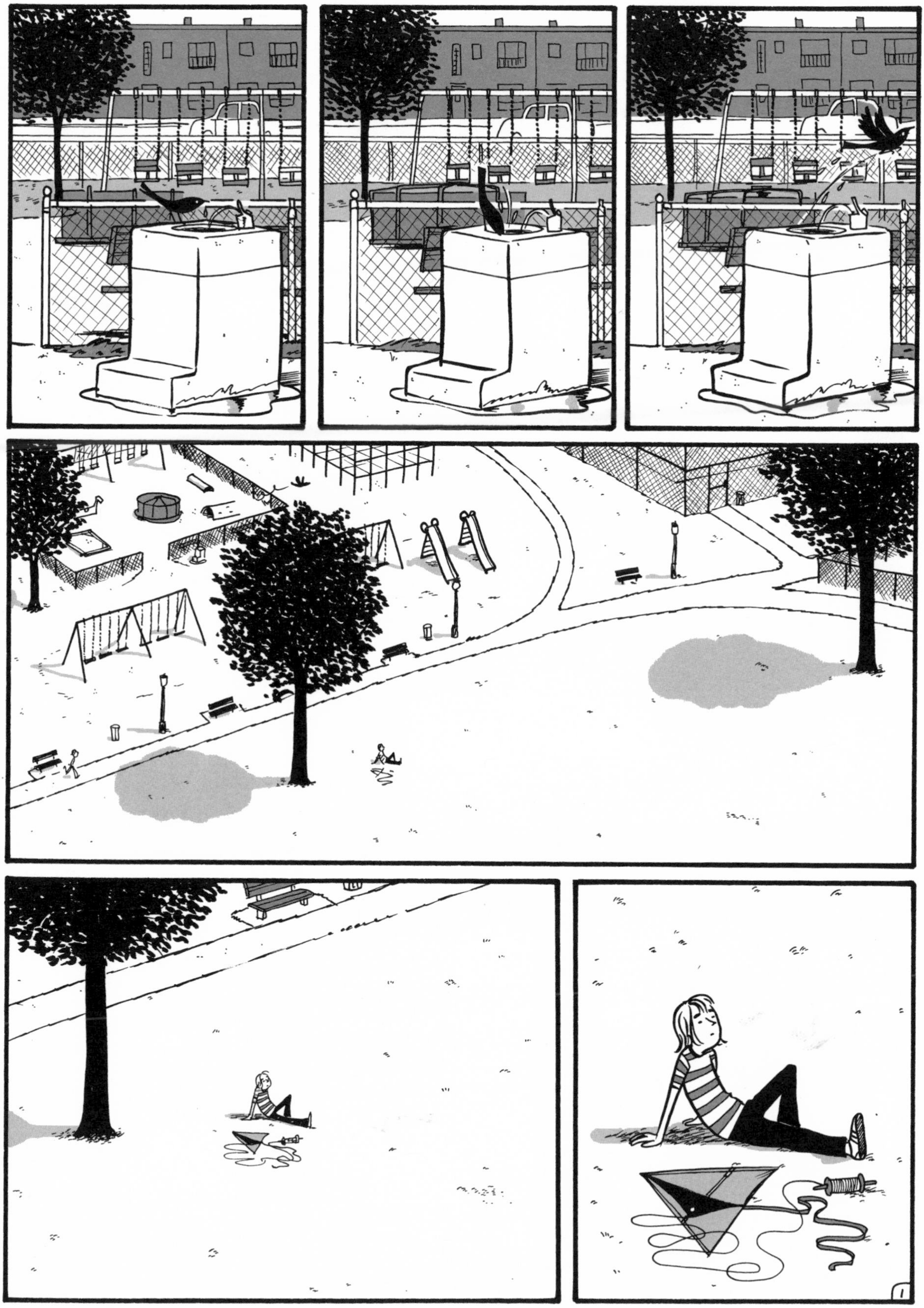

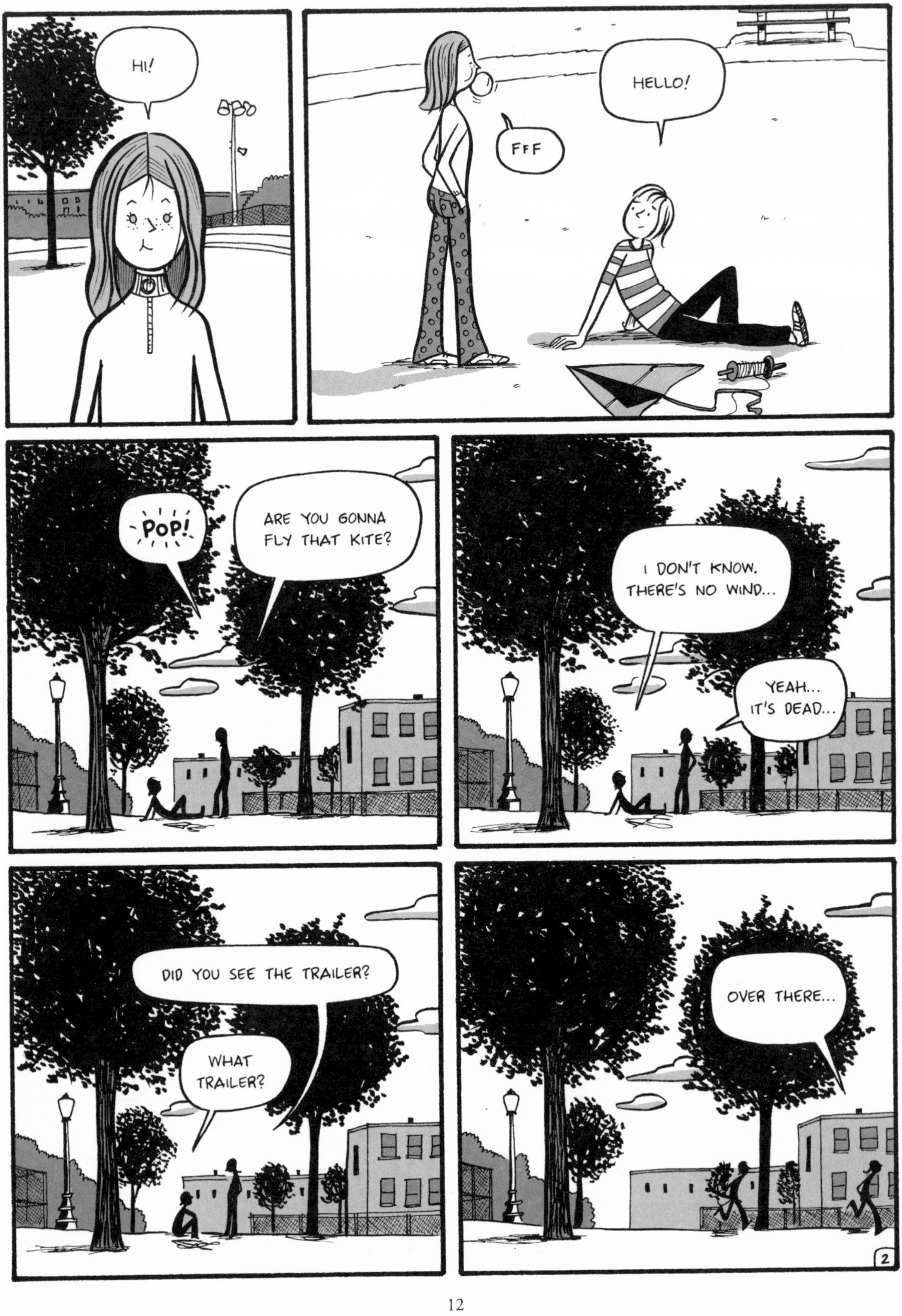
HI!
HELLO!
FFF
POP!
ARE YOU GONNA FLY THAT KITE?
I DON'T KNOW. THERE'S NO WIND...
YEAH... IT'S DEAD...
DID YOU SEE THE TRAILER?
WHAT TRAILER?
OVER THERE...
2

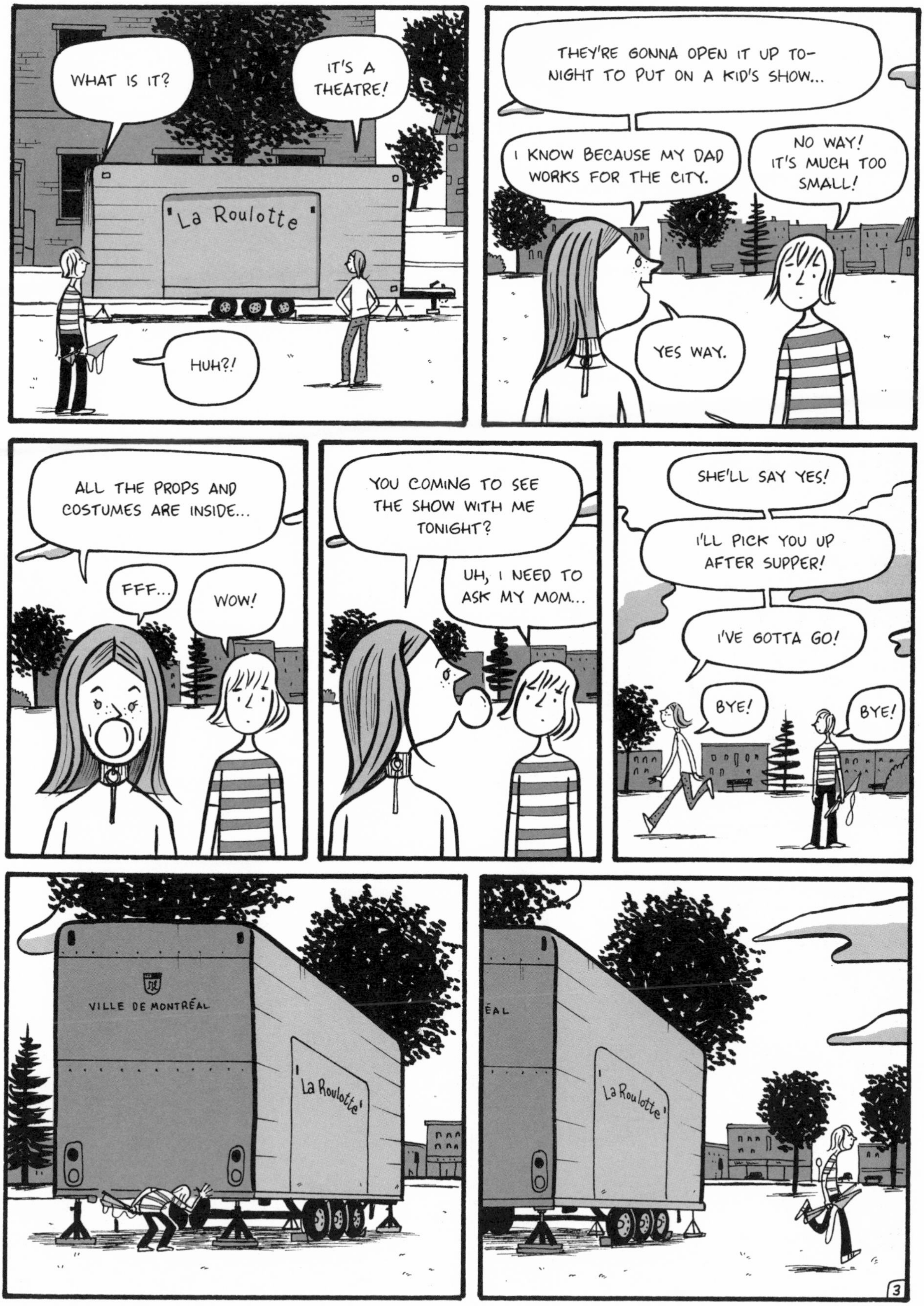
WHAT IS IT?
IT'S A THEATRE!
La Roulotte
HUH?!
THEY'RE GONNA OPEN IT UP TO-NIGHT TO PUT ON A KID'S SHOW...
I KNOW BECAUSE MY DAD WORKS FOR THE CITY.
NO WAY! IT'S MUCH TOO SMALL!
YES WAY.
ALL THE PROPS AND COSTUMES ARE INSIDE...
FFF...
WOW!
YOU COMING TO SEE THE SHOW WITH ME TONIGHT?
UH, I NEED TO ASK MY MOM...
SHE'LL SAY YES!
I'LL PICK YOU UP AFTER SUPPER!
I'VE GOTTA GO!
BYE!
BYE!
VILLE DE MONTRÉAL
'La Roulotte'
ÉAL
'La Roulotte'
3

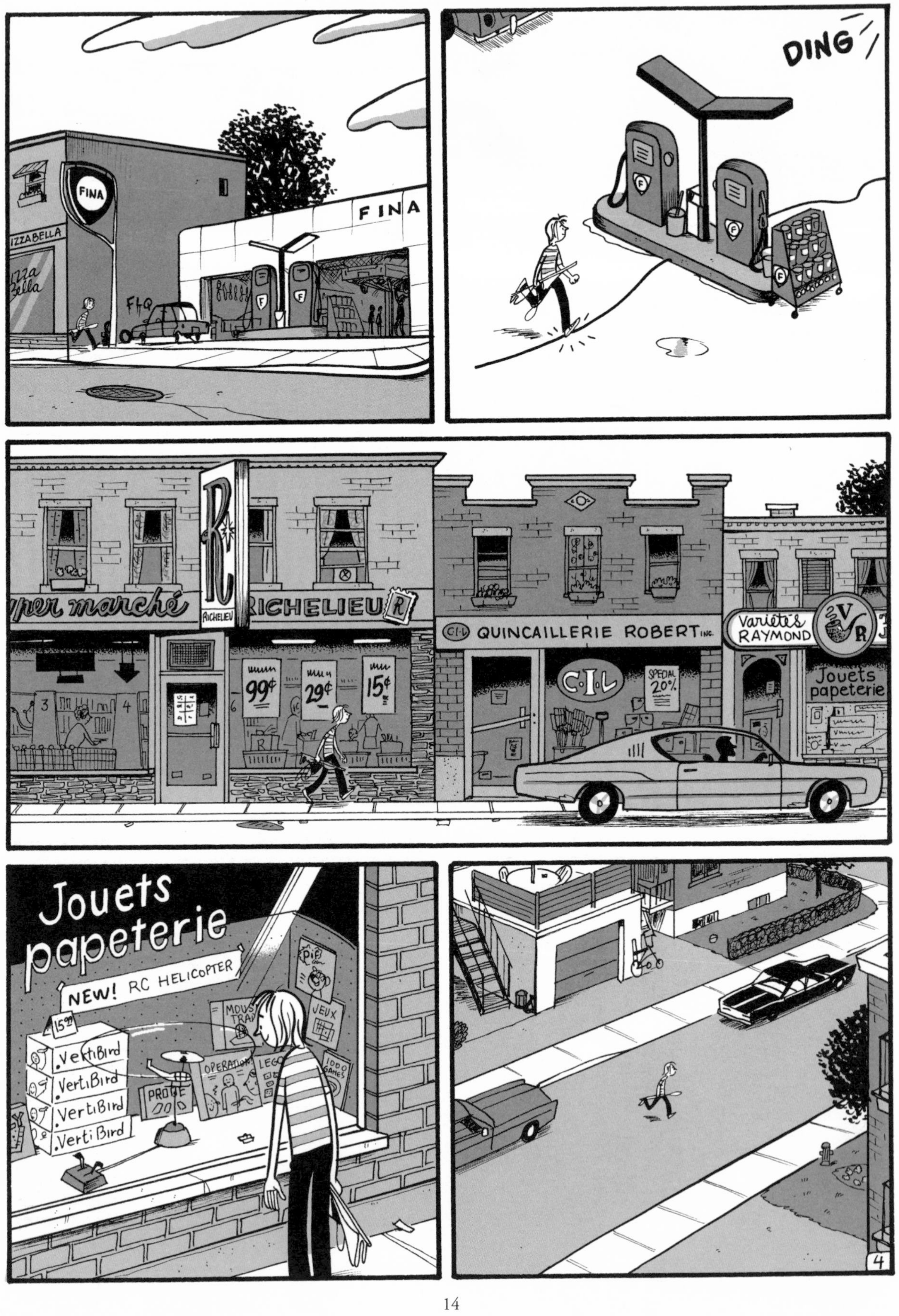
FINA
FINA
FLQ
DING
RICHELIEU
RICHELIEU
QUINCAILLERIE ROBERT INC.
C-I-L
99¢
29¢
15¢
C-I-L
SPECIAL 20%
Variétés RAYMOND
VR
Jouets papeterie
Jouets papeterie
NEW! RC HELICOPTER
15.99
VertiBird
VertiBird
VertiBird
VertiBird
OPERATION
LEGO
1000 GAMES
JEUX
PROBE
4

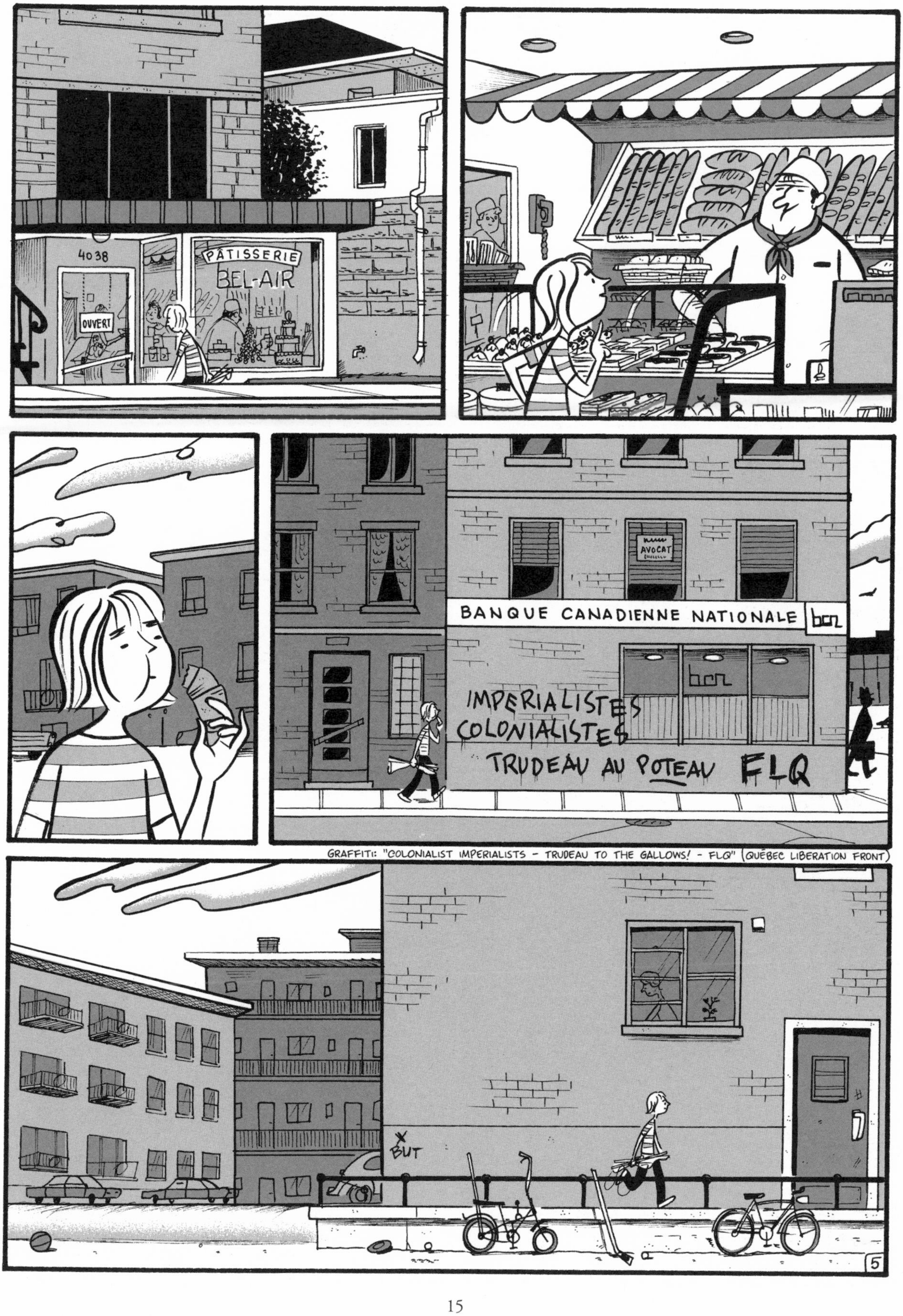
4038
OUVERT
PÂTISSERIE
BEL-AIR
AVOCAT
BANQUE CANADIENNE NATIONALE
bcn
bcn
IMPERIALISTES
COLONIALISTES
TRUDEAU AU POTEAU
FLQ
GRAFFITI: "COLONIALIST IMPERIALISTS - TRUDEAU TO THE GALLOWS! - FLQ" (QUÉBEC LIBERATION FRONT)
BUT
5

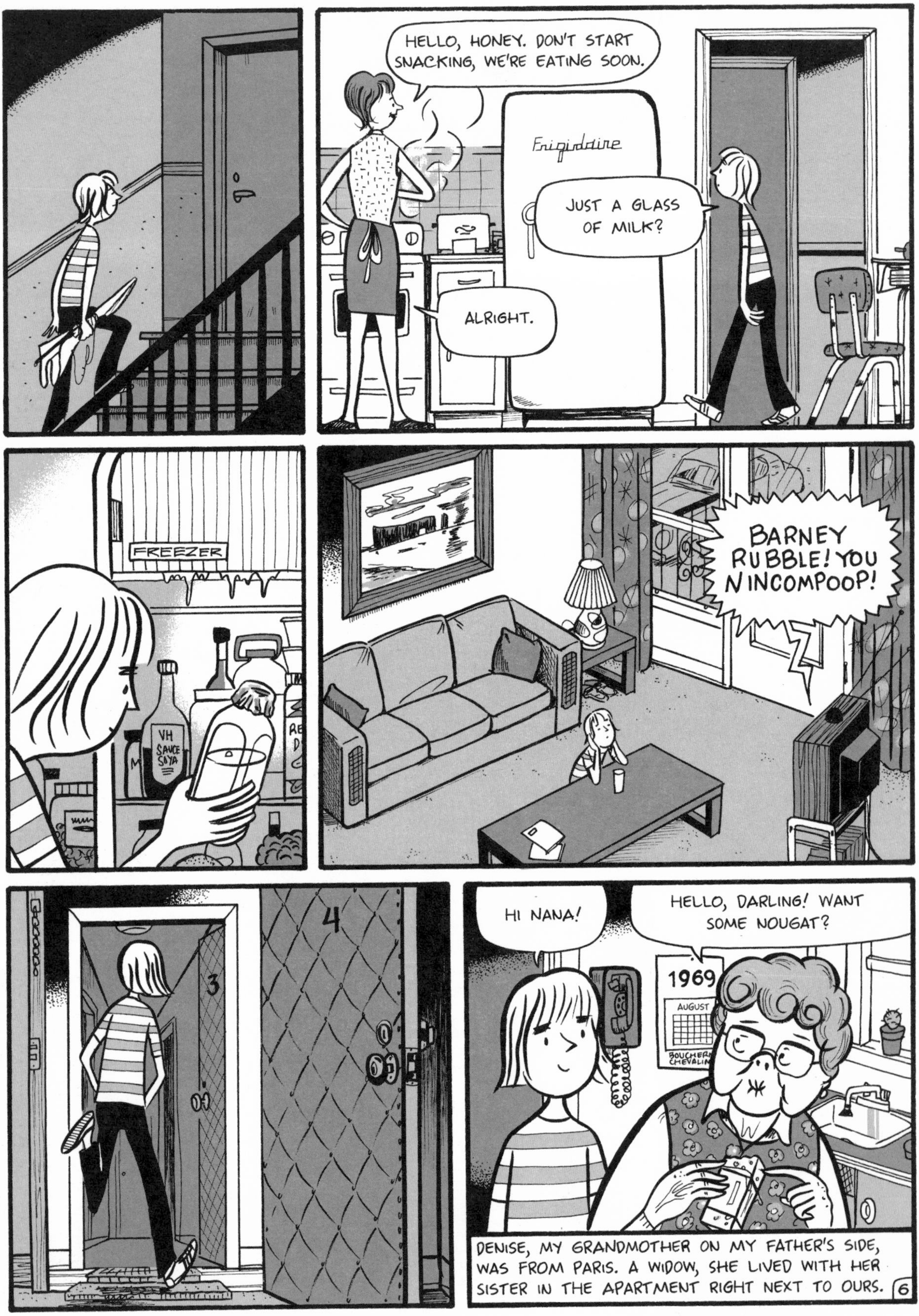
HELLO, HONEY. DON'T START SNACKING, WE'RE EATING SOON.
Frigidaire
JUST A GLASS OF MILK?
ALRIGHT.
FREEZER
VH SAUCE SOYA
BARNEY RUBBLE! YOU NINCOMPOOP!
4
3
HI NANA!
HELLO, DARLING! WANT SOME NOUGAT?
1969
AUGUST
DENISE, MY GRANDMOTHER ON MY FATHER'S SIDE, WAS FROM PARIS. A WIDOW, SHE LIVED WITH HER SISTER IN THE APARTMENT RIGHT NEXT TO OURS.
6

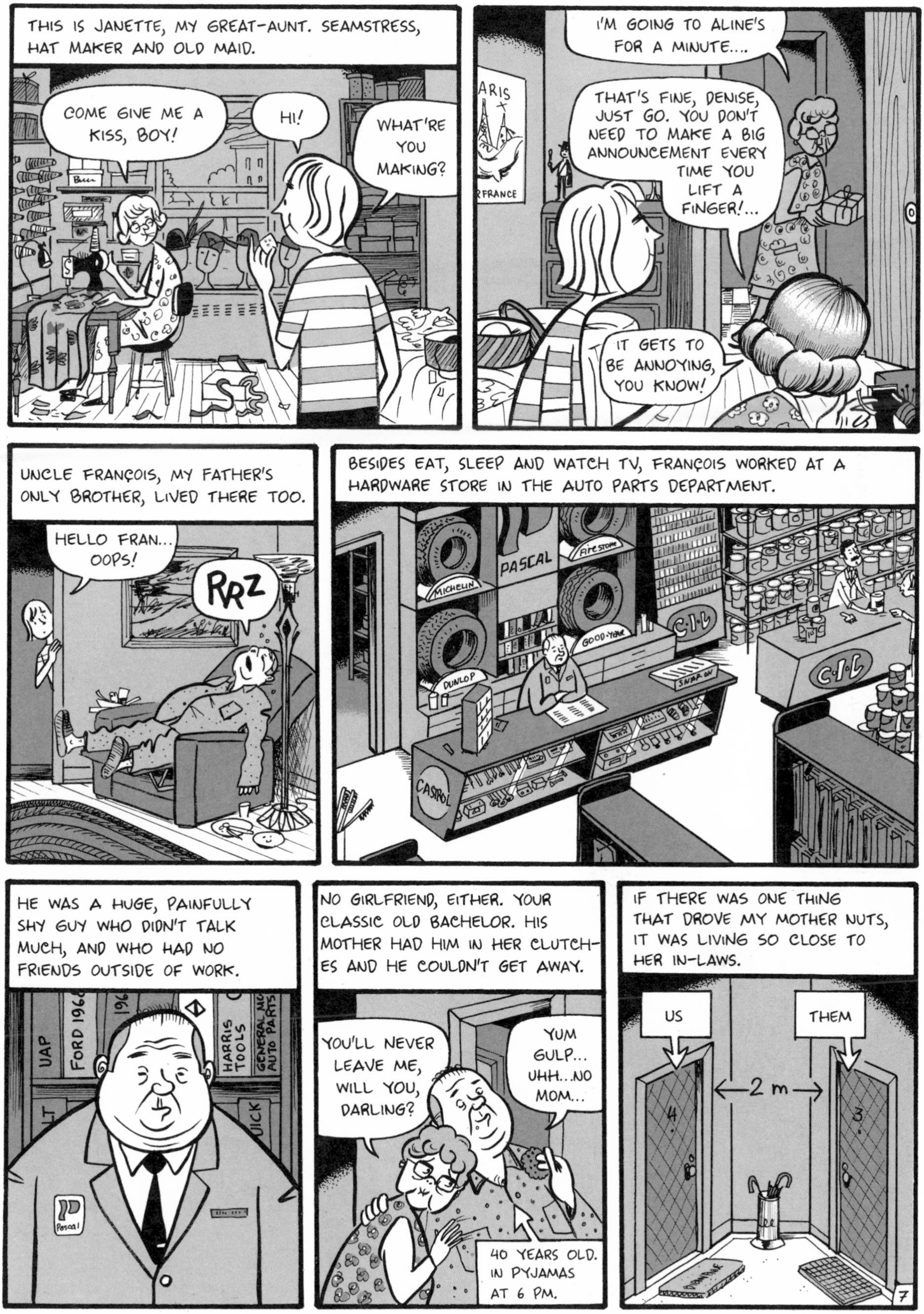
THIS IS JANETTE, MY GREAT-AUNT. SEAMSTRESS, HAT MAKER AND OLD MAID.
COME GIVE ME A KISS, BOY!
HI!
WHAT'RE YOU MAKING?
I'M GOING TO ALINE'S FOR A MINUTE....
THAT'S FINE, DENISE, JUST GO. YOU DON'T NEED TO MAKE A BIG ANNOUNCEMENT EVERY TIME YOU LIFT A FINGER!...
IT GETS TO BE ANNOYING, YOU KNOW!
UNCLE FRANÇOIS, MY FATHER'S ONLY BROTHER, LIVED THERE TOO.
HELLO FRAN... OOPS!
RRZ
BESIDES EAT, SLEEP AND WATCH TV, FRANÇOIS WORKED AT A HARDWARE STORE IN THE AUTO PARTS DEPARTMENT.
PASCAL
MICHELIN
Firestone
GOOD-YEAR
DUNLOP
C-I-L
SNAP-ON
CASTROL
HE WAS A HUGE, PAINFULLY SHY GUY WHO DIDN'T TALK MUCH, AND WHO HAD NO FRIENDS OUTSIDE OF WORK.
UAP
FORD 196
HARRIS TOOLS
GENERAL MO AUTO PARTS
Pascal
NO GIRLFRIEND, EITHER. YOUR CLASSIC OLD BACHELOR. HIS MOTHER HAD HIM IN HER CLUTCHES AND HE COULDN'T GET AWAY.
YOU'LL NEVER LEAVE ME, WILL YOU, DARLING?
YUM GULP... UHH...NO MOM...
40 YEARS OLD. IN PYJAMAS AT 6 PM.
IF THERE WAS ONE THING THAT DROVE MY MOTHER NUTS, IT WAS LIVING SO CLOSE TO HER IN-LAWS.
US
THEM
2 m
4
3
7

OUR APARTMENTS FACED EACH OTHER. NANA DENISE HAD FOUND THEM BEFORE I WAS BORN AND MOM ALWAYS REGRETTED THE ARRANGEMENT. WITH THE TWO FRONT DOORS OPEN ALL THE TIME, THE TWO APARTMENTS HAD QUICKLY MERGED INTO ONE.

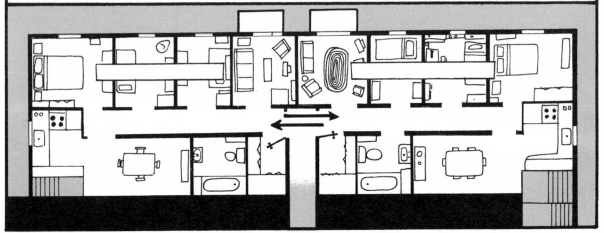

BOO!

AAH!

SORRY I MADE YOU JUMP, ALINE... HEE HEE!

HERE, NO NEED TO BOTHER WITH DESSERT TONIGHT. I BOUGHT SOME PASTRIES.

BUT... I JUST MADE TWO APPLE PIES...

YOU CAN EAT THEM SOME OTHER TIME! BESIDES, FRANÇOIS DOESN'T LIKE PIE...

OH, WELL! IF THAT BIG BABY DOESN'T LIKE PIE...

SEE YOU LATER! ♪

HERE'S THE LAMB. NOW WHERE'S FRANÇOIS?

YOU'LL HAVE TO EXCUSE HIM, ALINE, HE STAYED ON THE OTHER SIDE. HE WANTS TO WATCH THE BALLGAME...

WOULD YOU MIND MAKING A PLATE FOR HIM?

HONESTLY, DENISE, HE'S TOO MUCH!... ALINE AND ROBERT ARE HAVING US OVER FOR SUPPER, AND THAT LOUT DOESN'T EVEN GET UP OUT OF HIS ARMCHAIR!...

HE'S EXHAUSTED, JEANNE! AND HE WANTS TO WATCH THE GAME... LET HIM HAVE HIS LITTLE PLEASURES, WHY DON'T YOU?

YOU CAN'T BE SERIOUS!

DON'T WORRY ABOUT IT...

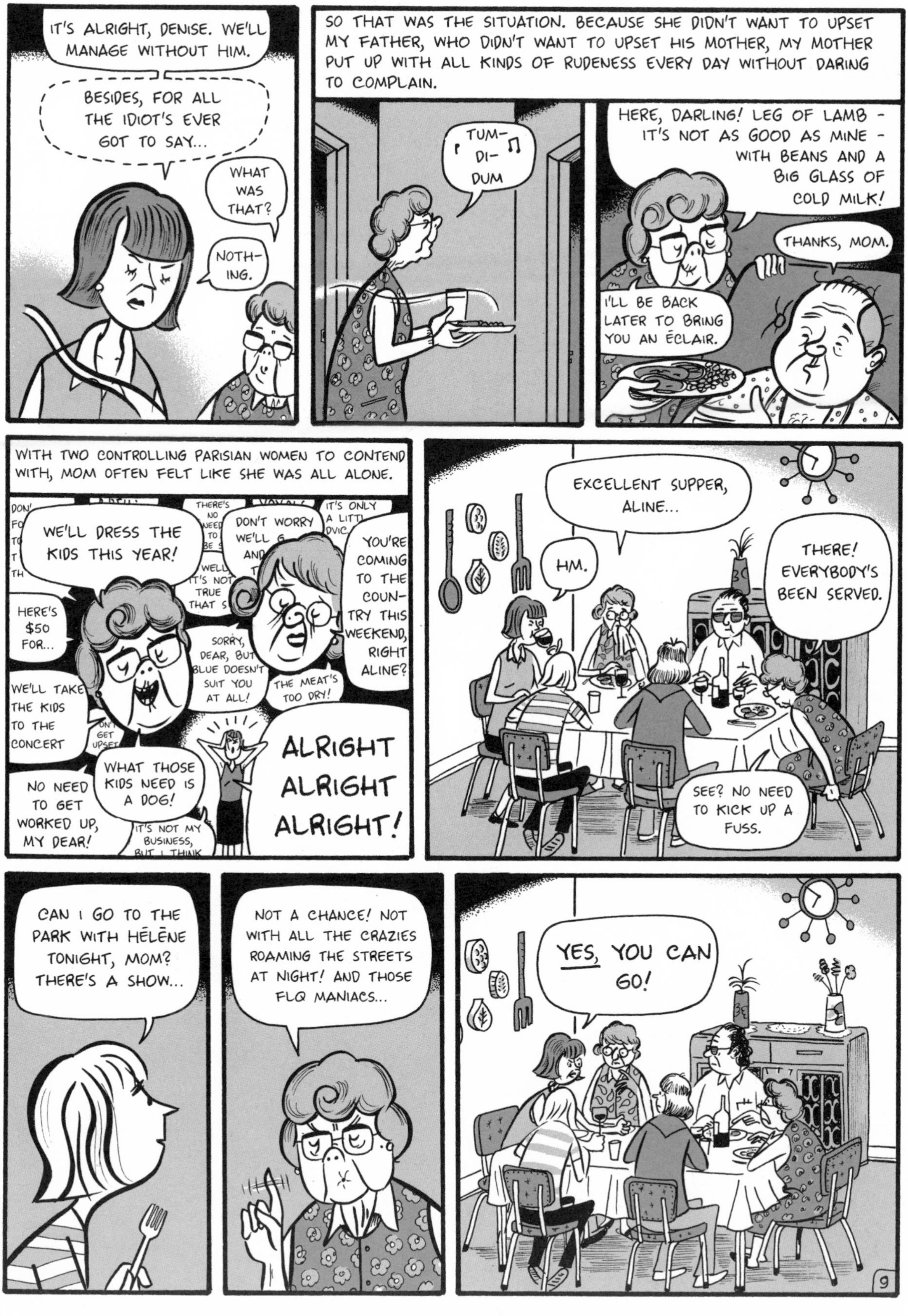
IT'S ALRIGHT, DENISE. WE'LL MANAGE WITHOUT HIM.
BESIDES, FOR ALL THE IDIOT'S EVER GOT TO SAY...
WHAT WAS THAT?
NOTH-ING.
SO THAT WAS THE SITUATION. BECAUSE SHE DIDN'T WANT TO UPSET MY FATHER, WHO DIDN'T WANT TO UPSET HIS MOTHER, MY MOTHER PUT UP WITH ALL KINDS OF RUDENESS EVERY DAY WITHOUT DARING TO COMPLAIN.
TUM-DI-DUM
HERE, DARLING! LEG OF LAMB - IT'S NOT AS GOOD AS MINE - WITH BEANS AND A BIG GLASS OF COLD MILK!
THANKS, MOM.
I'LL BE BACK LATER TO BRING YOU AN ÉCLAIR.
WITH TWO CONTROLLING PARISIAN WOMEN TO CONTEND WITH, MOM OFTEN FELT LIKE SHE WAS ALL ALONE.
WE'LL DRESS THE KIDS THIS YEAR!
YOU'RE COMING TO THE COUNTRY THIS WEEKEND, RIGHT ALINE?
HERE'S $50 FOR...
SORRY, DEAR, BUT BLUE DOESN'T SUIT YOU AT ALL!
THE MEAT'S TOO DRY!
WE'LL TAKE THE KIDS TO THE CONCERT
WHAT THOSE KIDS NEED IS A DOG!
NO NEED TO GET WORKED UP, MY DEAR!
ALRIGHT ALRIGHT ALRIGHT!
EXCELLENT SUPPER, ALINE...
HM.
THERE! EVERYBODY'S BEEN SERVED.
SEE? NO NEED TO KICK UP A FUSS.
CAN I GO TO THE PARK WITH HÉLÈNE TONIGHT, MOM? THERE'S A SHOW...
NOT A CHANCE! NOT WITH ALL THE CRAZIES ROAMING THE STREETS AT NIGHT! AND THOSE FLQ MANIACS...
YES, YOU CAN GO!
9

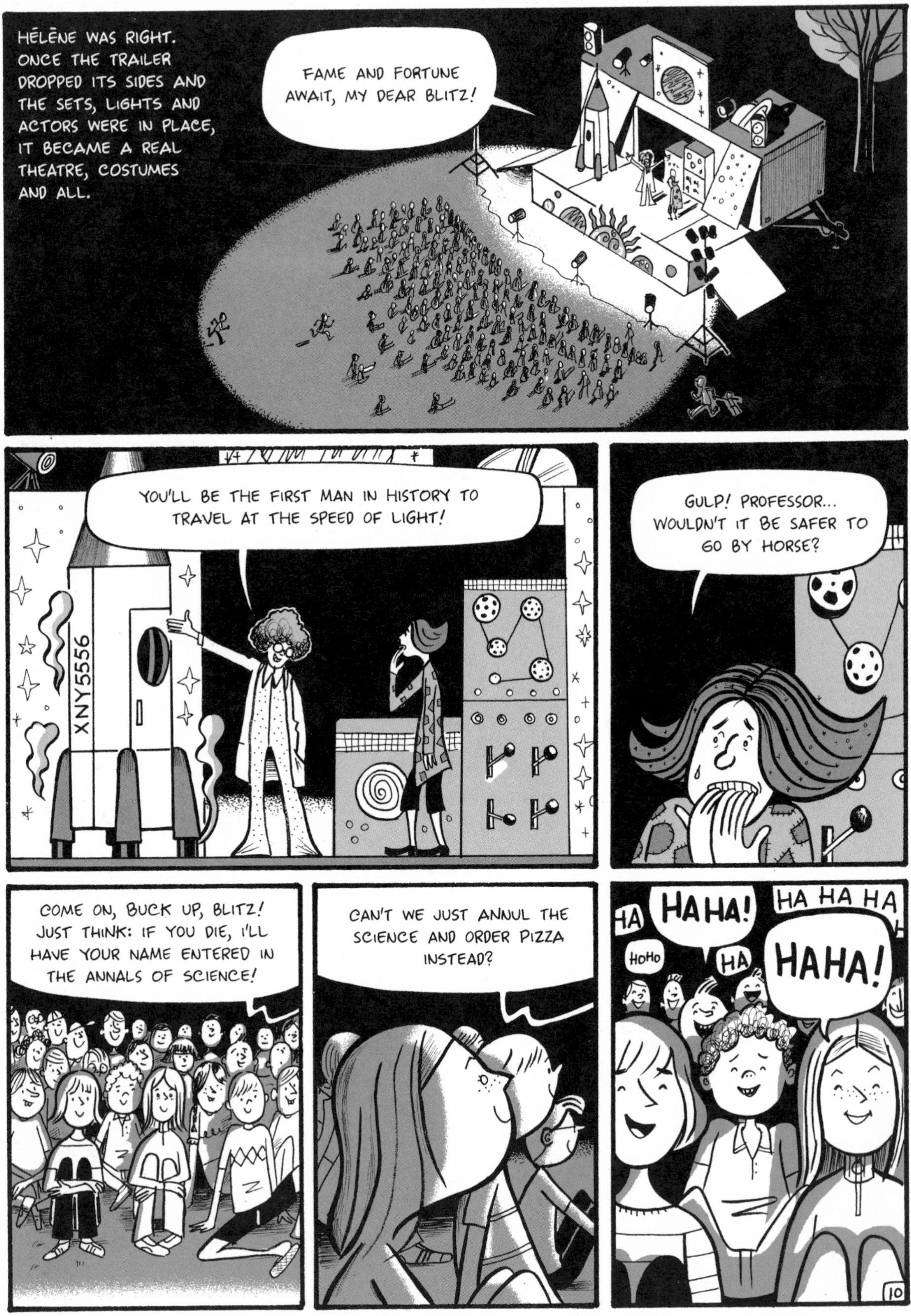
HÉLÈNE WAS RIGHT. ONCE THE TRAILER DROPPED ITS SIDES AND THE SETS, LIGHTS AND ACTORS WERE IN PLACE, IT BECAME A REAL THEATRE, COSTUMES AND ALL.
FAME AND FORTUNE AWAIT, MY DEAR BLITZ!
YOU'LL BE THE FIRST MAN IN HISTORY TO TRAVEL AT THE SPEED OF LIGHT!
XNY5556
GULP! PROFESSOR... WOULDN'T IT BE SAFER TO GO BY HORSE?
COME ON, BUCK UP, BLITZ! JUST THINK: IF YOU DIE, I'LL HAVE YOUR NAME ENTERED IN THE ANNALS OF SCIENCE!
CAN'T WE JUST ANNUL THE SCIENCE AND ORDER PIZZA INSTEAD?
HAHA!
HA HA HA
HOHO
HA
HAHA!
10

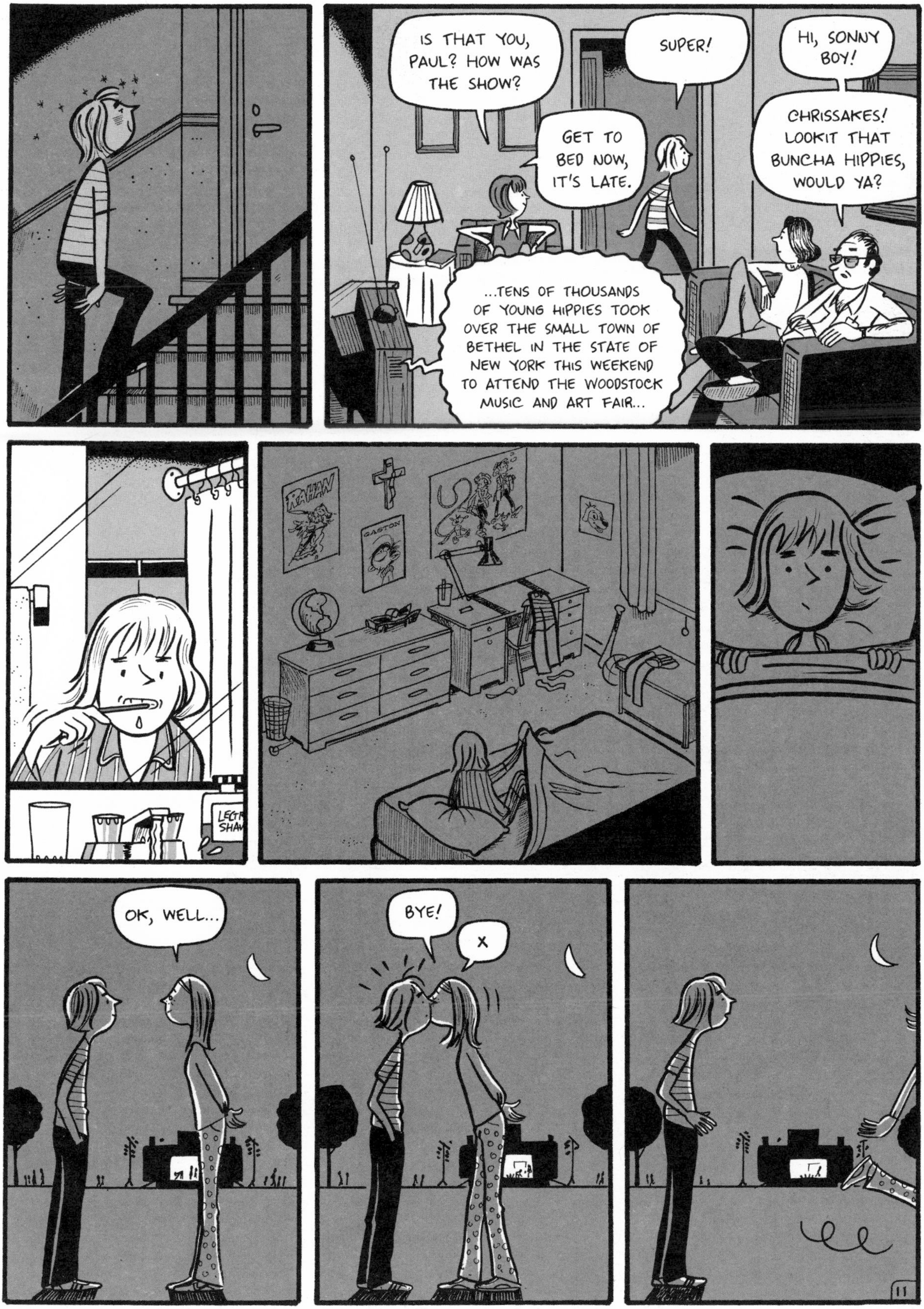
IS THAT YOU, PAUL? HOW WAS THE SHOW?
SUPER!
GET TO BED NOW, IT'S LATE.
HI, SONNY BOY!
CHRISSAKES! LOOKIT THAT BUNCHA HIPPIES, WOULD YA?
...TENS OF THOUSANDS OF YOUNG HIPPIES TOOK OVER THE SMALL TOWN OF BETHEL IN THE STATE OF NEW YORK THIS WEEKEND TO ATTEND THE WOODSTOCK MUSIC AND ART FAIR...
RAHAN
GASTON
LECTR
SHAV
OK, WELL...
BYE!
X
11

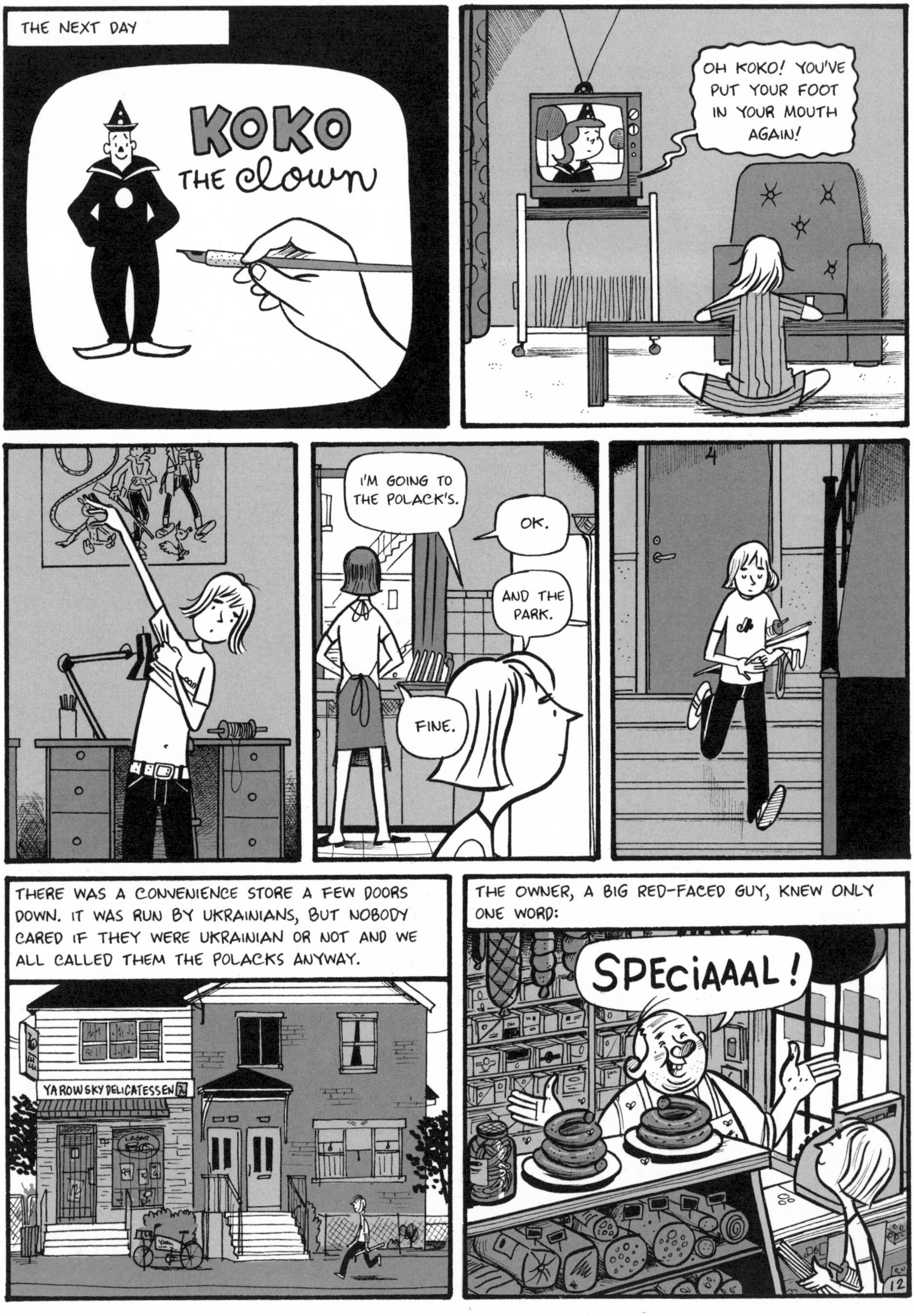
THE NEXT DAY
KOKO THE clown
OH KOKO! YOU'VE PUT YOUR FOOT IN YOUR MOUTH AGAIN!
I'M GOING TO THE POLACK'S.
OK.
AND THE PARK.
FINE.
THERE WAS A CONVENIENCE STORE A FEW DOORS DOWN. IT WAS RUN BY UKRAINIANS, BUT NOBODY CARED IF THEY WERE UKRAINIAN OR NOT AND WE ALL CALLED THEM THE POLACKS ANYWAY.
YAROWSKY DELICATESSEN
THE OWNER, A BIG RED-FACED GUY, KNEW ONLY ONE WORD:
SPECiAAAL!

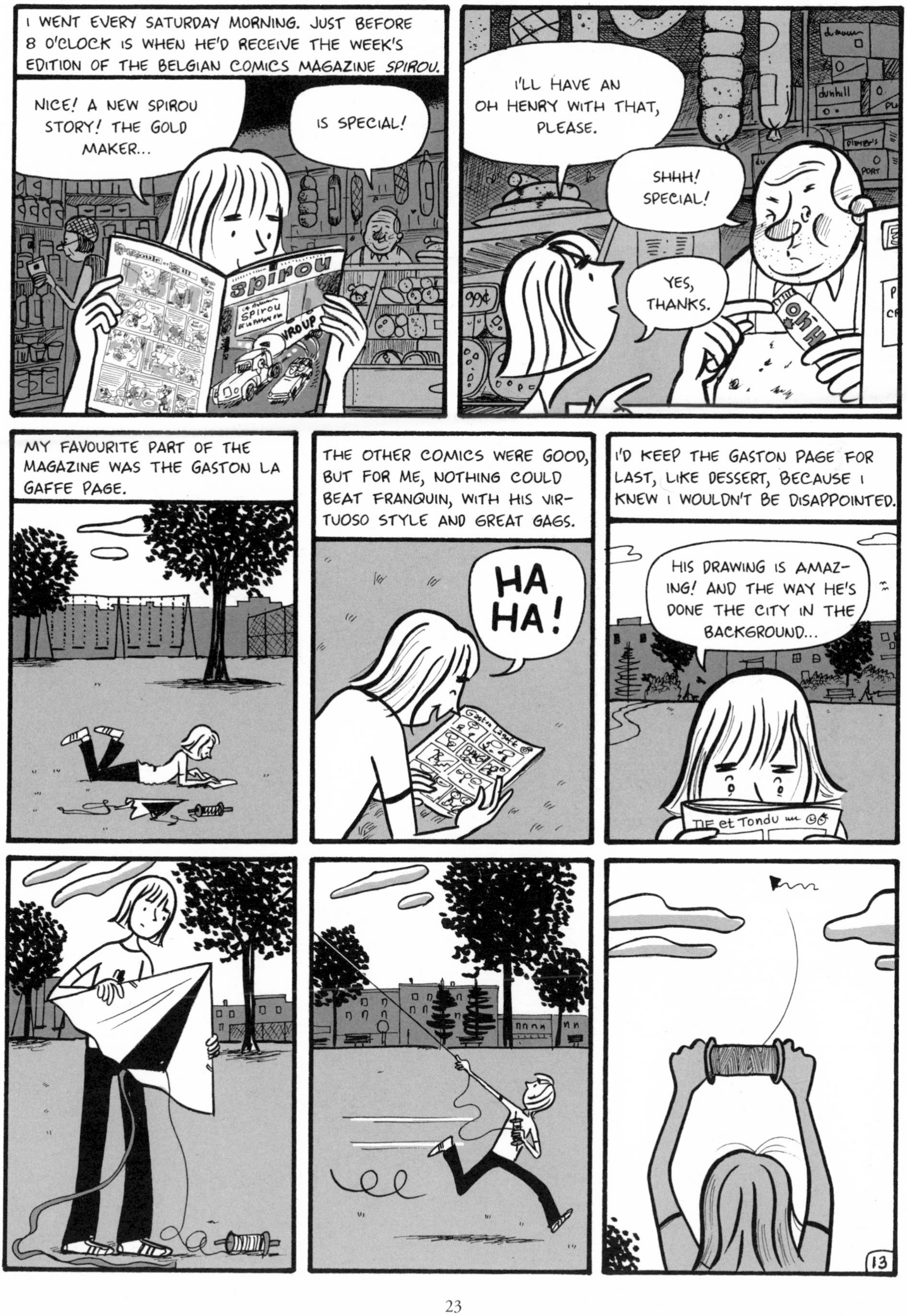
I WENT EVERY SATURDAY MORNING. JUST BEFORE 8 O'CLOCK IS WHEN HE'D RECEIVE THE WEEK'S EDITION OF THE BELGIAN COMICS MAGAZINE SPIROU.
NICE! A NEW SPIROU STORY! THE GOLD MAKER...
IS SPECIAL!
Spirou
I'LL HAVE AN OH HENRY WITH THAT, PLEASE.
SHHH! SPECIAL!
YES, THANKS.
99¢
OH HENRY
MY FAVOURITE PART OF THE MAGAZINE WAS THE GASTON LA GAFFE PAGE.
THE OTHER COMICS WERE GOOD, BUT FOR ME, NOTHING COULD BEAT FRANQUIN, WITH HIS VIRTUOSO STYLE AND GREAT GAGS.
HA HA!
I'D KEEP THE GASTON PAGE FOR LAST, LIKE DESSERT, BECAUSE I KNEW I WOULDN'T BE DISAPPOINTED.
HIS DRAWING IS AMAZING! AND THE WAY HE'S DONE THE CITY IN THE BACKGROUND...
Tif et Tondu
13

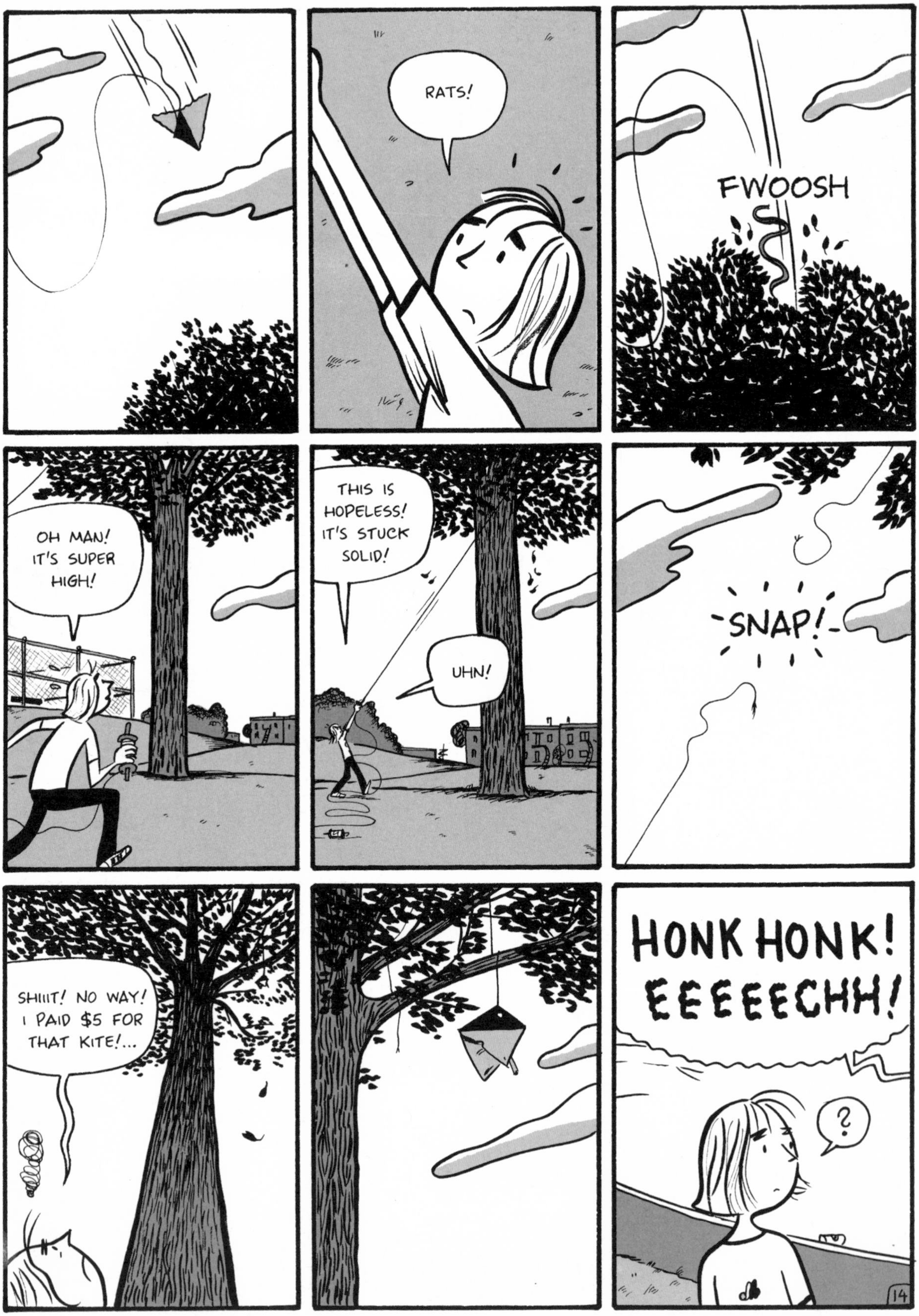
RATS!
FWOOSH
OH MAN! IT'S SUPER HIGH!
THIS IS HOPELESS! IT'S STUCK SOLID!
UHN!
SNAP!
SHIIIT! NO WAY! I PAID $5 FOR THAT KITE!...
HONK HONK! EEEEECHH!
?
14

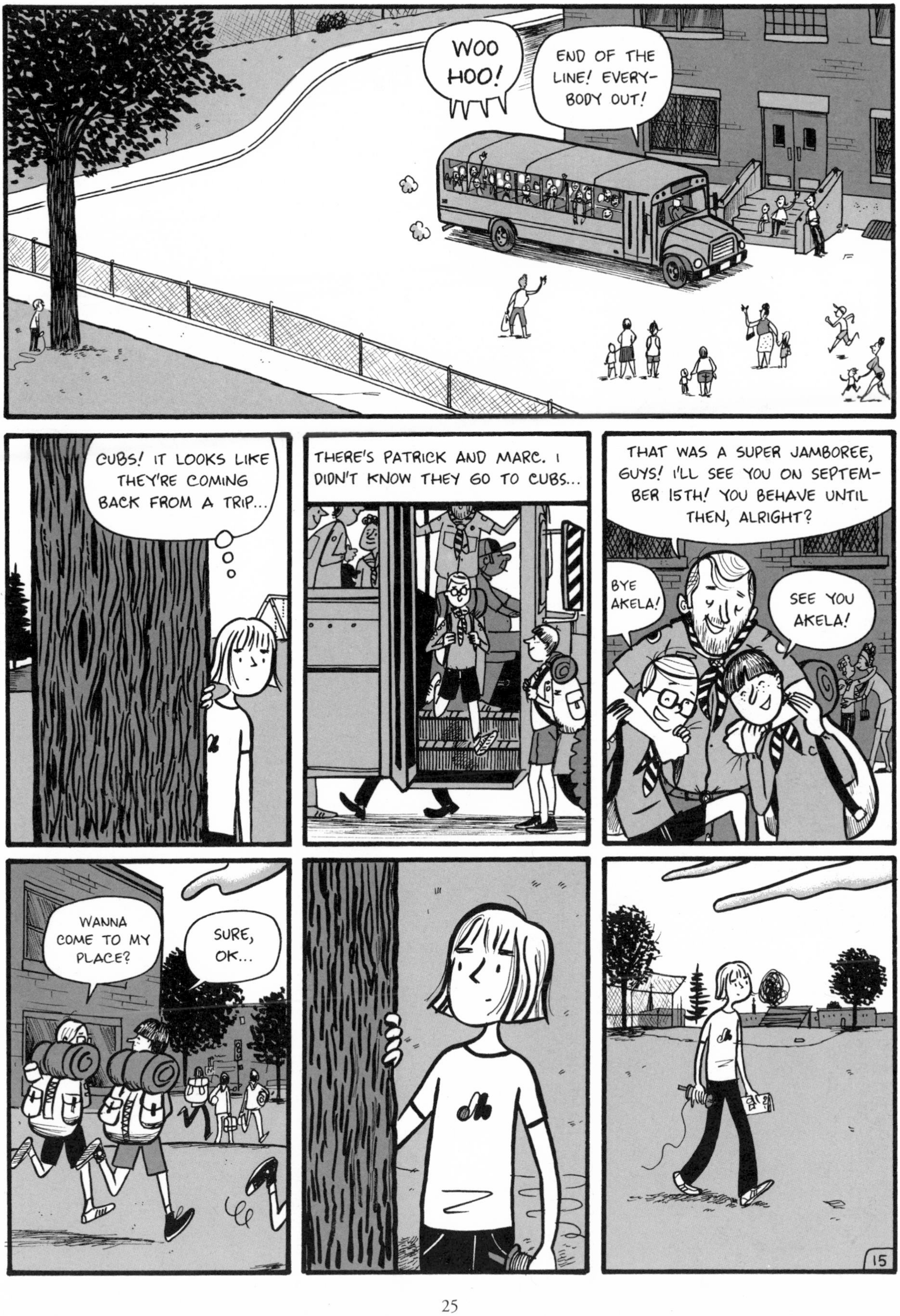
WOO HOO!
END OF THE LINE! EVERYBODY OUT!
CUBS! IT LOOKS LIKE THEY'RE COMING BACK FROM A TRIP...
THERE'S PATRICK AND MARC. I DIDN'T KNOW THEY GO TO CUBS...
THAT WAS A SUPER JAMBOREE, GUYS! I'LL SEE YOU ON SEPTEMBER 15TH! YOU BEHAVE UNTIL THEN, ALRIGHT?
BYE AKELA!
SEE YOU AKELA!
WANNA COME TO MY PLACE?
SURE, OK...
15

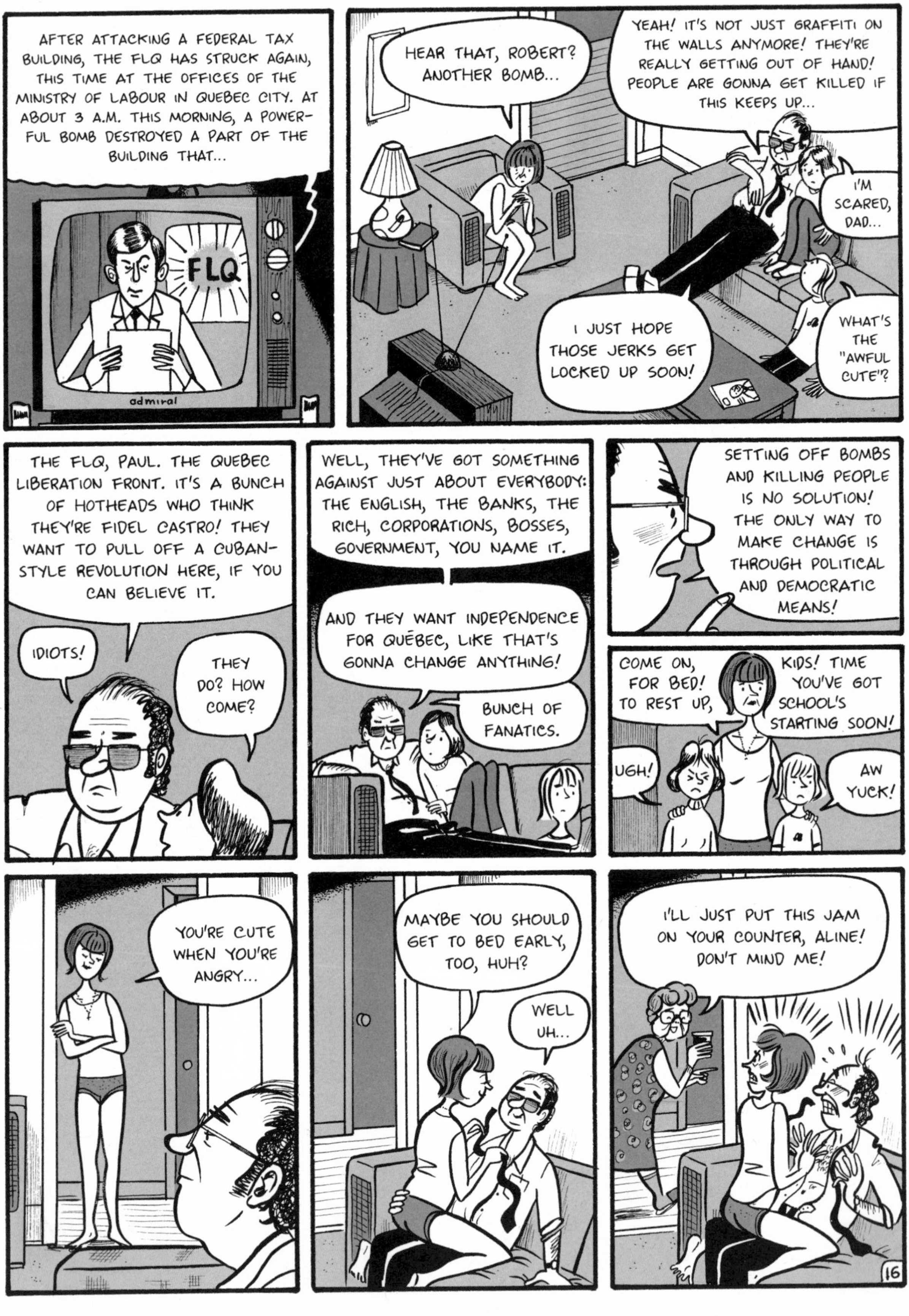
AFTER ATTACKING A FEDERAL TAX BUILDING, THE FLQ HAS STRUCK AGAIN, THIS TIME AT THE OFFICES OF THE MINISTRY OF LABOUR IN QUEBEC CITY. AT ABOUT 3 A.M. THIS MORNING, A POWERFUL BOMB DESTROYED A PART OF THE BUILDING THAT...
FLQ
admiral
HEAR THAT, ROBERT? ANOTHER BOMB...
YEAH! IT'S NOT JUST GRAFFITI ON THE WALLS ANYMORE! THEY'RE REALLY GETTING OUT OF HAND! PEOPLE ARE GONNA GET KILLED IF THIS KEEPS UP...
I'M SCARED, DAD...
I JUST HOPE THOSE JERKS GET LOCKED UP SOON!
WHAT'S THE "AWFUL CUTE"?
THE FLQ, PAUL. THE QUEBEC LIBERATION FRONT. IT'S A BUNCH OF HOTHEADS WHO THINK THEY'RE FIDEL CASTRO! THEY WANT TO PULL OFF A CUBAN-STYLE REVOLUTION HERE, IF YOU CAN BELIEVE IT.
IDIOTS!
THEY DO? HOW COME?
WELL, THEY'VE GOT SOMETHING AGAINST JUST ABOUT EVERYBODY: THE ENGLISH, THE BANKS, THE RICH, CORPORATIONS, BOSSES, GOVERNMENT, YOU NAME IT.
AND THEY WANT INDEPENDENCE FOR QUÉBEC, LIKE THAT'S GONNA CHANGE ANYTHING!
BUNCH OF FANATICS.
SETTING OFF BOMBS AND KILLING PEOPLE IS NO SOLUTION! THE ONLY WAY TO MAKE CHANGE IS THROUGH POLITICAL AND DEMOCRATIC MEANS!
COME ON, KIDS! TIME FOR BED! YOU'VE GOT TO REST UP, SCHOOL'S STARTING SOON!
UGH!
AW YUCK!
YOU'RE CUTE WHEN YOU'RE ANGRY...
MAYBE YOU SHOULD GET TO BED EARLY, TOO, HUH?
WELL UH...
I'LL JUST PUT THIS JAM ON YOUR COUNTER, ALINE! DON'T MIND ME!
16

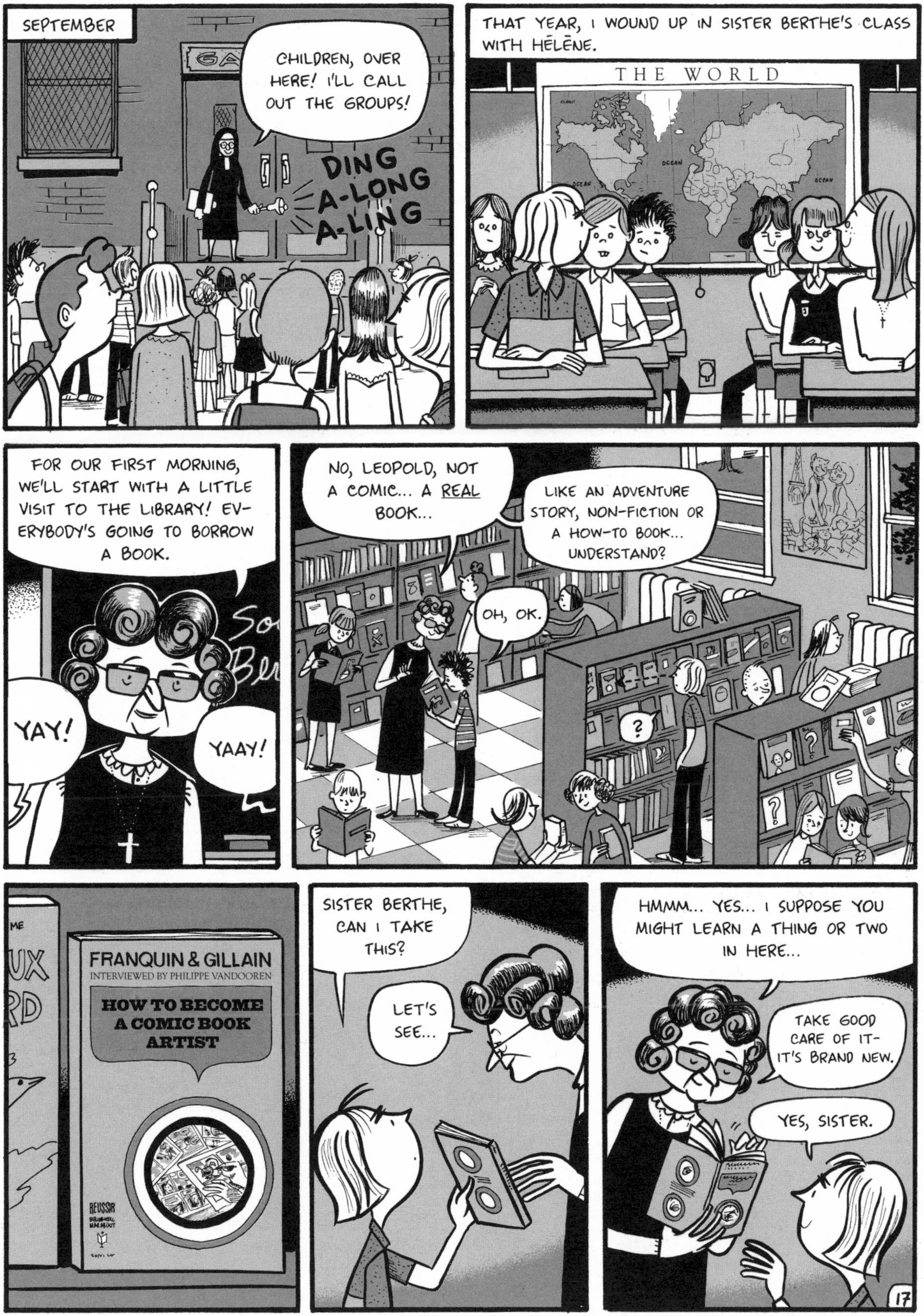
SEPTEMBER
CHILDREN, OVER HERE! I'LL CALL OUT THE GROUPS!
DING A-LONG A-LING
THAT YEAR, I WOUND UP IN SISTER BERTHE'S CLASS WITH HÉLÈNE.
THE WORLD
FOR OUR FIRST MORNING, WE'LL START WITH A LITTLE VISIT TO THE LIBRARY! EVERYBODY'S GOING TO BORROW A BOOK.
YAY!
YAAY!
NO, LEOPOLD, NOT A COMIC... A REAL BOOK...
LIKE AN ADVENTURE STORY, NON-FICTION OR A HOW-TO BOOK... UNDERSTAND?
OH, OK.
?
FRANQUIN & GILLAIN
INTERVIEWED BY PHILIPPE VANDOOREN
HOW TO BECOME A COMIC BOOK ARTIST
SISTER BERTHE, CAN I TAKE THIS?
LET'S SEE...
HMMM... YES... I SUPPOSE YOU MIGHT LEARN A THING OR TWO IN HERE...
TAKE GOOD CARE OF IT- IT'S BRAND NEW.
YES, SISTER.
17

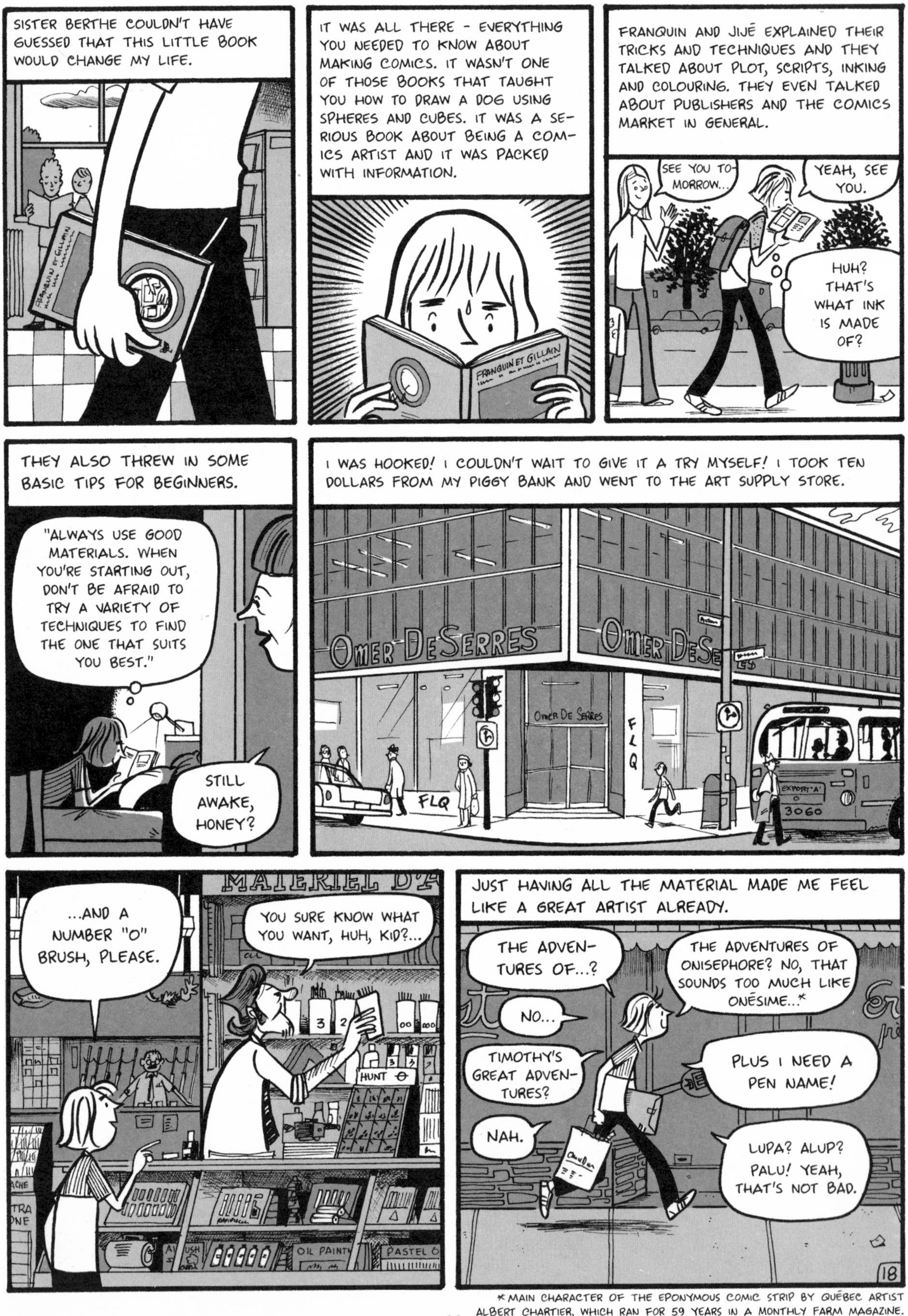
SISTER BERTHE COULDN'T HAVE GUESSED THAT THIS LITTLE BOOK WOULD CHANGE MY LIFE.
FRANQUIN ET GILLAIN
IT WAS ALL THERE - EVERYTHING YOU NEEDED TO KNOW ABOUT MAKING COMICS. IT WASN'T ONE OF THOSE BOOKS THAT TAUGHT YOU HOW TO DRAW A DOG USING SPHERES AND CUBES. IT WAS A SERIOUS BOOK ABOUT BEING A COMICS ARTIST AND IT WAS PACKED WITH INFORMATION.
FRANQUIN ET GILLAIN
FRANQUIN AND JIJÉ EXPLAINED THEIR TRICKS AND TECHNIQUES AND THEY TALKED ABOUT PLOT, SCRIPTS, INKING AND COLOURING. THEY EVEN TALKED ABOUT PUBLISHERS AND THE COMICS MARKET IN GENERAL.
SEE YOU TOMORROW...
YEAH, SEE YOU.
HUH? THAT'S WHAT INK IS MADE OF?
THEY ALSO THREW IN SOME BASIC TIPS FOR BEGINNERS.
"ALWAYS USE GOOD MATERIALS. WHEN YOU'RE STARTING OUT, DON'T BE AFRAID TO TRY A VARIETY OF TECHNIQUES TO FIND THE ONE THAT SUITS YOU BEST."
STILL AWAKE, HONEY?
I WAS HOOKED! I COULDN'T WAIT TO GIVE IT A TRY MYSELF! I TOOK TEN DOLLARS FROM MY PIGGY BANK AND WENT TO THE ART SUPPLY STORE.
OMER DESERRES
OMER DESE
OMER DE SERRES
FLQ
FLQ
EXPORT 'A'
3060
MATERIEL D'A
...AND A NUMBER "O" BRUSH, PLEASE.
YOU SURE KNOW WHAT YOU WANT, HUH, KID?...
HUNT
OIL PAINT
PASTEL
JUST HAVING ALL THE MATERIAL MADE ME FEEL LIKE A GREAT ARTIST ALREADY.
THE ADVENTURES OF...?
NO...
THE ADVENTURES OF ONISEPHORE? NO, THAT SOUNDS TOO MUCH LIKE ONÉSIME...*
TIMOTHY'S GREAT ADVENTURES?
PLUS I NEED A PEN NAME!
NAH.
LUPA? ALUP? PALU! YEAH, THAT'S NOT BAD.
18

*MAIN CHARACTER OF THE EPONYMOUS COMIC STRIP BY QUÉBEC ARTIST ALBERT CHARTIER, WHICH RAN FOR 59 YEARS IN A MONTHLY FARM MAGAZINE.

THE FIRST THING I DID WAS SKETCH A CHARACTER BASED ON GASTON.
ABOUT 5 HEADS HIGH
BIG HEAD, BIG NOSE
SKINNY NECK
SPAGHETTI ARMS
OVAL BELLY
BIG HANDS
LONG SPAGHETTI LEGS
HUGE FEET
Da!u
THEN I CREATED ANOTHER CHARACTER TO KEEP THE FIRST ONE COMPANY. HE WAS FANTASIO'S DOUBLE.
let's go Julot!!!
Arghhh can't you give it a Break Gaspar Grmbl...
Da!u
WITH PRACTICE, IT GOT PRETTY EASY TO CHURN OUT CHARACTERS USING THIS TECHNIQUE.
HEH HEH! THAT'S NOT BAD AT ALL, PAUL!
THANKS!
BUT PLACING THEM IN A SETTING AND MAKING THEM HAVE ADVENTURES WAS A WHOLE OTHER STORY.
Suddenly...!!!
Take that Nazi scum BAG!!!
No!!! AhhHH!!!
BANG
POW
Look out!!! A Grenade!!!
CATACLATPA
CLAC
glog glog
pccchhh
Da!u
BUT WHAT'S WRONG WITH HIS FOOT?
NOTHING! THAT'S A GERMAN HELMET IN FRONT OF HIS FOOT...
AND WHAT'S THIS BLACK TRIANGLE SUPPOSED TO BE?
THAT'S BLOOD FLOWING FROM THE GUY'S HEAD. THIS IS WHERE JULOT COMES TO DEACTIVATE THE GRENADE!
WHAT GRENADE?
AND THOSE ARE THE TANKS ROLLING UP AND...
YOU CAN LOOK AT THAT AFTER CHURCH. WE NEED TO GO!
OH YEAH, YOU'RE RIGHT...
I DON'T WANT TO GO!
MOOOOM! WHY DO WE ALWAYS HAVE TO GO TO CHURCH?
YEAH! HOW COME?
NO COMPLAINING, KIDS. SUNDAY IS THE DAY OF THE LORD AND THAT'S THAT.
THAT'S RIGHT. IT'S NOT UP FOR NEGOTIATION.
19

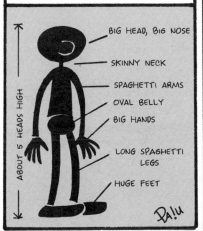

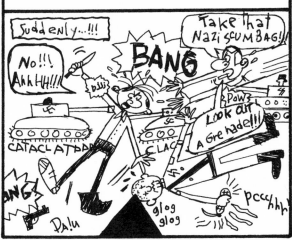

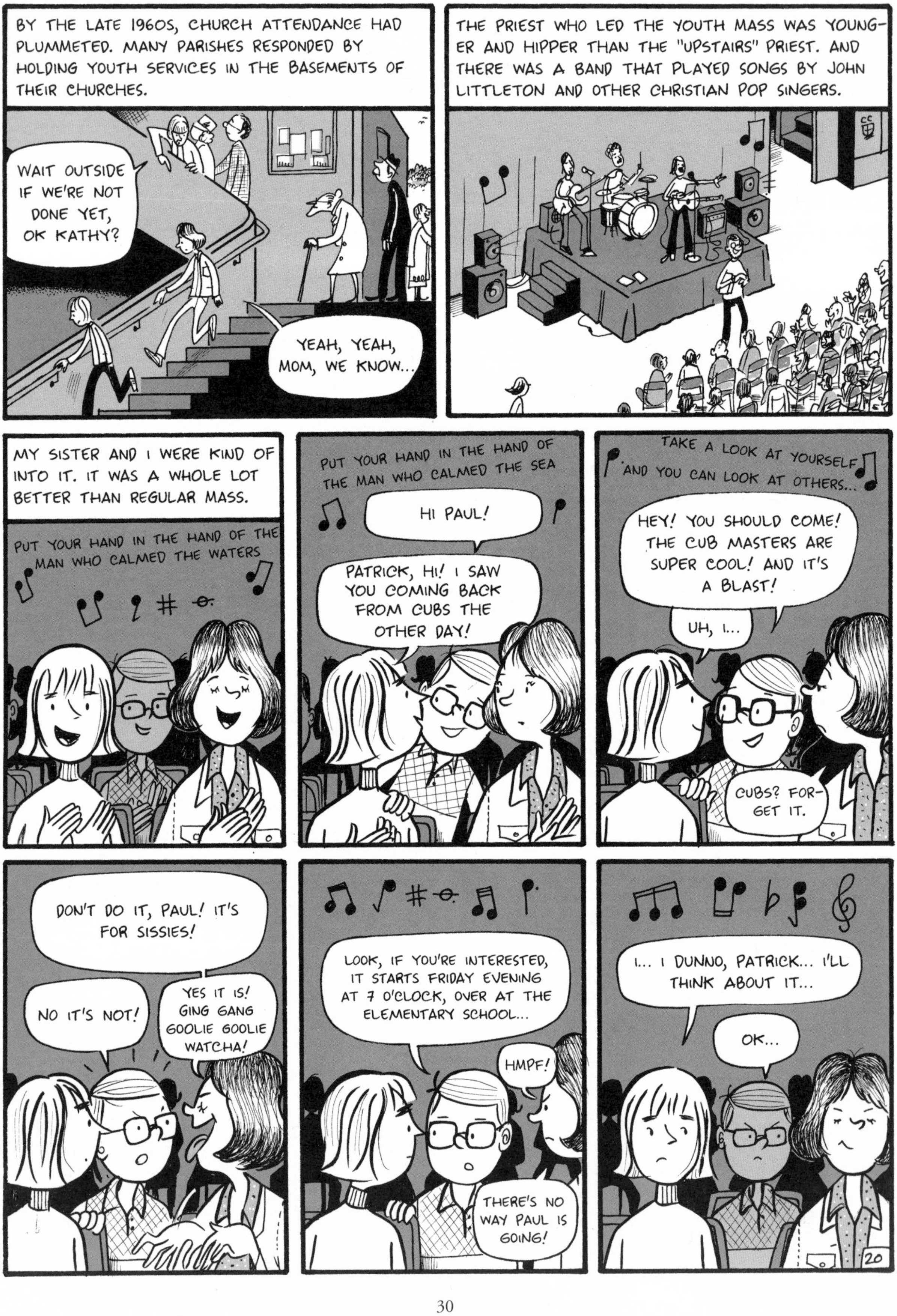
BY THE LATE 1960S, CHURCH ATTENDANCE HAD PLUMMETED. MANY PARISHES RESPONDED BY HOLDING YOUTH SERVICES IN THE BASEMENTS OF THEIR CHURCHES.
WAIT OUTSIDE IF WE'RE NOT DONE YET, OK KATHY?
YEAH, YEAH, MOM, WE KNOW...
THE PRIEST WHO LED THE YOUTH MASS WAS YOUNGER AND HIPPER THAN THE "UPSTAIRS" PRIEST. AND THERE WAS A BAND THAT PLAYED SONGS BY JOHN LITTLETON AND OTHER CHRISTIAN POP SINGERS.
MY SISTER AND I WERE KIND OF INTO IT. IT WAS A WHOLE LOT BETTER THAN REGULAR MASS.
PUT YOUR HAND IN THE HAND OF THE MAN WHO CALMED THE WATERS
PUT YOUR HAND IN THE HAND OF THE MAN WHO CALMED THE SEA
HI PAUL!
PATRICK, HI! I SAW YOU COMING BACK FROM CUBS THE OTHER DAY!
TAKE A LOOK AT YOURSELF AND YOU CAN LOOK AT OTHERS...
HEY! YOU SHOULD COME! THE CUB MASTERS ARE SUPER COOL! AND IT'S A BLAST!
UH, I...
CUBS? FORGET IT.
DON'T DO IT, PAUL! IT'S FOR SISSIES!
NO IT'S NOT!
YES IT IS! GING GANG GOOLIE GOOLIE WATCHA!
LOOK, IF YOU'RE INTERESTED, IT STARTS FRIDAY EVENING AT 7 O'CLOCK, OVER AT THE ELEMENTARY SCHOOL...
HMPF!
THERE'S NO WAY PAUL IS GOING!
I... I DUNNO, PATRICK... I'LL THINK ABOUT IT...
OK...
20

Raymond

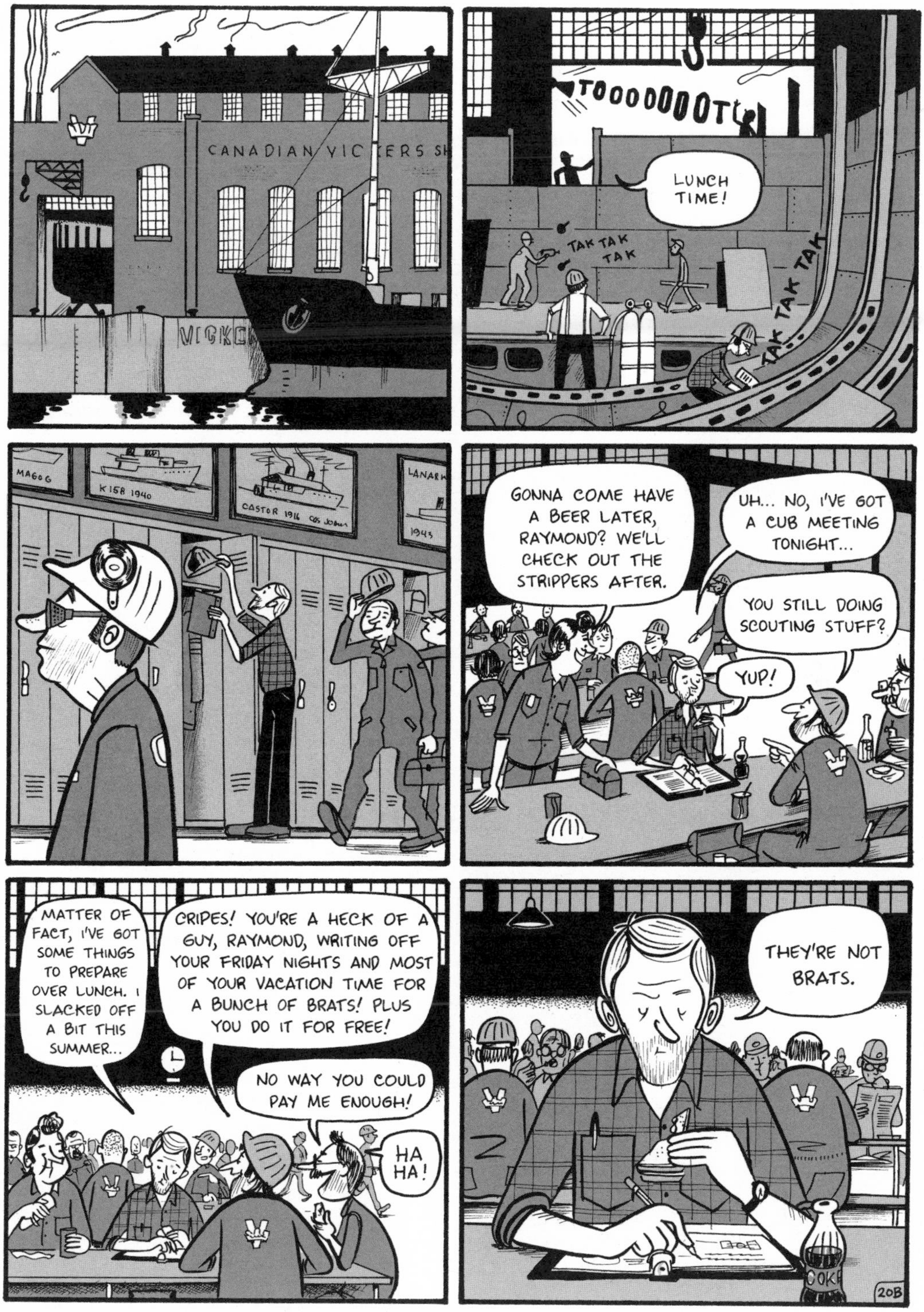
CANADIAN VICKERS SH
VICKER
TOOOOOOOOT
LUNCH TIME!
TAK TAK TAK
TAK TAK TAK TAK
MAGOG
K158 1940
CASTOR 1916
LANARK
1943
GONNA COME HAVE A BEER LATER, RAYMOND? WE'LL CHECK OUT THE STRIPPERS AFTER.
UH... NO, I'VE GOT A CUB MEETING TONIGHT...
YOU STILL DOING SCOUTING STUFF?
YUP!
MATTER OF FACT, I'VE GOT SOME THINGS TO PREPARE OVER LUNCH. I SLACKED OFF A BIT THIS SUMMER...
CRIPES! YOU'RE A HECK OF A GUY, RAYMOND, WRITING OFF YOUR FRIDAY NIGHTS AND MOST OF YOUR VACATION TIME FOR A BUNCH OF BRATS! PLUS YOU DO IT FOR FREE!
NO WAY YOU COULD PAY ME ENOUGH!
HA HA!
THEY'RE NOT BRATS.
COKE

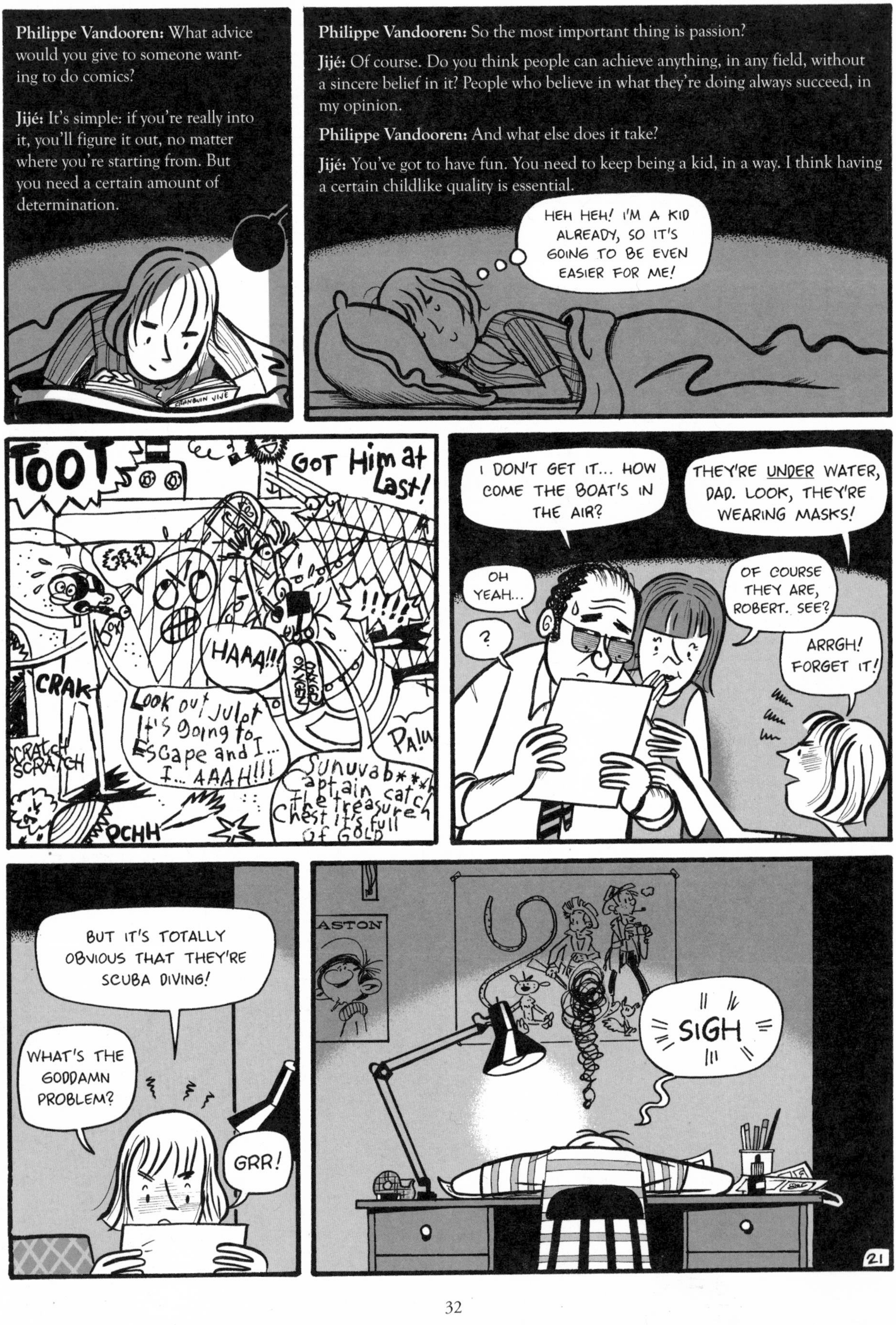
Philippe Vandooren: What advice would you give to someone wanting to do comics?
Jijé: It's simple: if you're really into it, you'll figure it out, no matter where you're starting from. But you need a certain amount of determination.
Philippe Vandooren: So the most important thing is passion?
Jijé: Of course. Do you think people can achieve anything, in any field, without a sincere belief in it? People who believe in what they're doing always succeed, in my opinion.
Philippe Vandooren: And what else does it take?
Jijé: You've got to have fun. You need to keep being a kid, in a way. I think having a certain childlike quality is essential.
HEH HEH! I'M A KID ALREADY, SO IT'S GOING TO BE EVEN EASIER FOR ME!
TOOT
Got Him at Last!
GRR
!!!!!
HAAA!!!
OXYGEN
CRAK
Look out Julot It's going to Escape and I... I... AAAH!!!
PA!U
Sunuvab***h Captain catch the treasure Chest it's full of GOLD
SCRATCH SCRATCH
PCHH
I DON'T GET IT... HOW COME THE BOAT'S IN THE AIR?
THEY'RE UNDER WATER, DAD. LOOK, THEY'RE WEARING MASKS!
OH YEAH...
?
OF COURSE THEY ARE, ROBERT. SEE?
ARRGH! FORGET IT!
BUT IT'S TOTALLY OBVIOUS THAT THEY'RE SCUBA DIVING!
WHAT'S THE GODDAMN PROBLEM?
GRR!
ASTON
SIGH
21

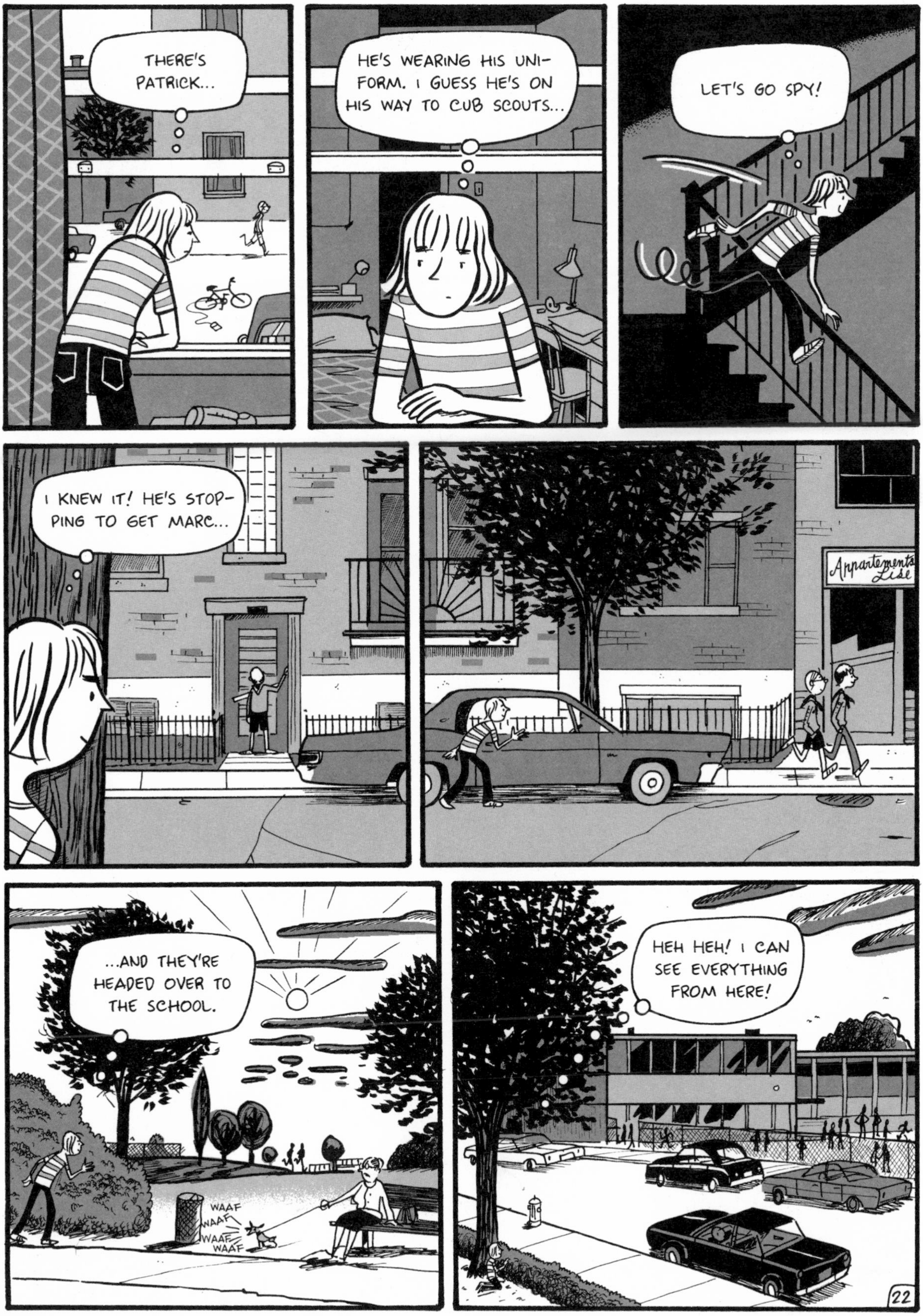
THERE'S PATRICK...
HE'S WEARING HIS UNI-FORM. I GUESS HE'S ON HIS WAY TO CUB SCOUTS...
LET'S GO SPY!
I KNEW IT! HE'S STOP-PING TO GET MARC...
Appartements Lise
...AND THEY'RE HEADED OVER TO THE SCHOOL.
WAAF
WAAF
WAAF
WAAF
HEH HEH! I CAN SEE EVERYTHING FROM HERE!
22

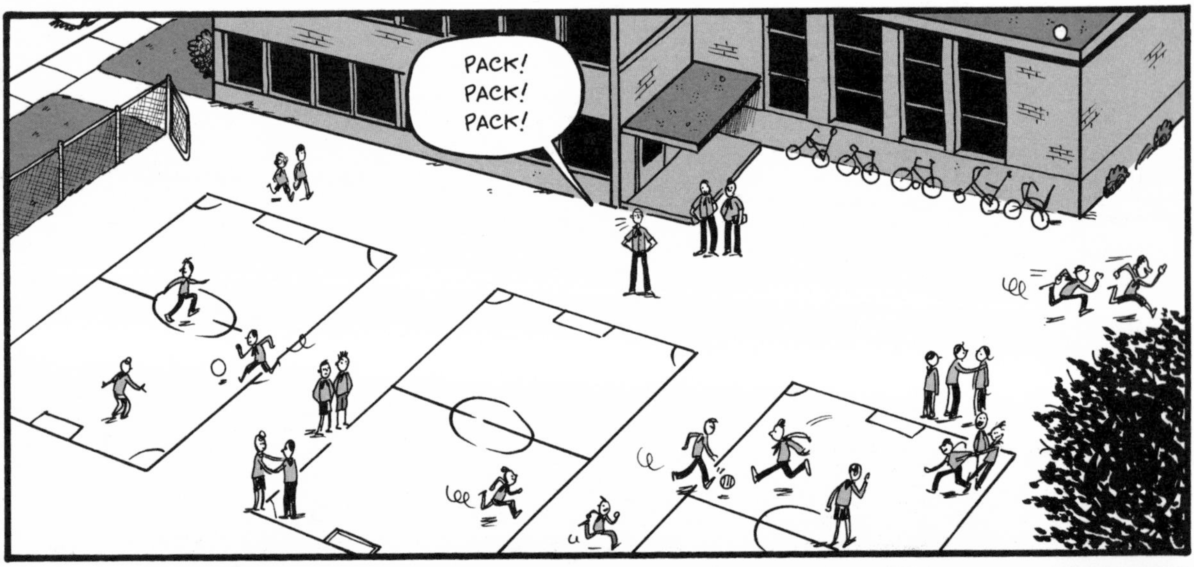
PACK!
PACK!
PACK!

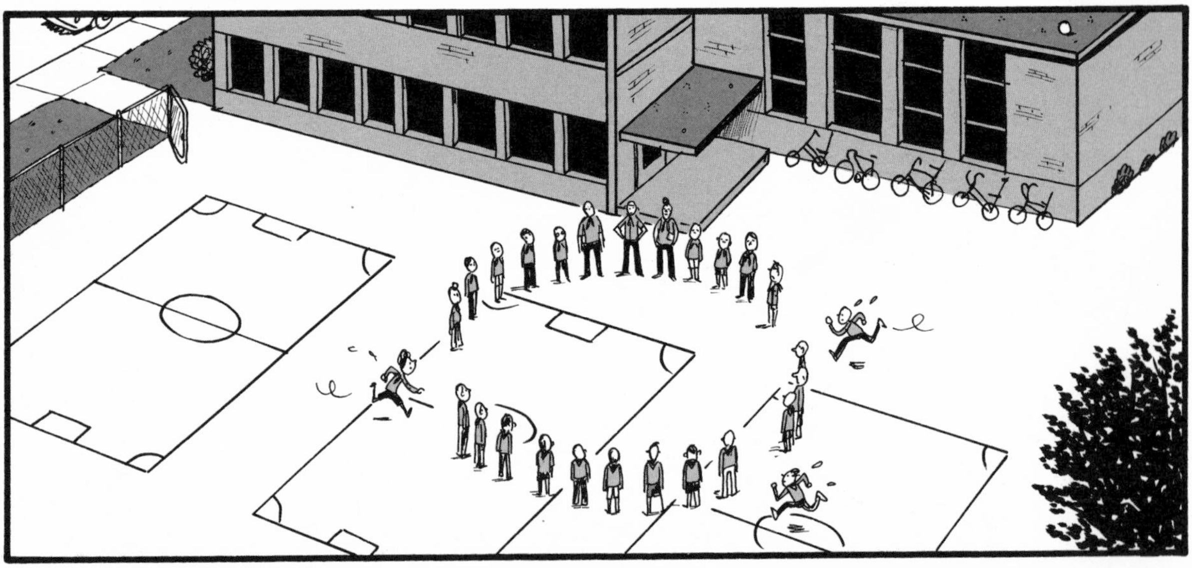

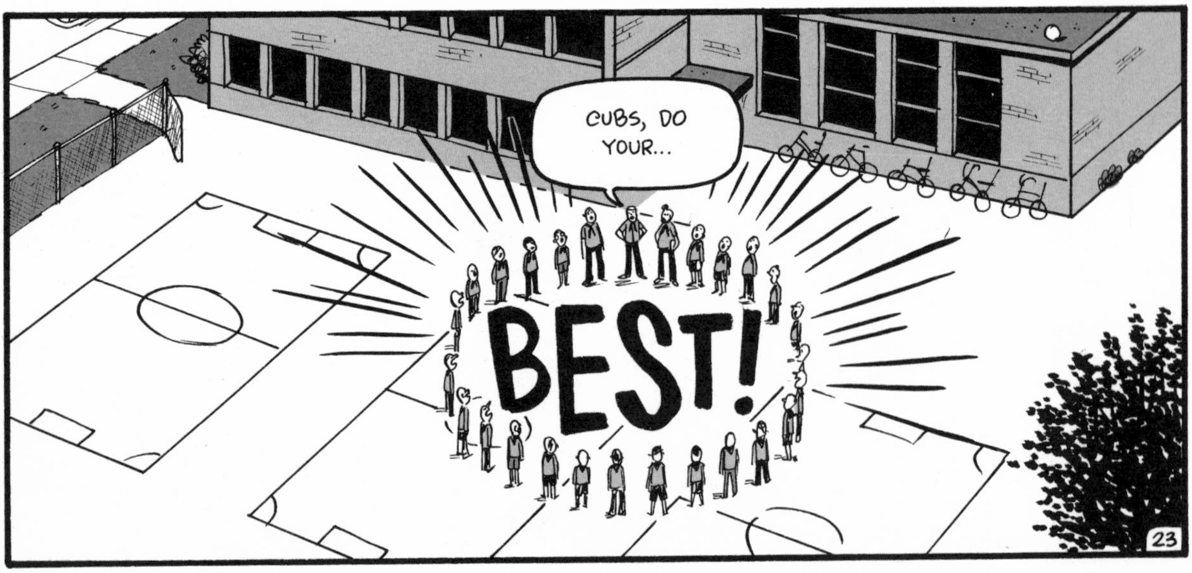
CUBS, DO YOUR...
BEST!
23

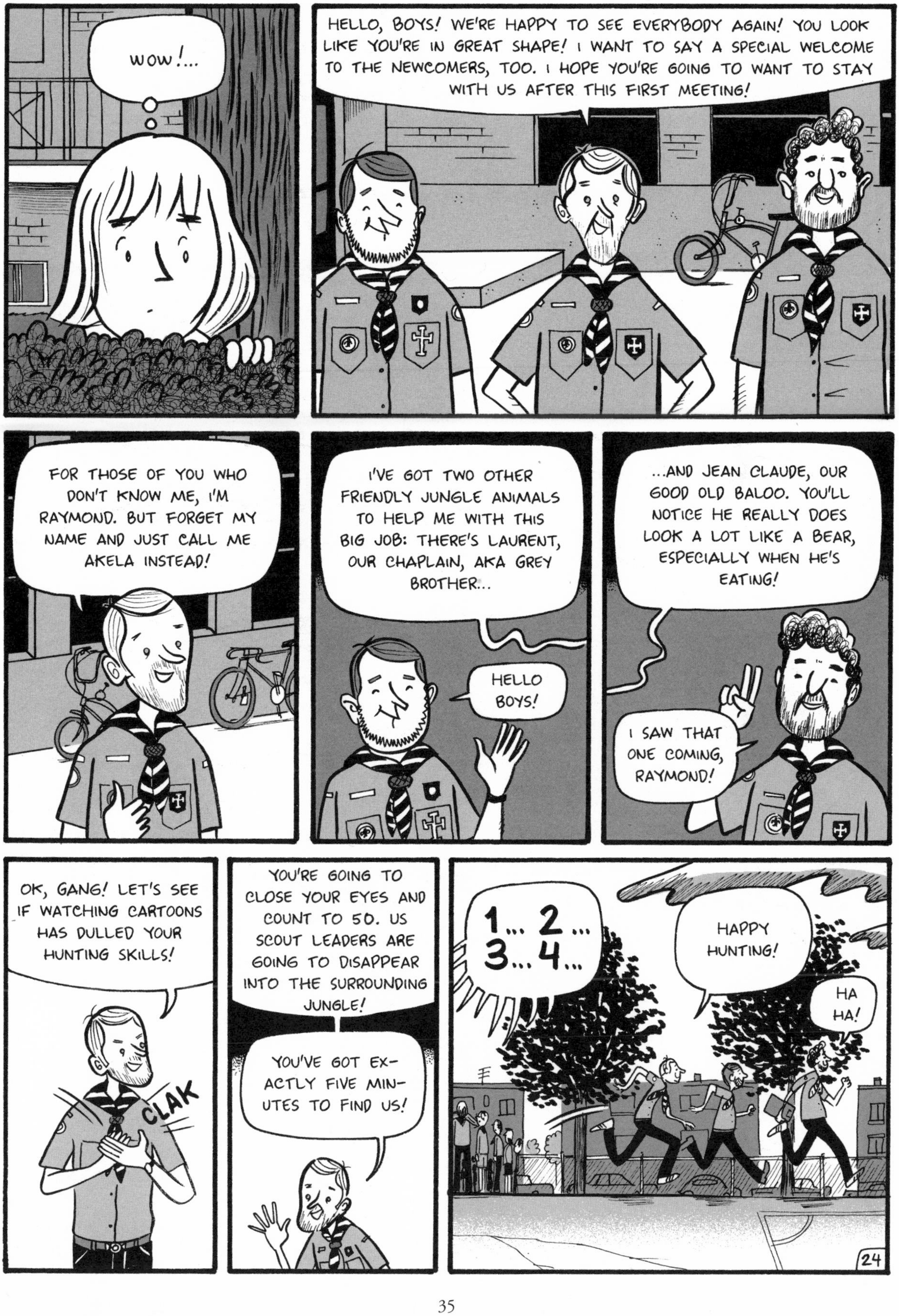
WOW!...
HELLO, BOYS! WE'RE HAPPY TO SEE EVERYBODY AGAIN! YOU LOOK LIKE YOU'RE IN GREAT SHAPE! I WANT TO SAY A SPECIAL WELCOME TO THE NEWCOMERS, TOO. I HOPE YOU'RE GOING TO WANT TO STAY WITH US AFTER THIS FIRST MEETING!
FOR THOSE OF YOU WHO DON'T KNOW ME, I'M RAYMOND. BUT FORGET MY NAME AND JUST CALL ME AKELA INSTEAD!
I'VE GOT TWO OTHER FRIENDLY JUNGLE ANIMALS TO HELP ME WITH THIS BIG JOB: THERE'S LAURENT, OUR CHAPLAIN, AKA GREY BROTHER...
HELLO BOYS!
...AND JEAN CLAUDE, OUR GOOD OLD BALOO. YOU'LL NOTICE HE REALLY DOES LOOK A LOT LIKE A BEAR, ESPECIALLY WHEN HE'S EATING!
I SAW THAT ONE COMING, RAYMOND!
OK, GANG! LET'S SEE IF WATCHING CARTOONS HAS DULLED YOUR HUNTING SKILLS!
CLAK
YOU'RE GOING TO CLOSE YOUR EYES AND COUNT TO 50. US SCOUT LEADERS ARE GOING TO DISAPPEAR INTO THE SURROUNDING JUNGLE!
YOU'VE GOT EX-ACTLY FIVE MIN-UTES TO FIND US!
1... 2... 3... 4...
HAPPY HUNTING!
HA HA!
24

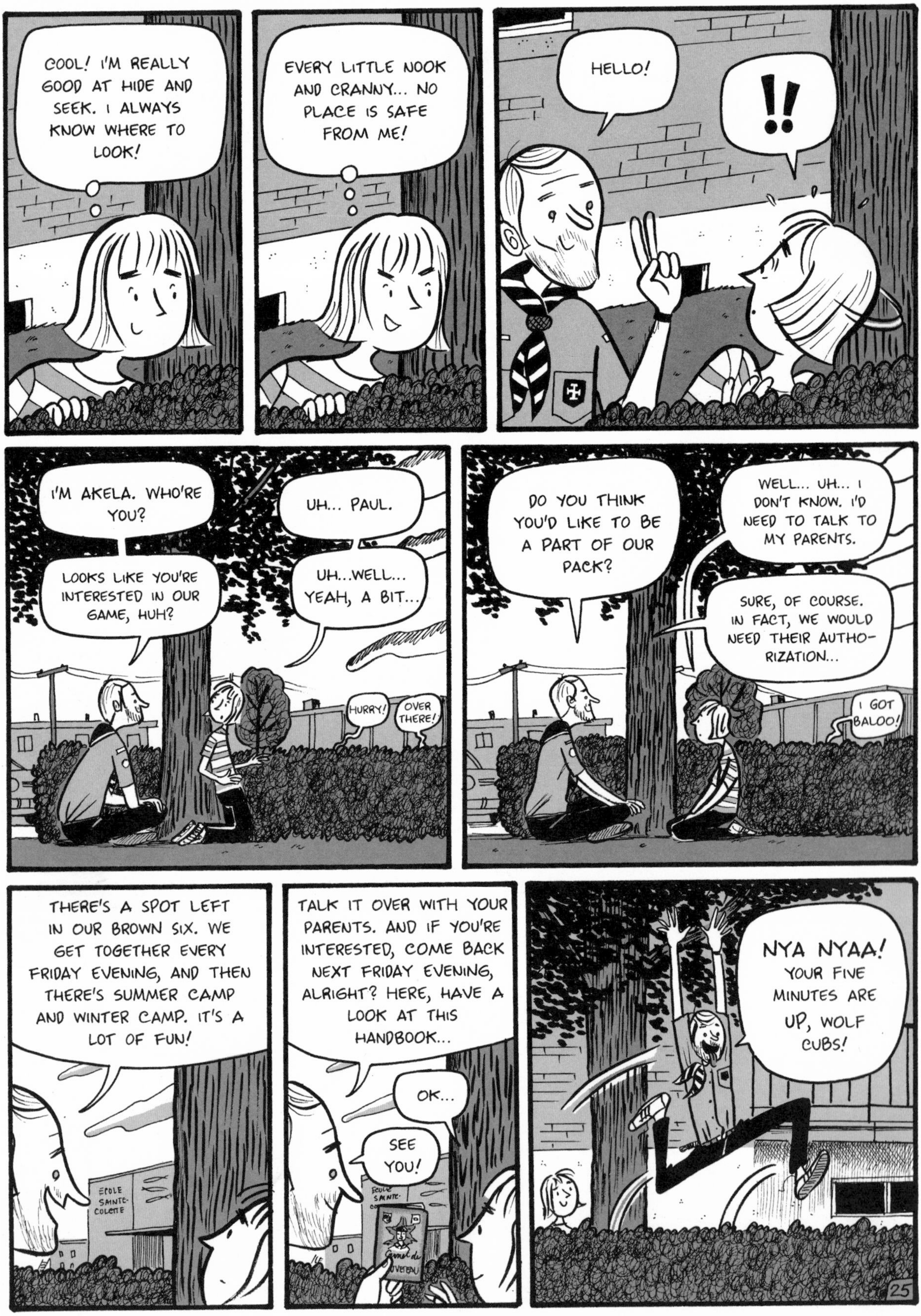
COOL! I'M REALLY GOOD AT HIDE AND SEEK. I ALWAYS KNOW WHERE TO LOOK!
EVERY LITTLE NOOK AND CRANNY... NO PLACE IS SAFE FROM ME!
HELLO!
!!
I'M AKELA. WHO'RE YOU?
UH... PAUL.
LOOKS LIKE YOU'RE INTERESTED IN OUR GAME, HUH?
UH...WELL... YEAH, A BIT...
HURRY!
OVER THERE!
DO YOU THINK YOU'D LIKE TO BE A PART OF OUR PACK?
WELL... UH... I DON'T KNOW. I'D NEED TO TALK TO MY PARENTS.
SURE, OF COURSE. IN FACT, WE WOULD NEED THEIR AUTHORIZATION...
I GOT BALOO!
THERE'S A SPOT LEFT IN OUR BROWN SIX. WE GET TOGETHER EVERY FRIDAY EVENING, AND THEN THERE'S SUMMER CAMP AND WINTER CAMP. IT'S A LOT OF FUN!
ECOLE SAINTE-COLETTE
TALK IT OVER WITH YOUR PARENTS. AND IF YOU'RE INTERESTED, COME BACK NEXT FRIDAY EVENING, ALRIGHT? HERE, HAVE A LOOK AT THIS HANDBOOK...
OK...
SEE YOU!
NYA NYAA! YOUR FIVE MINUTES ARE UP, WOLF CUBS!
25

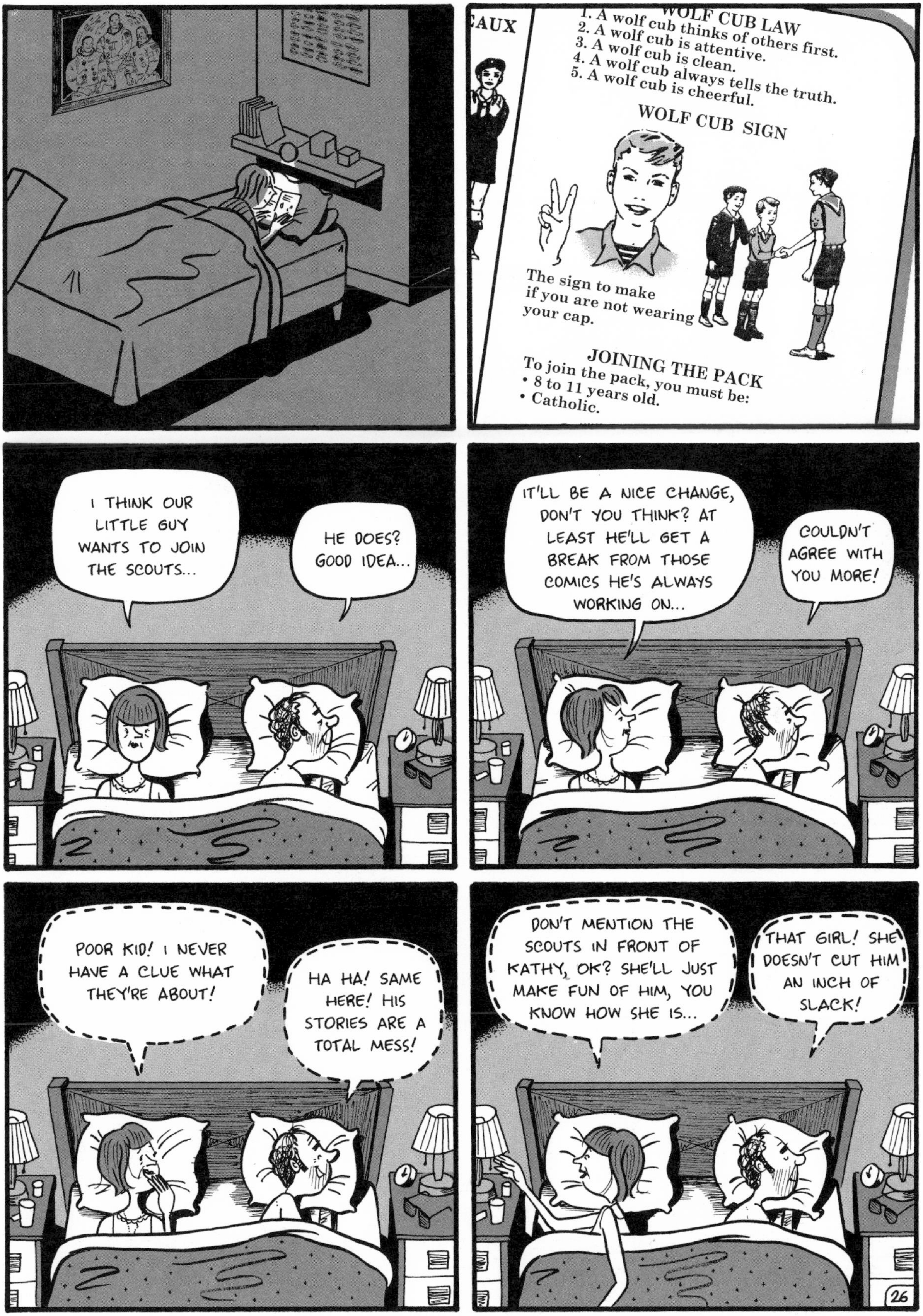
EAUX
WOLF CUB LAW
1. A wolf cub thinks of others first.
2. A wolf cub is attentive.
3. A wolf cub is clean.
4. A wolf cub always tells the truth.
5. A wolf cub is cheerful.
WOLF CUB SIGN
The sign to make if you are not wearing your cap.
JOINING THE PACK
To join the pack, you must be:
• 8 to 11 years old.
• Catholic.
I THINK OUR LITTLE GUY WANTS TO JOIN THE SCOUTS...
HE DOES? GOOD IDEA...
IT'LL BE A NICE CHANGE, DON'T YOU THINK? AT LEAST HE'LL GET A BREAK FROM THOSE COMICS HE'S ALWAYS WORKING ON...
COULDN'T AGREE WITH YOU MORE!
POOR KID! I NEVER HAVE A CLUE WHAT THEY'RE ABOUT!
HA HA! SAME HERE! HIS STORIES ARE A TOTAL MESS!
DON'T MENTION THE SCOUTS IN FRONT OF KATHY, OK? SHE'LL JUST MAKE FUN OF HIM, YOU KNOW HOW SHE IS...
THAT GIRL! SHE DOESN'T CUT HIM AN INCH OF SLACK!
26

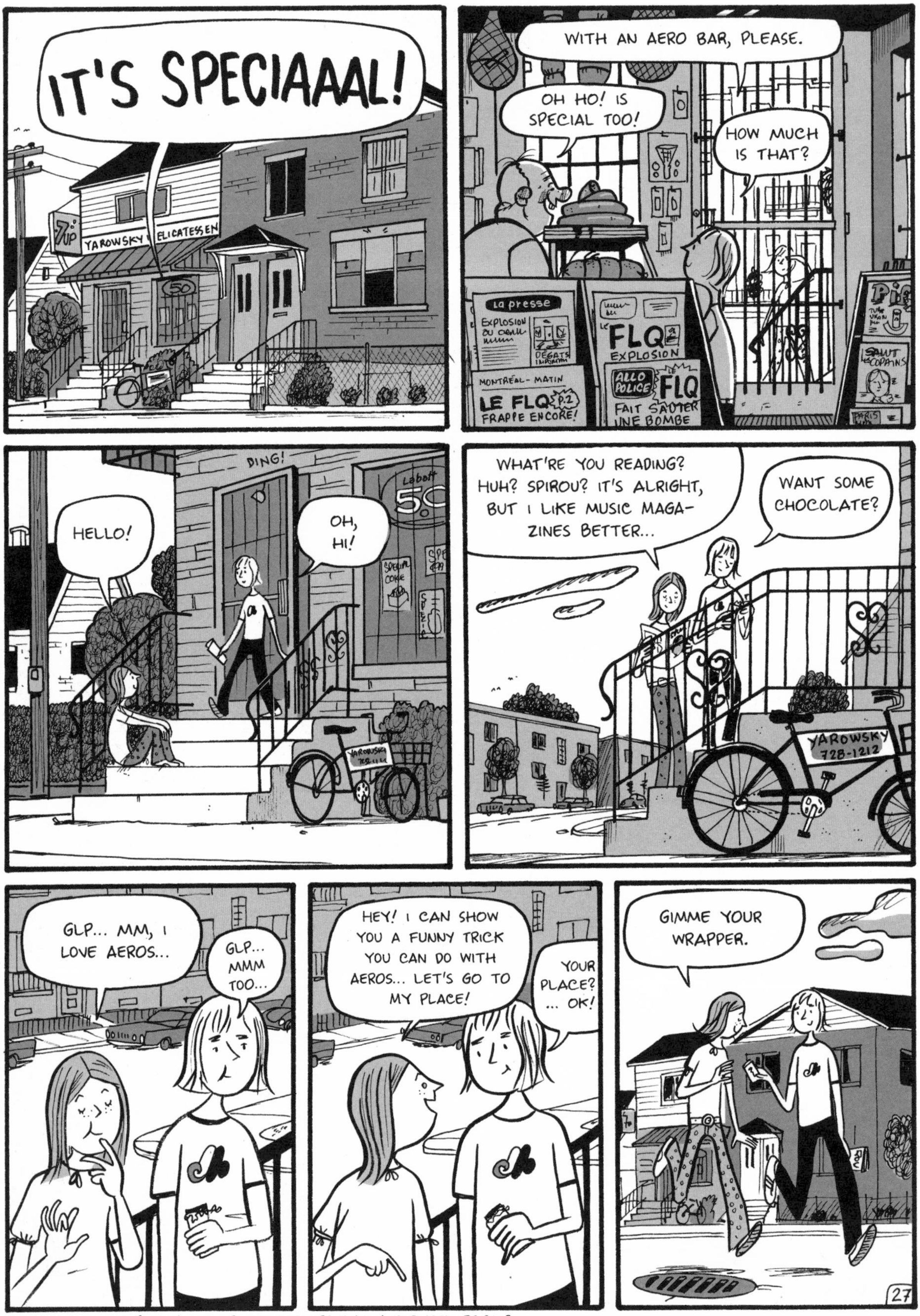
IT'S SPECIAAAL!
7UP
YAROWSKY ELICATESSEN
50
WITH AN AERO BAR, PLEASE.
OH HO! IS SPECIAL TOO!
HOW MUCH IS THAT?
la presse
EXPLOSION
DÉGATS
FLQ EXPLOSION
MONTRÉAL-MATIN
LE FLQ P.2 FRAPPE ENCORE!
ALLO POLICE
FLQ FAIT SAUTER UNE BOMBE
SALUT LES COPAINS
DING!
HELLO!
OH, HI!
YAROWSKY
WHAT'RE YOU READING? HUH? SPIROU? IT'S ALRIGHT, BUT I LIKE MUSIC MAGAZINES BETTER...
WANT SOME CHOCOLATE?
YAROWSKY 728-1212
GLP... MM, I LOVE AEROS...
GLP... MMM TOO...
HEY! I CAN SHOW YOU A FUNNY TRICK YOU CAN DO WITH AEROS... LET'S GO TO MY PLACE!
YOUR PLACE? ... OK!
GIMME YOUR WRAPPER.
27

PANEL 2 HEADLINES: EXPLOSION, FLQ EXPLOSION, FLQ STRIKES AGAIN, FLQ SETS OFF BOMB

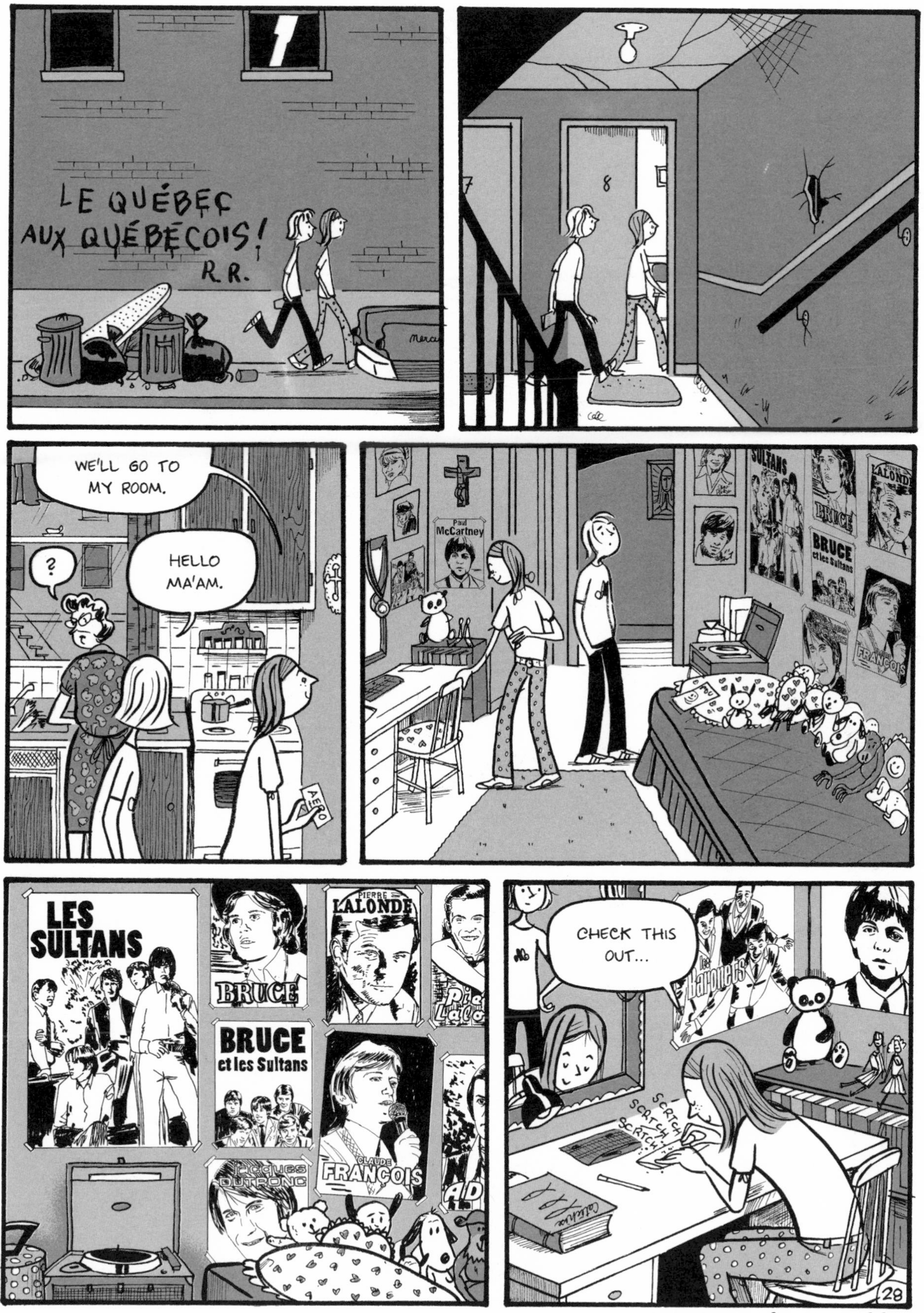
LE QUÉBEC AUX QUÉBÉCOIS!
R.R.
WE'LL GO TO MY ROOM.
?
HELLO MA'AM.
AERO
Paul McCartney
SULTANS
BRUCE
BRUCE et les Sultans
LALONDE
FRANÇOIS
LES SULTANS
BRUCE
PIERRE LALONDE
BRUCE et les Sultans
CLAUDE FRANÇOIS
JACQUES DUTRONC
CHECK THIS OUT...
SCRTCH SCRTCH SCRTCH

PANEL 1 GRAFFITI: QUÉBEC FOR THE QUÉBÉCOIS!

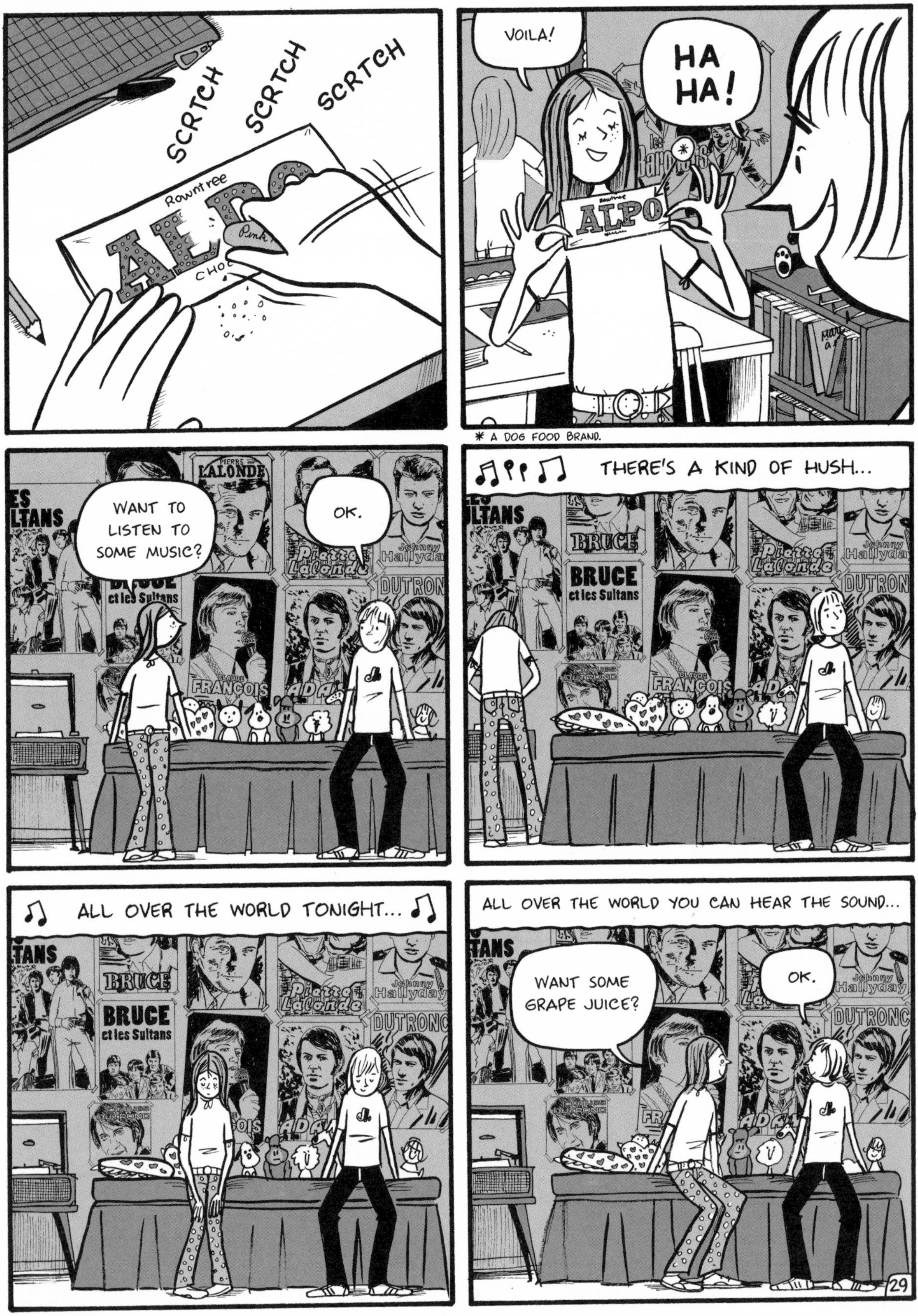
SCRTCH SCRTCH SCRTCH
Rowntree ALPO
Pink
CHOC
VOILA!
HA HA!
Rowntree ALPO*
* A DOG FOOD BRAND.
WANT TO LISTEN TO SOME MUSIC?
OK.
♫ THERE'S A KIND OF HUSH...
♫ ALL OVER THE WORLD TONIGHT... ♫
ALL OVER THE WORLD YOU CAN HEAR THE SOUND...
WANT SOME GRAPE JUICE?
OK.
BRUCE et les Sultans
Pierre Lalonde
Johnny Hallyday
DUTRONC
CLAUDE FRANCOIS
29

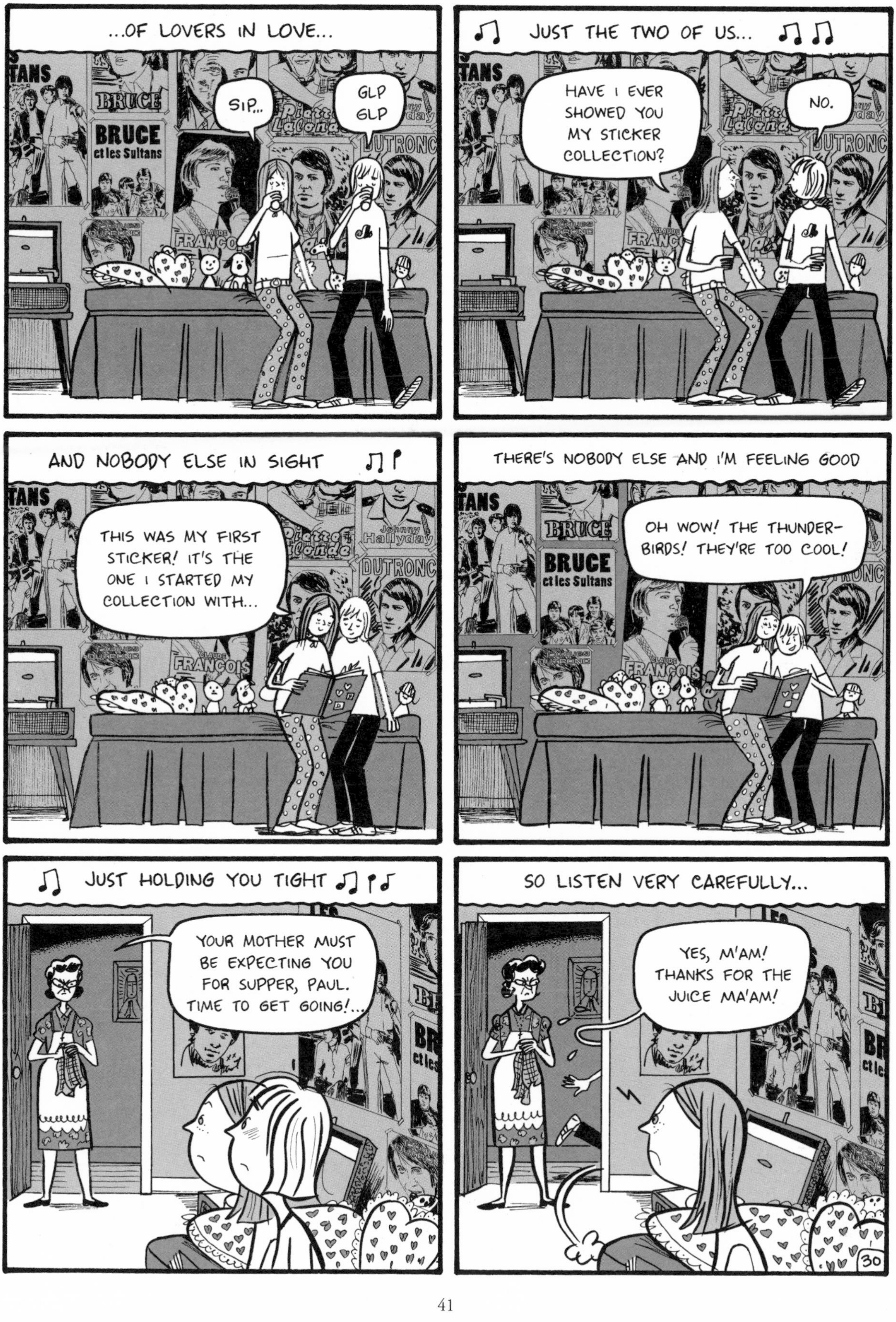
...OF LOVERS IN LOVE...
SIP...
GLP GLP
JUST THE TWO OF US...
HAVE I EVER SHOWED YOU MY STICKER COLLECTION?
NO.
AND NOBODY ELSE IN SIGHT
THIS WAS MY FIRST STICKER! IT'S THE ONE I STARTED MY COLLECTION WITH...
THERE'S NOBODY ELSE AND I'M FEELING GOOD
OH WOW! THE THUNDER-BIRDS! THEY'RE TOO COOL!
JUST HOLDING YOU TIGHT
YOUR MOTHER MUST BE EXPECTING YOU FOR SUPPER, PAUL. TIME TO GET GOING!...
SO LISTEN VERY CAREFULLY...
YES, M'AM! THANKS FOR THE JUICE MA'AM!
30

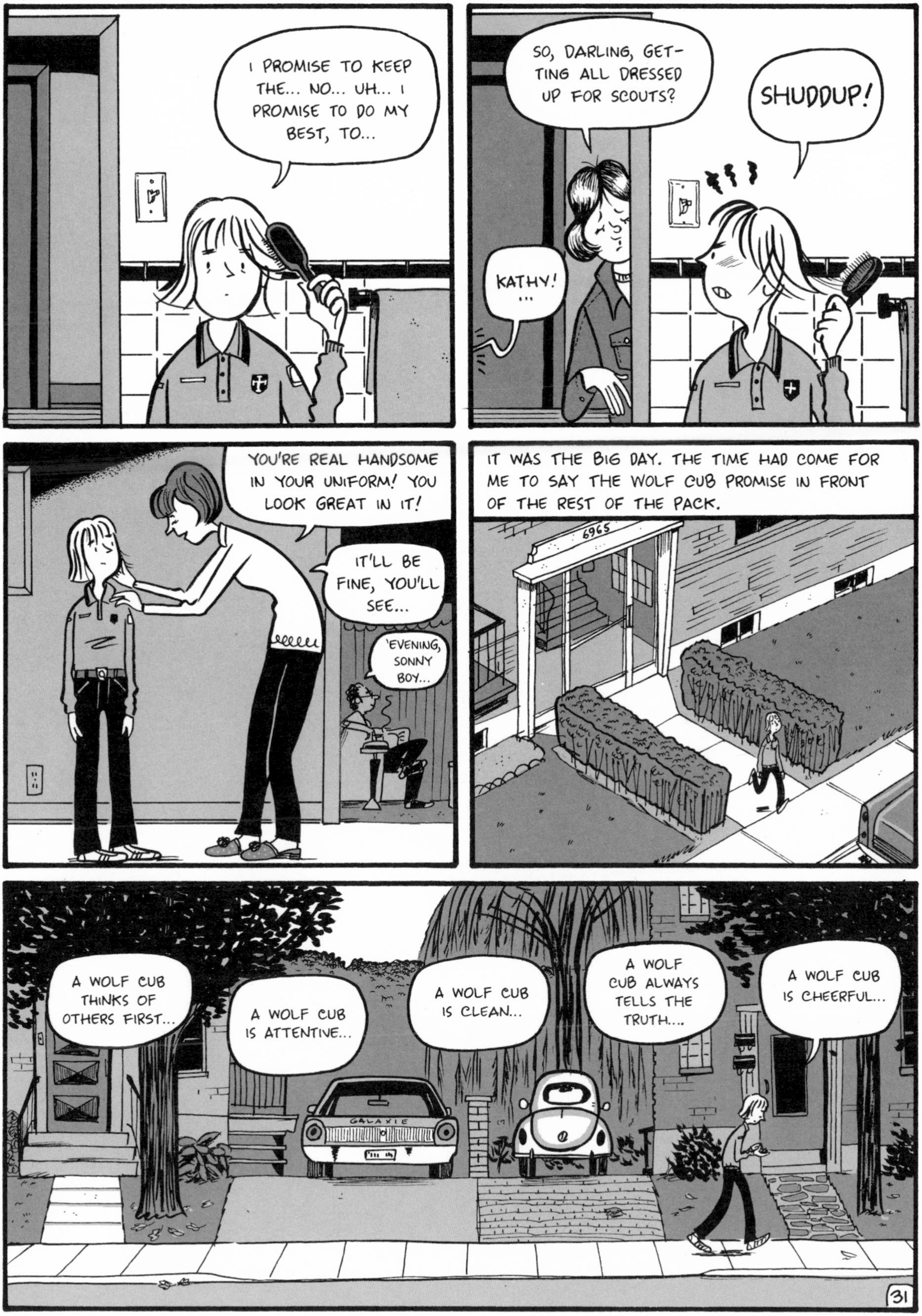
I PROMISE TO KEEP THE... NO... UH... I PROMISE TO DO MY BEST, TO...
SO, DARLING, GETTING ALL DRESSED UP FOR SCOUTS?
KATHY! ...
SHUDDUP!
YOU'RE REAL HANDSOME IN YOUR UNIFORM! YOU LOOK GREAT IN IT!
IT'LL BE FINE, YOU'LL SEE...
'EVENING, SONNY BOY...
IT WAS THE BIG DAY. THE TIME HAD COME FOR ME TO SAY THE WOLF CUB PROMISE IN FRONT OF THE REST OF THE PACK.
6965
A WOLF CUB THINKS OF OTHERS FIRST...
A WOLF CUB IS ATTENTIVE...
A WOLF CUB IS CLEAN...
A WOLF CUB ALWAYS TELLS THE TRUTH....
A WOLF CUB IS CHEERFUL...
GALAXIE
31

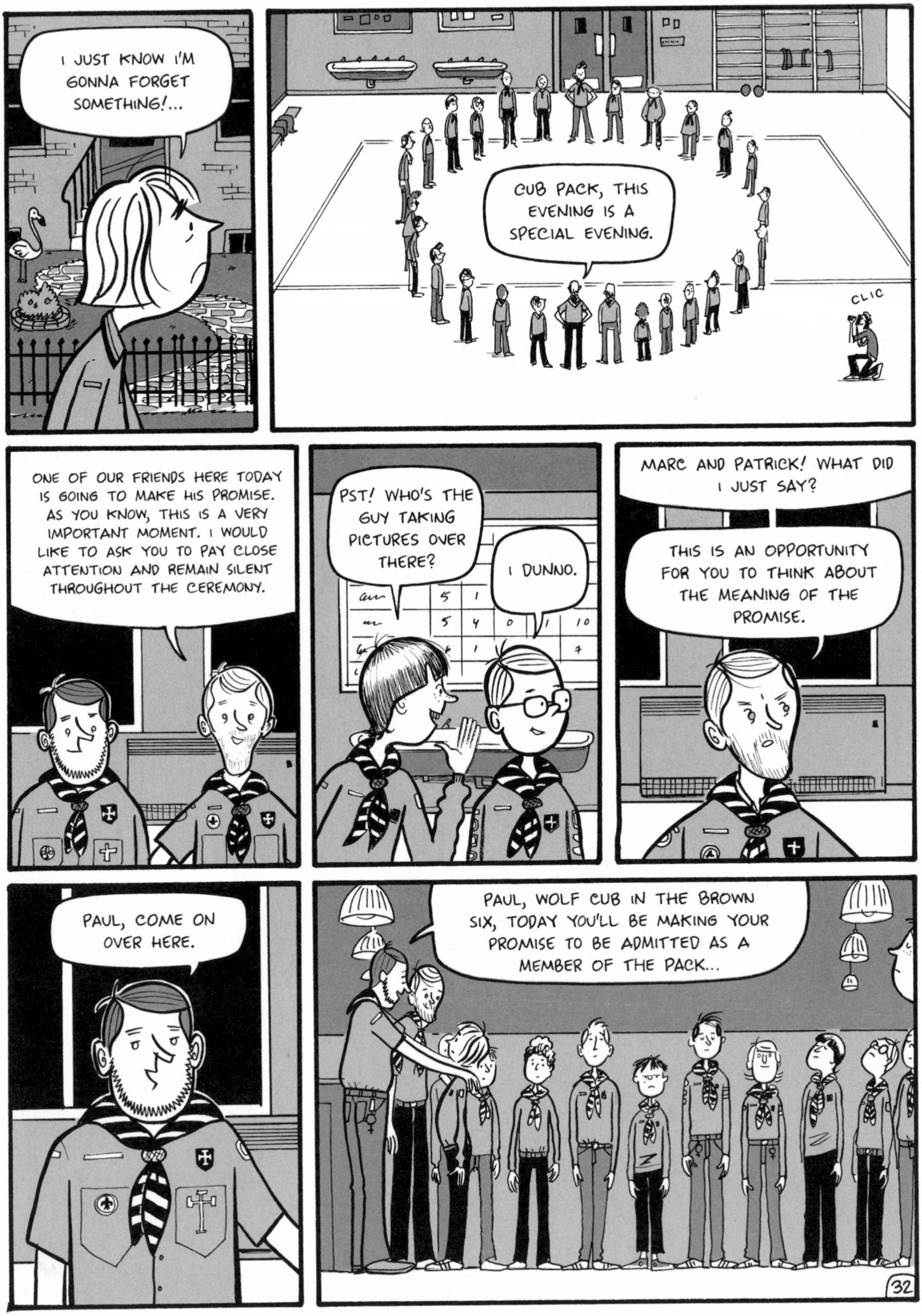
I JUST KNOW I'M GONNA FORGET SOMETHING!...
CUB PACK, THIS EVENING IS A SPECIAL EVENING.
CLIC
ONE OF OUR FRIENDS HERE TODAY IS GOING TO MAKE HIS PROMISE. AS YOU KNOW, THIS IS A VERY IMPORTANT MOMENT. I WOULD LIKE TO ASK YOU TO PAY CLOSE ATTENTION AND REMAIN SILENT THROUGHOUT THE CEREMONY.
PST! WHO'S THE GUY TAKING PICTURES OVER THERE?
I DUNNO.
MARC AND PATRICK! WHAT DID I JUST SAY?
THIS IS AN OPPORTUNITY FOR YOU TO THINK ABOUT THE MEANING OF THE PROMISE.
PAUL, COME ON OVER HERE.
PAUL, WOLF CUB IN THE BROWN SIX, TODAY YOU'LL BE MAKING YOUR PROMISE TO BE ADMITTED AS A MEMBER OF THE PACK...
32

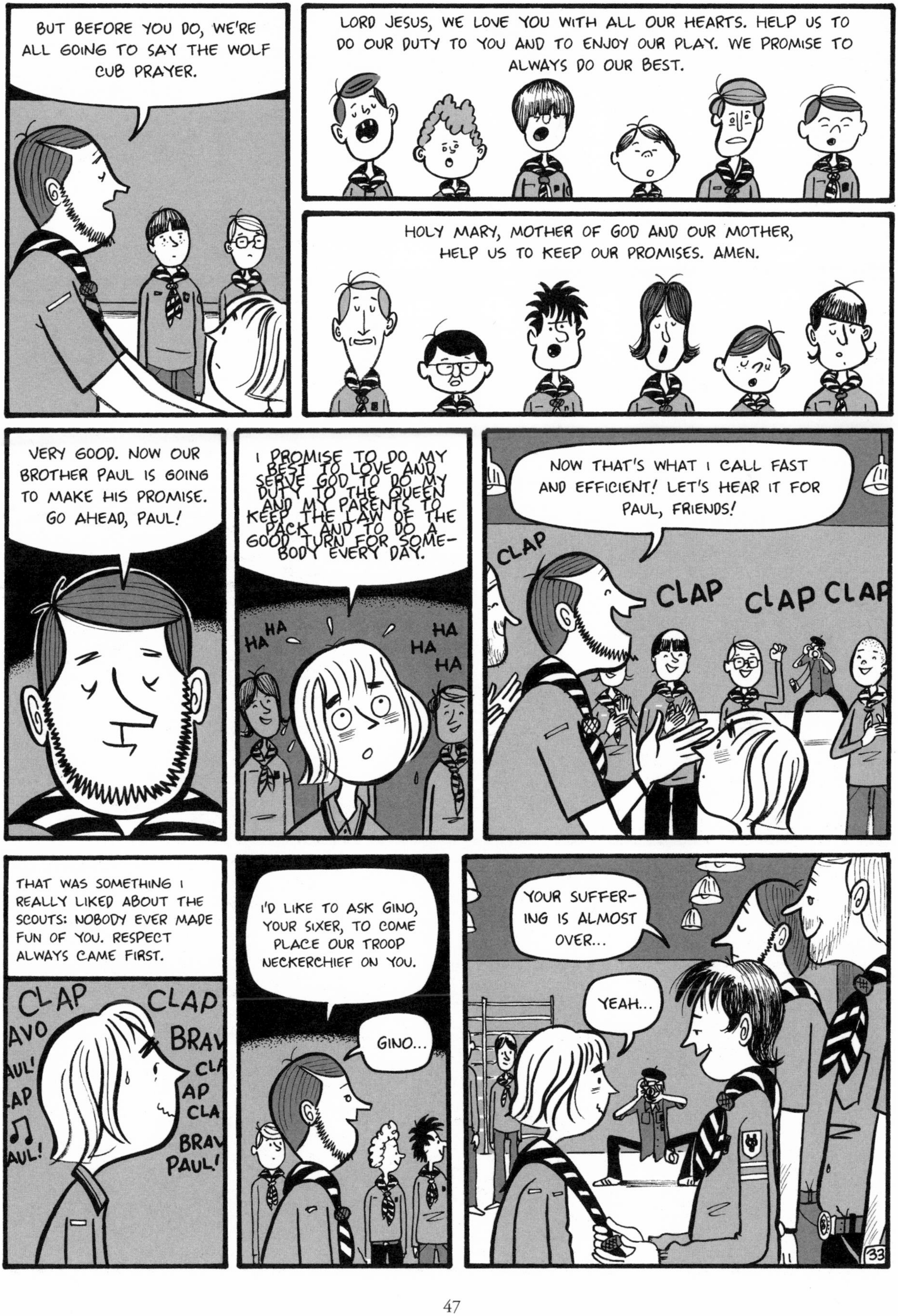
BUT BEFORE YOU DO, WE'RE ALL GOING TO SAY THE WOLF CUB PRAYER.
LORD JESUS, WE LOVE YOU WITH ALL OUR HEARTS. HELP US TO DO OUR DUTY TO YOU AND TO ENJOY OUR PLAY. WE PROMISE TO ALWAYS DO OUR BEST.
HOLY MARY, MOTHER OF GOD AND OUR MOTHER, HELP US TO KEEP OUR PROMISES. AMEN.
VERY GOOD. NOW OUR BROTHER PAUL IS GOING TO MAKE HIS PROMISE. GO AHEAD, PAUL!
I PROMISE TO DO MY BEST TO LOVE AND SERVE GOD TO DO MY DUTY TO THE QUEEN AND MY PARENTS TO KEEP THE LAW OF THE PACK AND TO DO A GOOD TURN FOR SOME-BODY EVERY DAY.
HA HA
HA HA HA
NOW THAT'S WHAT I CALL FAST AND EFFICIENT! LET'S HEAR IT FOR PAUL, FRIENDS!
CLAP
CLAP
CLAP CLAP
THAT WAS SOMETHING I REALLY LIKED ABOUT THE SCOUTS: NOBODY EVER MADE FUN OF YOU. RESPECT ALWAYS CAME FIRST.
CLAP
CLAP
BRAV
PAUL!
BRAV
PAUL!
I'D LIKE TO ASK GINO, YOUR SIXER, TO COME PLACE OUR TROOP NECKERCHIEF ON YOU.
GINO...
YOUR SUFFER-ING IS ALMOST OVER...
YEAH...

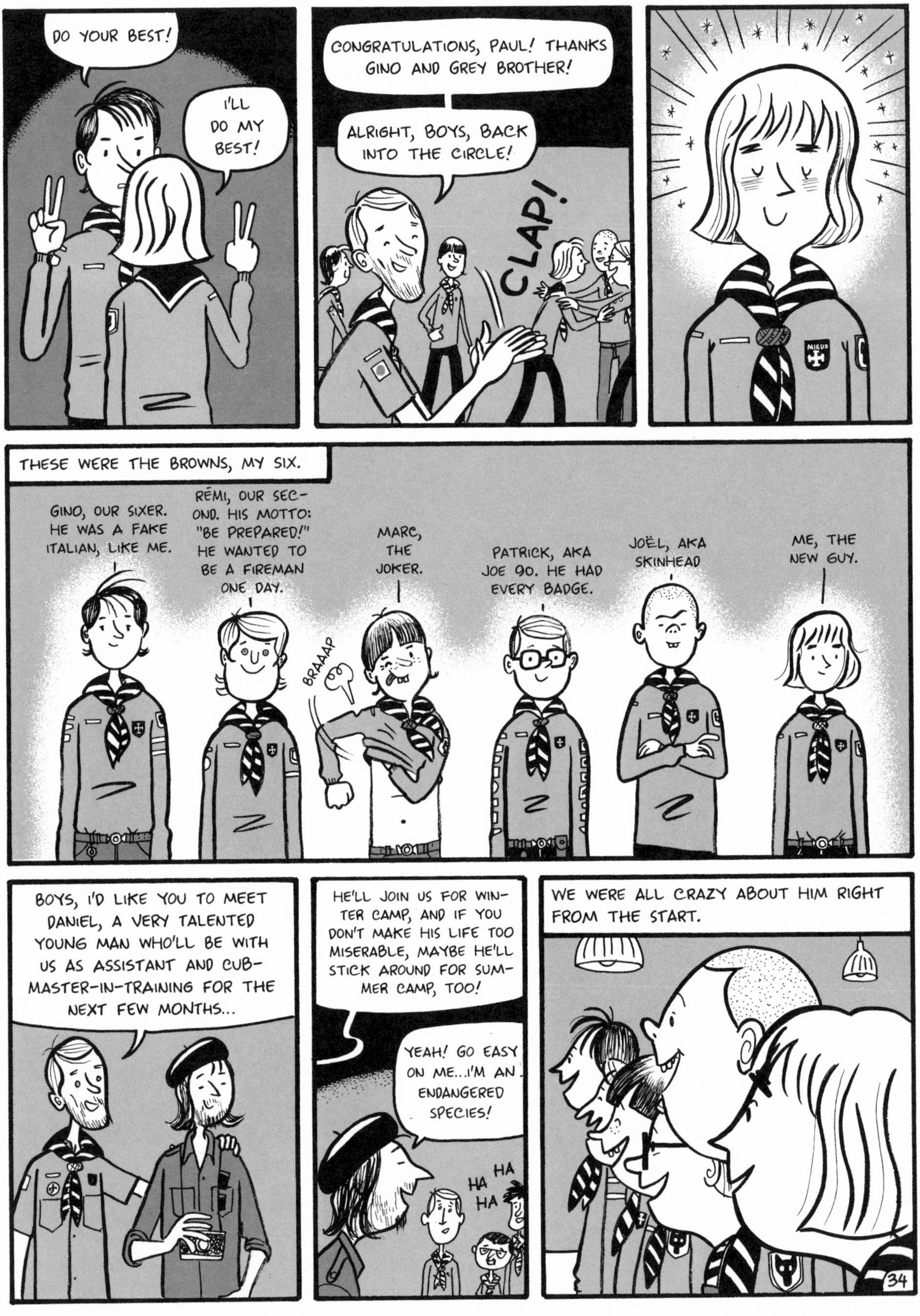
DO YOUR BEST!
I'LL DO MY BEST!
CONGRATULATIONS, PAUL! THANKS GINO AND GREY BROTHER!
ALRIGHT, BOYS, BACK INTO THE CIRCLE!
CLAP!
MIEUX
THESE WERE THE BROWNS, MY SIX.
GINO, OUR SIXER. HE WAS A FAKE ITALIAN, LIKE ME.
RÉMI, OUR SECOND. HIS MOTTO: "BE PREPARED!" HE WANTED TO BE A FIREMAN ONE DAY.
MARC, THE JOKER.
BRAAAP
PATRICK, AKA JOE 90. HE HAD EVERY BADGE.
JOËL, AKA SKINHEAD
ME, THE NEW GUY.
BOYS, I'D LIKE YOU TO MEET DANIEL, A VERY TALENTED YOUNG MAN WHO'LL BE WITH US AS ASSISTANT AND CUB-MASTER-IN-TRAINING FOR THE NEXT FEW MONTHS...
HE'LL JOIN US FOR WINTER CAMP, AND IF YOU DON'T MAKE HIS LIFE TOO MISERABLE, MAYBE HE'LL STICK AROUND FOR SUMMER CAMP, TOO!
YEAH! GO EASY ON ME...I'M AN ENDANGERED SPECIES!
HA HA HA
WE WERE ALL CRAZY ABOUT HIM RIGHT FROM THE START.
34

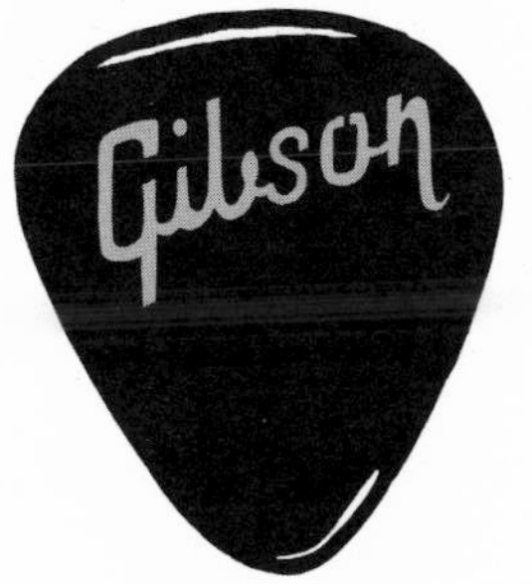
Gibson

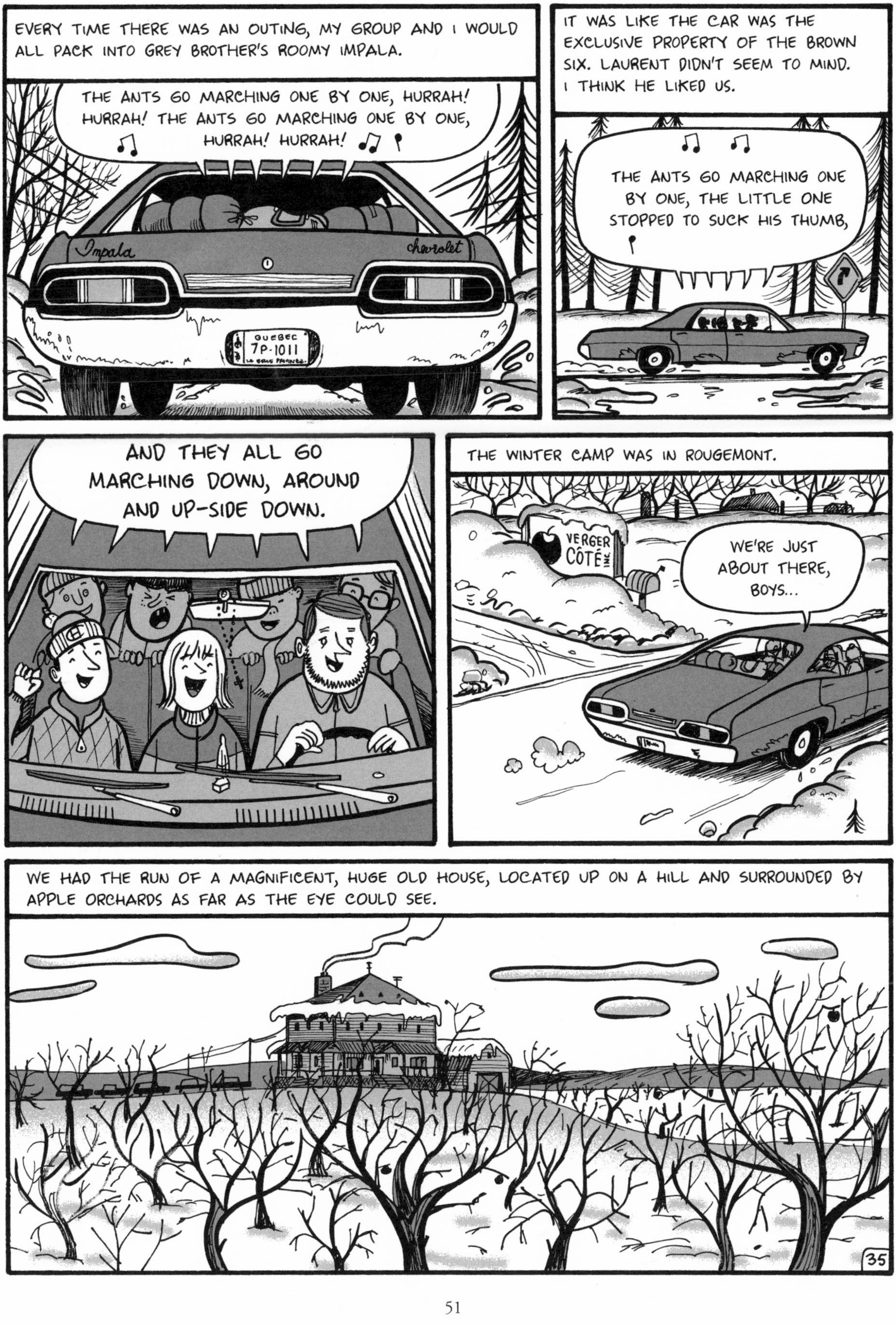
EVERY TIME THERE WAS AN OUTING, MY GROUP AND I WOULD ALL PACK INTO GREY BROTHER'S ROOMY IMPALA.
THE ANTS GO MARCHING ONE BY ONE, HURRAH! HURRAH! THE ANTS GO MARCHING ONE BY ONE, HURRAH! HURRAH!
Impala
Chevrolet
QUEBEC
7P-1011
IT WAS LIKE THE CAR WAS THE EXCLUSIVE PROPERTY OF THE BROWN SIX. LAURENT DIDN'T SEEM TO MIND. I THINK HE LIKED US.
THE ANTS GO MARCHING ONE BY ONE, THE LITTLE ONE STOPPED TO SUCK HIS THUMB,
AND THEY ALL GO MARCHING DOWN, AROUND AND UP-SIDE DOWN.
THE WINTER CAMP WAS IN ROUGEMONT.
VERGER CÔTÉ INC.
WE'RE JUST ABOUT THERE, BOYS...
WE HAD THE RUN OF A MAGNIFICENT, HUGE OLD HOUSE, LOCATED UP ON A HILL AND SURROUNDED BY APPLE ORCHARDS AS FAR AS THE EYE COULD SEE.
35

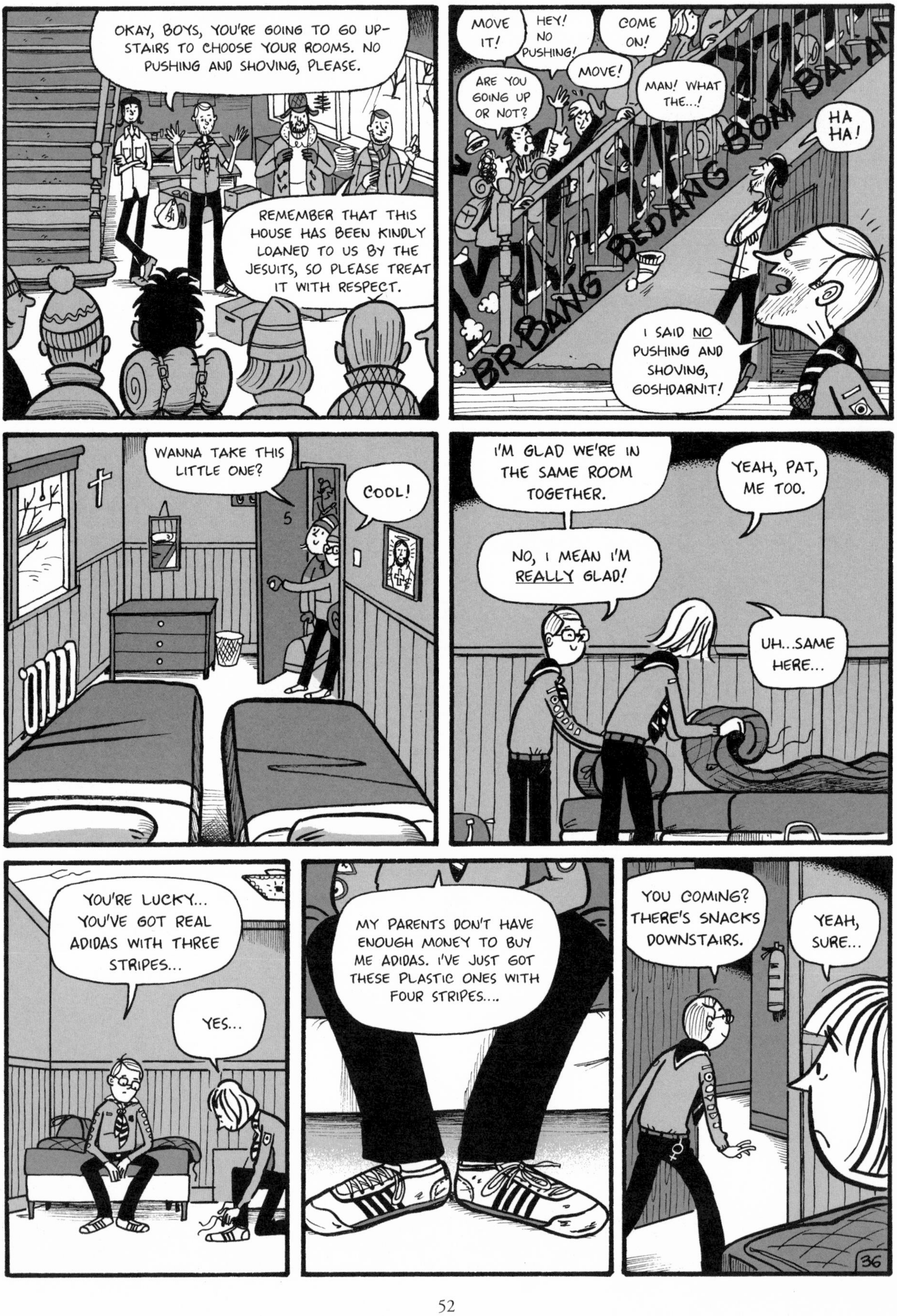
OKAY, BOYS, YOU'RE GOING TO GO UP-STAIRS TO CHOOSE YOUR ROOMS. NO PUSHING AND SHOVING, PLEASE.
REMEMBER THAT THIS HOUSE HAS BEEN KINDLY LOANED TO US BY THE JESUITS, SO PLEASE TREAT IT WITH RESPECT.
MOVE IT!
HEY! NO PUSHING!
COME ON!
ARE YOU GOING UP OR NOT?
MOVE!
MAN! WHAT THE...!
BR DANG BEDANG BOM BALAN
HA HA!
I SAID NO PUSHING AND SHOVING, GOSHDARNIT!
WANNA TAKE THIS LITTLE ONE?
COOL!
5
I'M GLAD WE'RE IN THE SAME ROOM TOGETHER.
YEAH, PAT, ME TOO.
NO, I MEAN I'M REALLY GLAD!
UH...SAME HERE...
YOU'RE LUCKY... YOU'VE GOT REAL ADIDAS WITH THREE STRIPES...
YES...
MY PARENTS DON'T HAVE ENOUGH MONEY TO BUY ME ADIDAS. I'VE JUST GOT THESE PLASTIC ONES WITH FOUR STRIPES....
YOU COMING? THERE'S SNACKS DOWNSTAIRS.
YEAH, SURE...
36

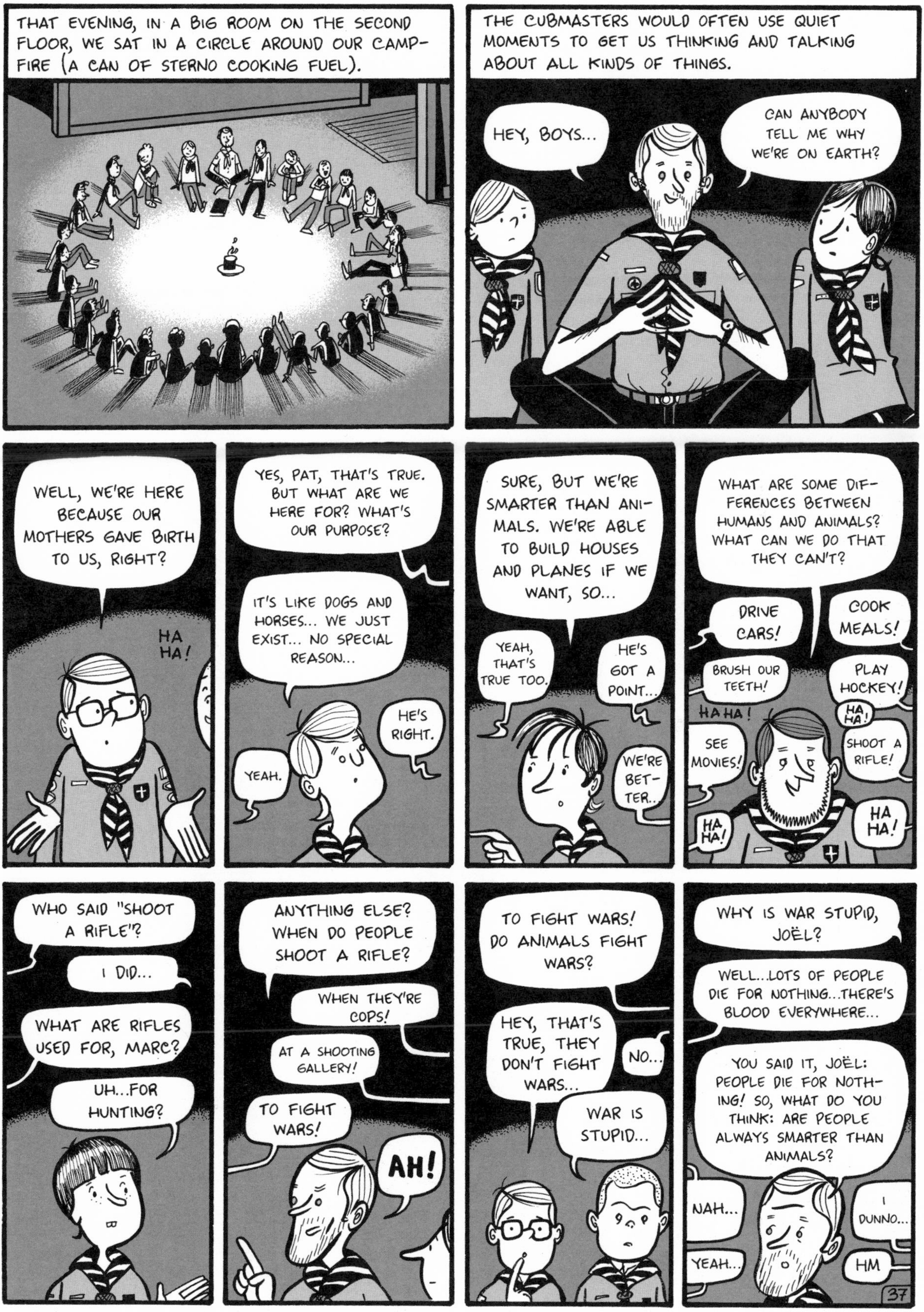

THAT EVENING, IN A BIG ROOM ON THE SECOND FLOOR, WE SAT IN A CIRCLE AROUND OUR CAMPFIRE (A CAN OF STERNO COOKING FUEL).
THE CUBMASTERS WOULD OFTEN USE QUIET MOMENTS TO GET US THINKING AND TALKING ABOUT ALL KINDS OF THINGS.
HEY, BOYS...
CAN ANYBODY TELL ME WHY WE'RE ON EARTH?
WELL, WE'RE HERE BECAUSE OUR MOTHERS GAVE BIRTH TO US, RIGHT?
HA HA!
YES, PAT, THAT'S TRUE. BUT WHAT ARE WE HERE FOR? WHAT'S OUR PURPOSE?
IT'S LIKE DOGS AND HORSES... WE JUST EXIST... NO SPECIAL REASON...
HE'S RIGHT.
YEAH.
SURE, BUT WE'RE SMARTER THAN ANIMALS. WE'RE ABLE TO BUILD HOUSES AND PLANES IF WE WANT, SO...
YEAH, THAT'S TRUE TOO.
HE'S GOT A POINT...
WE'RE BETTER...
WHAT ARE SOME DIFFERENCES BETWEEN HUMANS AND ANIMALS? WHAT CAN WE DO THAT THEY CAN'T?
DRIVE CARS!
COOK MEALS!
BRUSH OUR TEETH!
PLAY HOCKEY!
HA HA!
HA HA!
SEE MOVIES!
SHOOT A RIFLE!
HA HA!
HA HA!
WHO SAID "SHOOT A RIFLE"?
I DID...
WHAT ARE RIFLES USED FOR, MARC?
UH...FOR HUNTING?
ANYTHING ELSE? WHEN DO PEOPLE SHOOT A RIFLE?
WHEN THEY'RE COPS!
AT A SHOOTING GALLERY!
TO FIGHT WARS!
AH!
TO FIGHT WARS! DO ANIMALS FIGHT WARS?
HEY, THAT'S TRUE, THEY DON'T FIGHT WARS...
NO...
WAR IS STUPID...
WHY IS WAR STUPID, JOËL?
WELL...LOTS OF PEOPLE DIE FOR NOTHING...THERE'S BLOOD EVERYWHERE...
YOU SAID IT, JOËL: PEOPLE DIE FOR NOTHING! SO, WHAT DO YOU THINK: ARE PEOPLE ALWAYS SMARTER THAN ANIMALS?
NAH...
I DUNNO...
YEAH...
HM
37

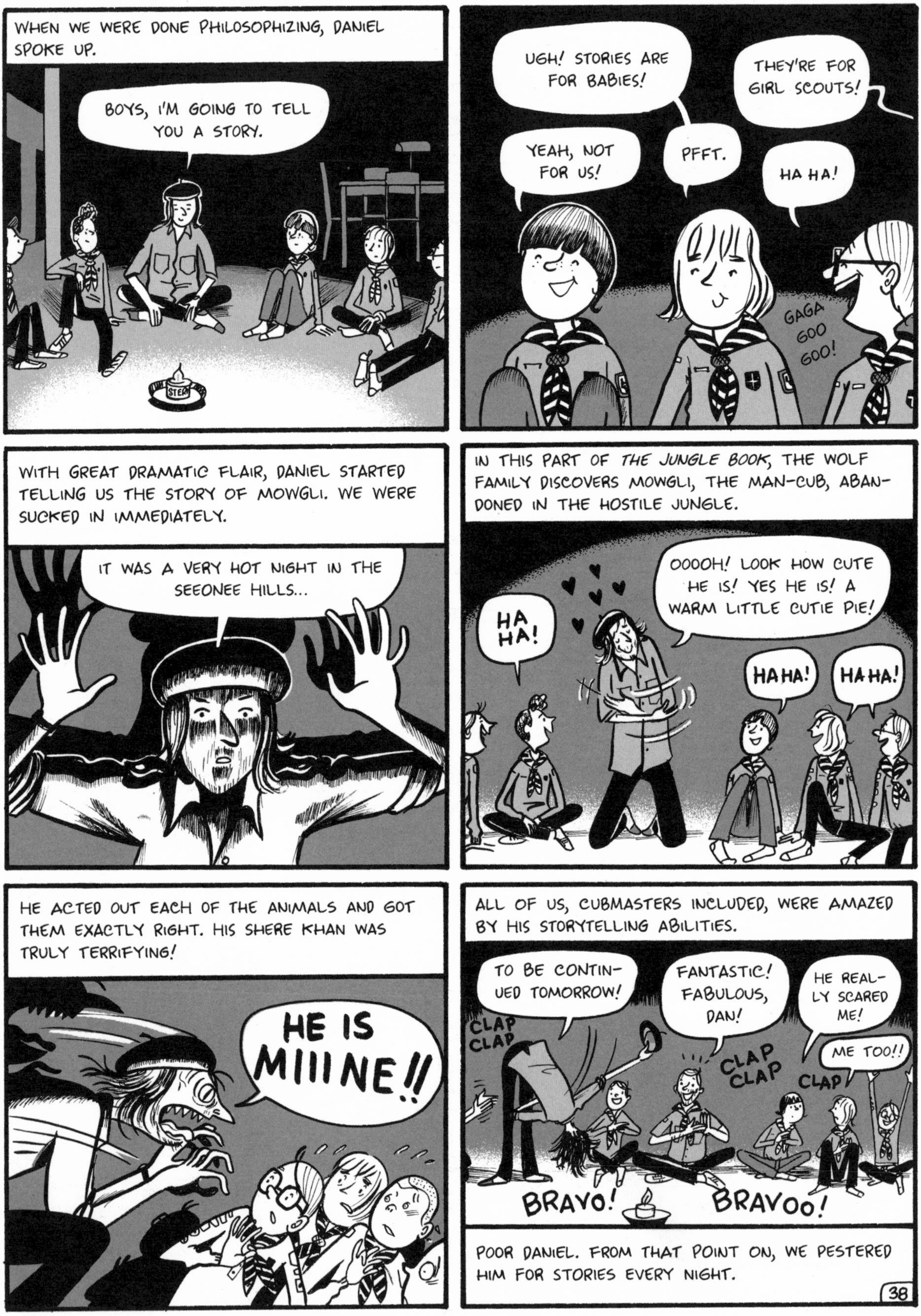

WHEN WE WERE DONE PHILOSOPHIZING, DANIEL SPOKE UP.
BOYS, I'M GOING TO TELL YOU A STORY.
UGH! STORIES ARE FOR BABIES!
THEY'RE FOR GIRL SCOUTS!
YEAH, NOT FOR US!
PFFT.
HA HA!
GAGA GOO GOO!
WITH GREAT DRAMATIC FLAIR, DANIEL STARTED TELLING US THE STORY OF MOWGLI. WE WERE SUCKED IN IMMEDIATELY.
IT WAS A VERY HOT NIGHT IN THE SEEONEE HILLS...
IN THIS PART OF *THE JUNGLE BOOK*, THE WOLF FAMILY DISCOVERS MOWGLI, THE MAN-CUB, ABANDONED IN THE HOSTILE JUNGLE.
HA HA!
OOOOH! LOOK HOW CUTE HE IS! YES HE IS! A WARM LITTLE CUTIE PIE!
HAHA!
HAHA!
HE ACTED OUT EACH OF THE ANIMALS AND GOT THEM EXACTLY RIGHT. HIS SHERE KHAN WAS TRULY TERRIFYING!
HE IS MIIINE!!
ALL OF US, CUBMASTERS INCLUDED, WERE AMAZED BY HIS STORYTELLING ABILITIES.
TO BE CONTINUED TOMORROW!
FANTASTIC! FABULOUS, DAN!
HE REALLY SCARED ME!
CLAP CLAP
CLAP CLAP
CLAP
ME TOO!!
BRAVO!
BRAVOO!
POOR DANIEL. FROM THAT POINT ON, WE PESTERED HIM FOR STORIES EVERY NIGHT.
38

Daniel

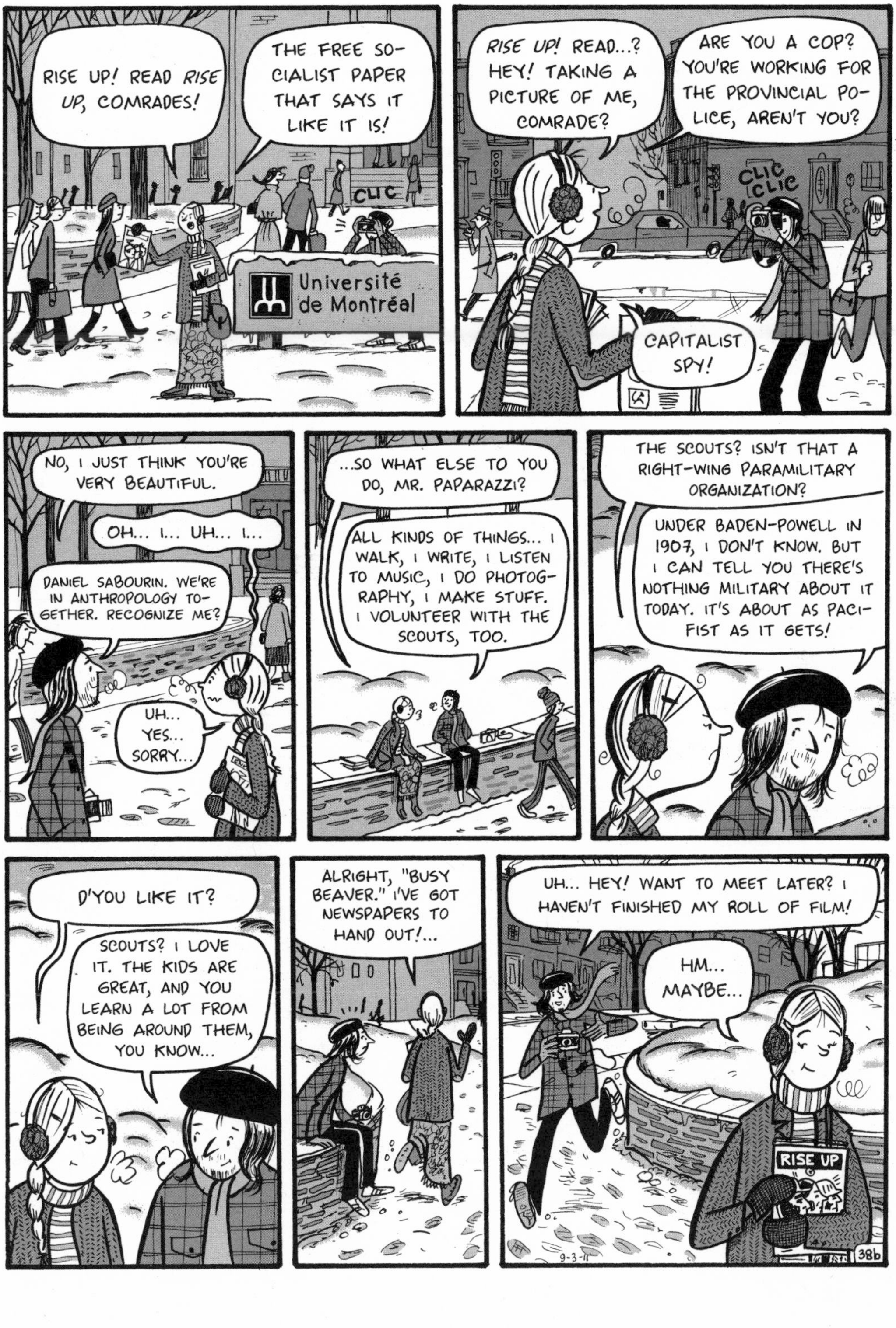

RISE UP! READ *RISE UP*, COMRADES!
THE FREE SOCIALIST PAPER THAT SAYS IT LIKE IT IS!
CLIC
Université de Montréal
RISE UP! READ...? HEY! TAKING A PICTURE OF ME, COMRADE?
ARE YOU A COP? YOU'RE WORKING FOR THE PROVINCIAL POLICE, AREN'T YOU?
CLIC CLIC
CAPITALIST SPY!
NO, I JUST THINK YOU'RE VERY BEAUTIFUL.
OH... I... UH... I...
DANIEL SABOURIN. WE'RE IN ANTHROPOLOGY TOGETHER. RECOGNIZE ME?
UH... YES... SORRY...
...SO WHAT ELSE TO YOU DO, MR. PAPARAZZI?
ALL KINDS OF THINGS... I WALK, I WRITE, I LISTEN TO MUSIC, I DO PHOTOGRAPHY, I MAKE STUFF. I VOLUNTEER WITH THE SCOUTS, TOO.
THE SCOUTS? ISN'T THAT A RIGHT-WING PARAMILITARY ORGANIZATION?
UNDER BADEN-POWELL IN 1907, I DON'T KNOW. BUT I CAN TELL YOU THERE'S NOTHING MILITARY ABOUT IT TODAY. IT'S ABOUT AS PACIFIST AS IT GETS!
D'YOU LIKE IT?
SCOUTS? I LOVE IT. THE KIDS ARE GREAT, AND YOU LEARN A LOT FROM BEING AROUND THEM, YOU KNOW...
ALRIGHT, "BUSY BEAVER." I'VE GOT NEWSPAPERS TO HAND OUT!...
UH... HEY! WANT TO MEET LATER? I HAVEN'T FINISHED MY ROLL OF FILM!
HM... MAYBE...
RISE UP
9-3-11
38b

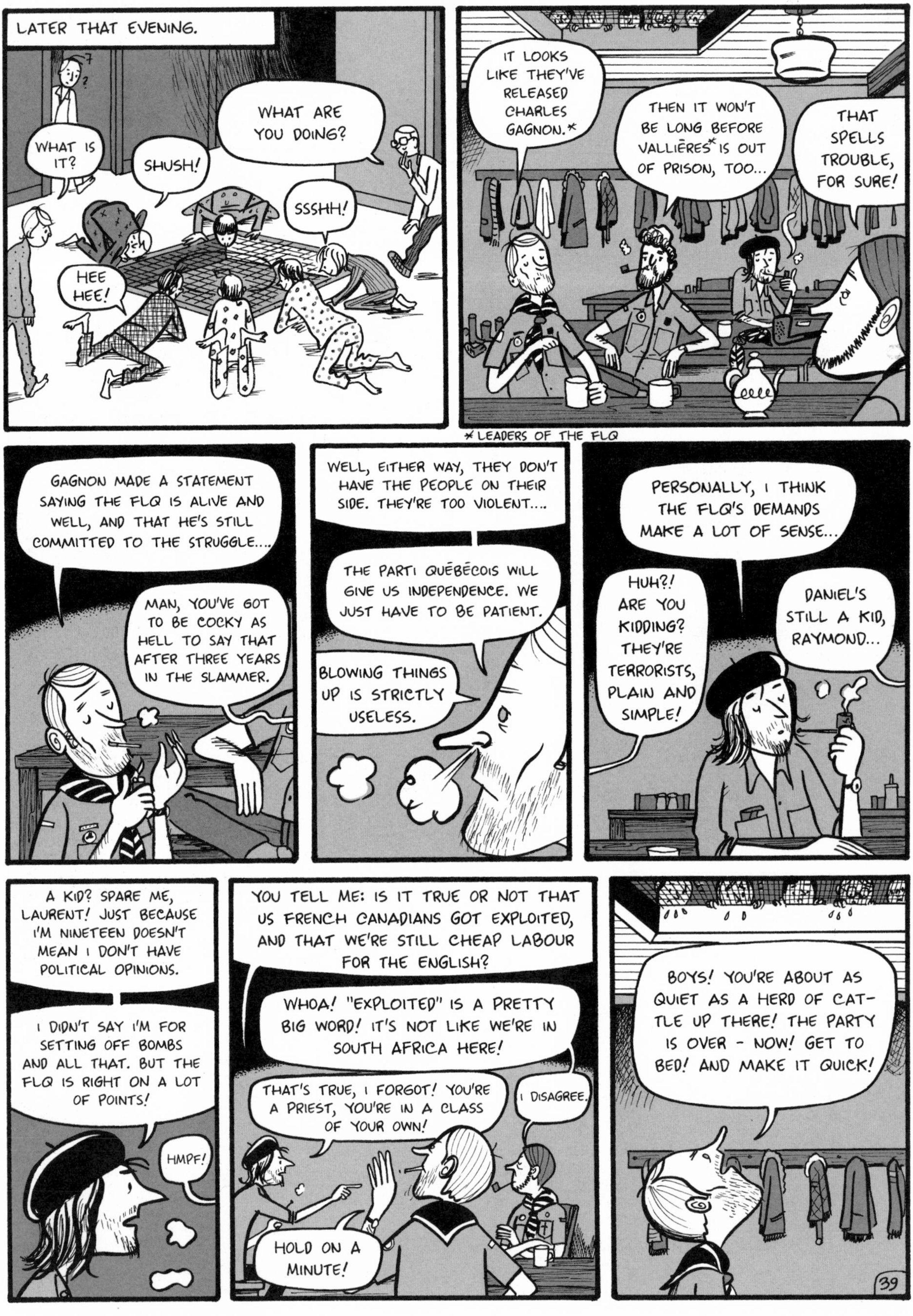

LATER THAT EVENING.
WHAT IS IT?
SHUSH!
WHAT ARE YOU DOING?
SSSHH!
HEE HEE!
IT LOOKS LIKE THEY'VE RELEASED CHARLES GAGNON.*
THEN IT WON'T BE LONG BEFORE VALLIÈRES* IS OUT OF PRISON, TOO...
THAT SPELLS TROUBLE, FOR SURE!
* LEADERS OF THE FLQ
GAGNON MADE A STATEMENT SAYING THE FLQ IS ALIVE AND WELL, AND THAT HE'S STILL COMMITTED TO THE STRUGGLE....
MAN, YOU'VE GOT TO BE COCKY AS HELL TO SAY THAT AFTER THREE YEARS IN THE SLAMMER.
WELL, EITHER WAY, THEY DON'T HAVE THE PEOPLE ON THEIR SIDE. THEY'RE TOO VIOLENT....
THE PARTI QUÉBÉCOIS WILL GIVE US INDEPENDENCE. WE JUST HAVE TO BE PATIENT.
BLOWING THINGS UP IS STRICTLY USELESS.
PERSONALLY, I THINK THE FLQ'S DEMANDS MAKE A LOT OF SENSE...
HUH?! ARE YOU KIDDING? THEY'RE TERRORISTS, PLAIN AND SIMPLE!
DANIEL'S STILL A KID, RAYMOND...
A KID? SPARE ME, LAURENT! JUST BECAUSE I'M NINETEEN DOESN'T MEAN I DON'T HAVE POLITICAL OPINIONS.
I DIDN'T SAY I'M FOR SETTING OFF BOMBS AND ALL THAT. BUT THE FLQ IS RIGHT ON A LOT OF POINTS!
HMPF!
YOU TELL ME: IS IT TRUE OR NOT THAT US FRENCH CANADIANS GOT EXPLOITED, AND THAT WE'RE STILL CHEAP LABOUR FOR THE ENGLISH?
WHOA! "EXPLOITED" IS A PRETTY BIG WORD! IT'S NOT LIKE WE'RE IN SOUTH AFRICA HERE!
THAT'S TRUE, I FORGOT! YOU'RE A PRIEST, YOU'RE IN A CLASS OF YOUR OWN!
I DISAGREE.
HOLD ON A MINUTE!
BOYS! YOU'RE ABOUT AS QUIET AS A HERD OF CAT-TLE UP THERE! THE PARTY IS OVER - NOW! GET TO BED! AND MAKE IT QUICK!
39

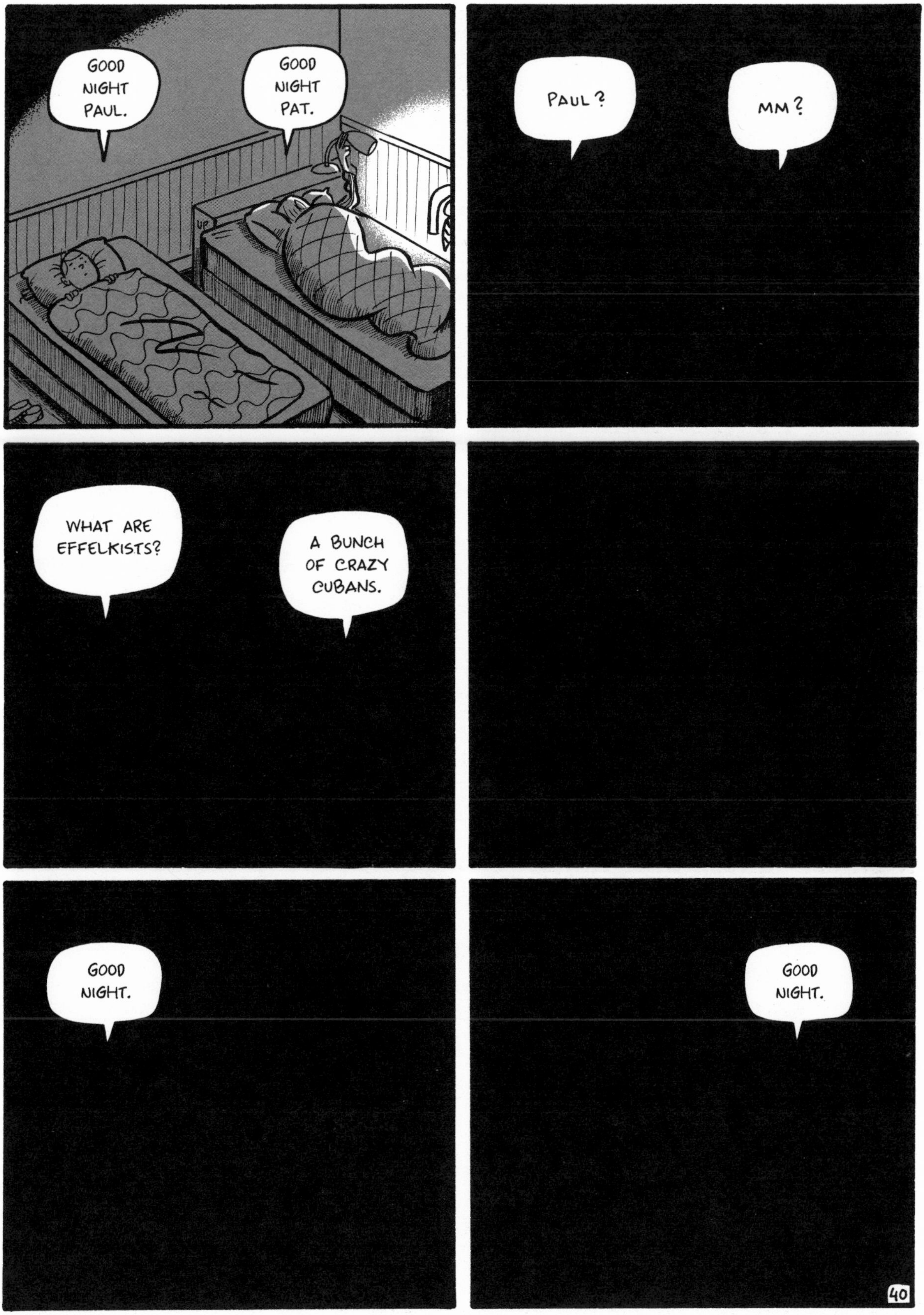
GOOD NIGHT PAUL.
GOOD NIGHT PAT.
PAUL?
MM?
WHAT ARE EFFELKISTS?
A BUNCH OF CRAZY CUBANS.
GOOD NIGHT.
GOOD NIGHT.
40

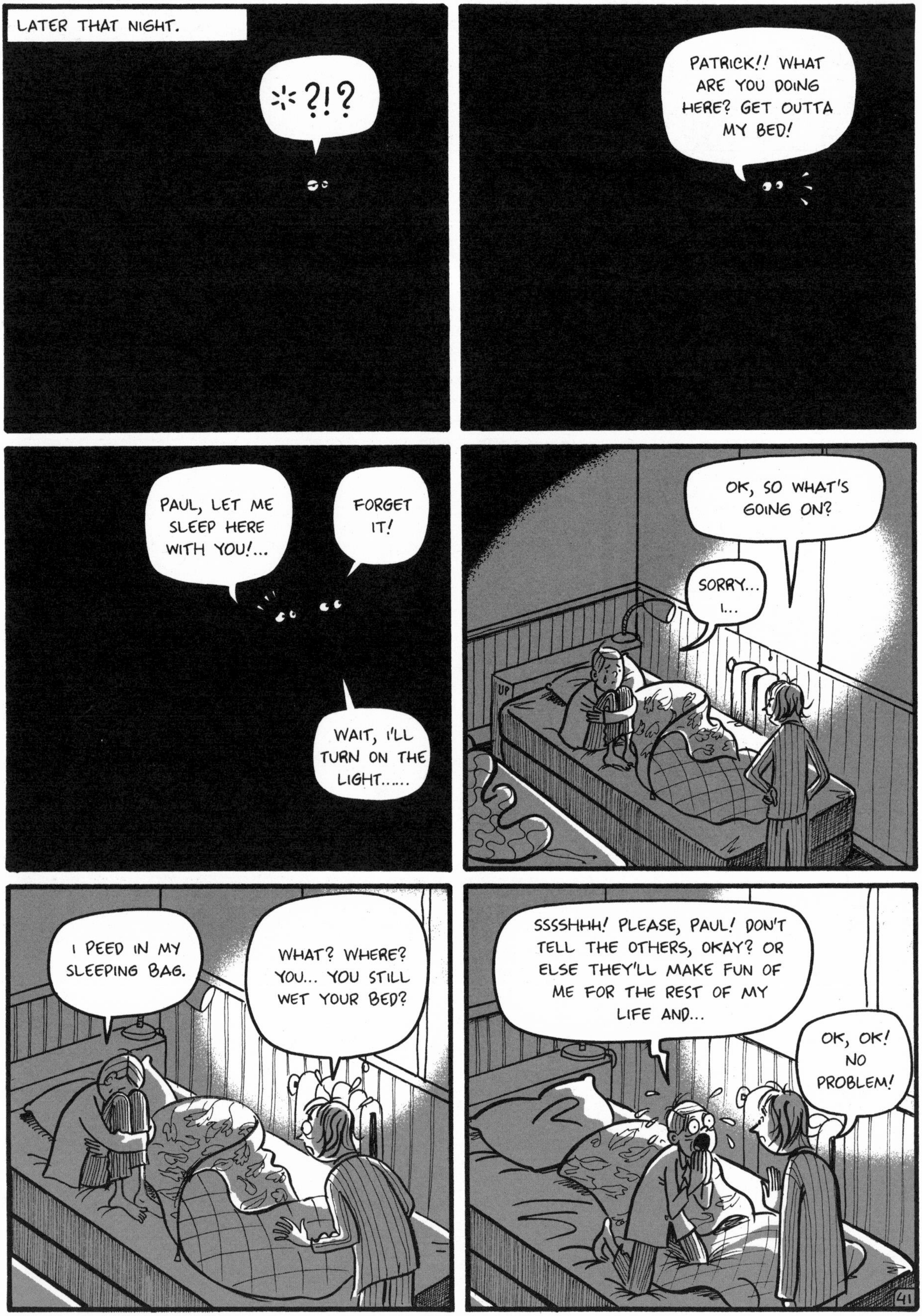
LATER THAT NIGHT.
*?!?
PATRICK!! WHAT ARE YOU DOING HERE? GET OUTTA MY BED!
PAUL, LET ME SLEEP HERE WITH YOU!...
FORGET IT!
WAIT, I'LL TURN ON THE LIGHT......
OK, SO WHAT'S GOING ON?
SORRY... I...
UP
I PEED IN MY SLEEPING BAG.
WHAT? WHERE? YOU... YOU STILL WET YOUR BED?
SSSSHHH! PLEASE, PAUL! DON'T TELL THE OTHERS, OKAY? OR ELSE THEY'LL MAKE FUN OF ME FOR THE REST OF MY LIFE AND...
OK, OK! NO PROBLEM!
41

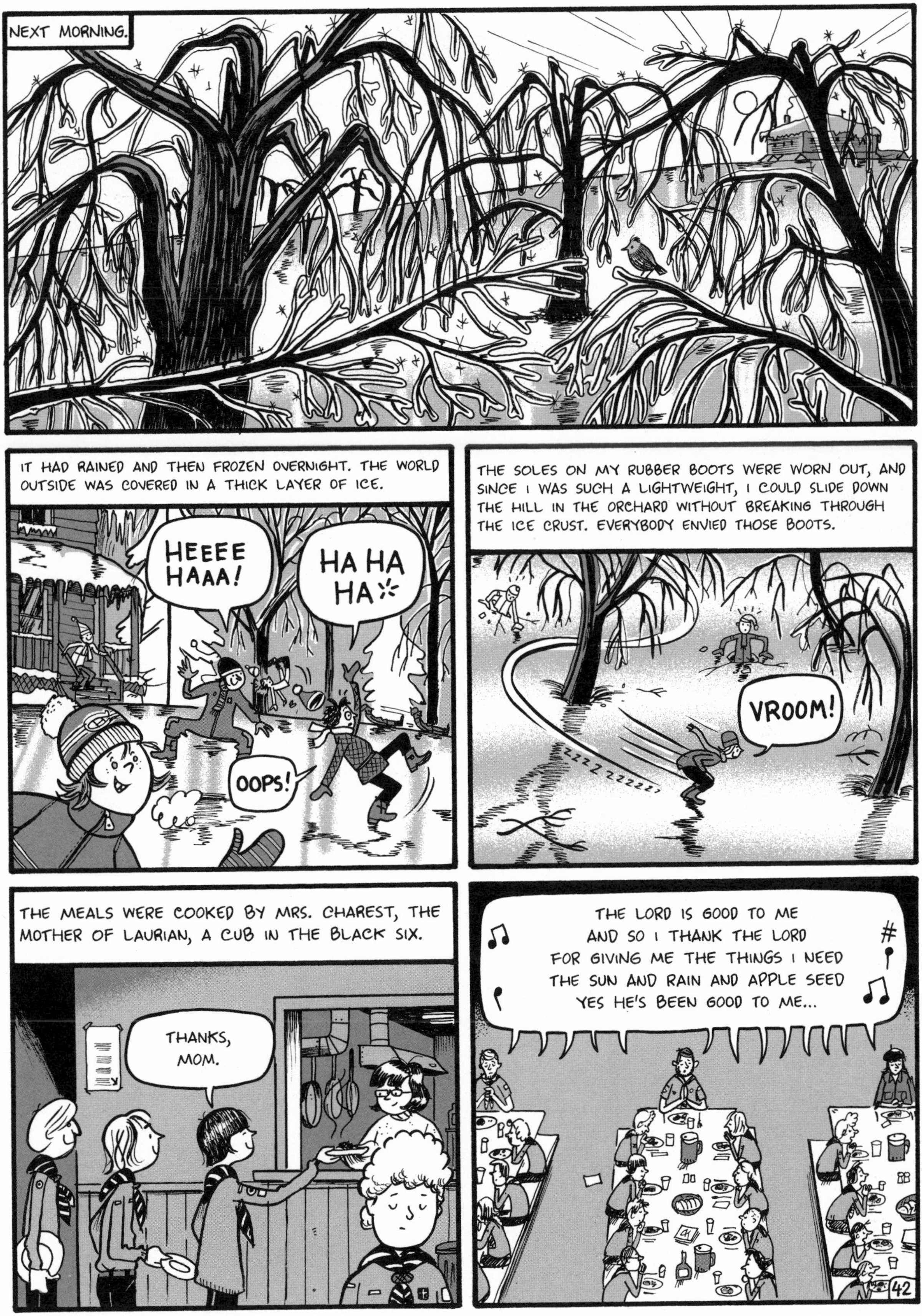
NEXT MORNING.
IT HAD RAINED AND THEN FROZEN OVERNIGHT. THE WORLD OUTSIDE WAS COVERED IN A THICK LAYER OF ICE.
HEEEE HAAA!
HA HA HA
OOPS!
THE SOLES ON MY RUBBER BOOTS WERE WORN OUT, AND SINCE I WAS SUCH A LIGHTWEIGHT, I COULD SLIDE DOWN THE HILL IN THE ORCHARD WITHOUT BREAKING THROUGH THE ICE CRUST. EVERYBODY ENVIED THOSE BOOTS.
VROOM!
THE MEALS WERE COOKED BY MRS. CHAREST, THE MOTHER OF LAURIAN, A CUB IN THE BLACK SIX.
THANKS, MOM.
THE LORD IS GOOD TO ME
AND SO I THANK THE LORD
FOR GIVING ME THE THINGS I NEED
THE SUN AND RAIN AND APPLE SEED
YES HE'S BEEN GOOD TO ME...
42

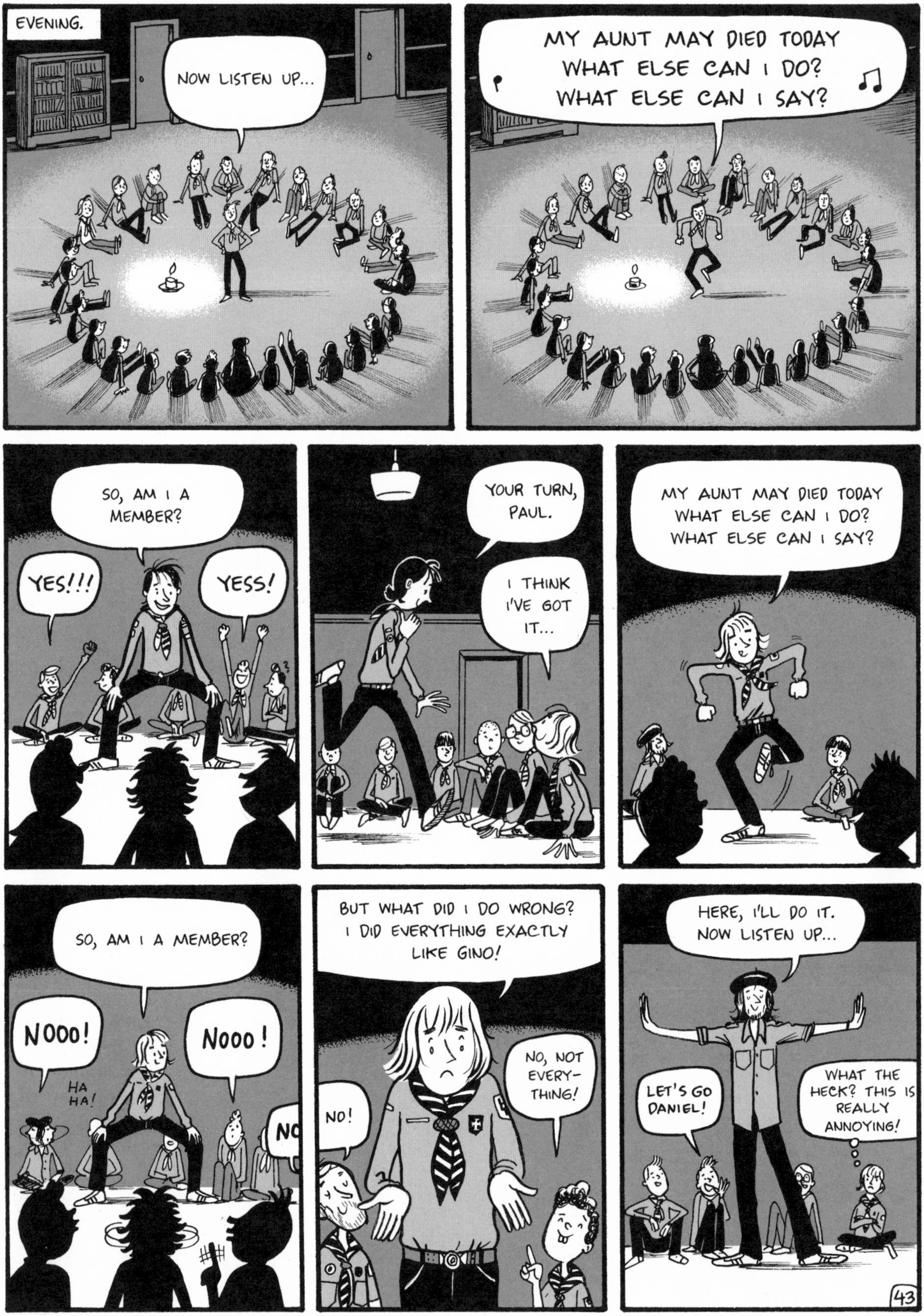

EVENING.
NOW LISTEN UP...
MY AUNT MAY DIED TODAY
WHAT ELSE CAN I DO?
WHAT ELSE CAN I SAY?
SO, AM I A MEMBER?
YES!!!
YESS!
YOUR TURN, PAUL.
I THINK I'VE GOT IT...
MY AUNT MAY DIED TODAY
WHAT ELSE CAN I DO?
WHAT ELSE CAN I SAY?
SO, AM I A MEMBER?
NOOO!
HA HA!
NOOO!
BUT WHAT DID I DO WRONG? I DID EVERYTHING EXACTLY LIKE GINO!
NO!
NO, NOT EVERY-THING!
HERE, I'LL DO IT. NOW LISTEN UP...
LET'S GO DANIEL!
WHAT THE HECK? THIS IS REALLY ANNOYING!
43

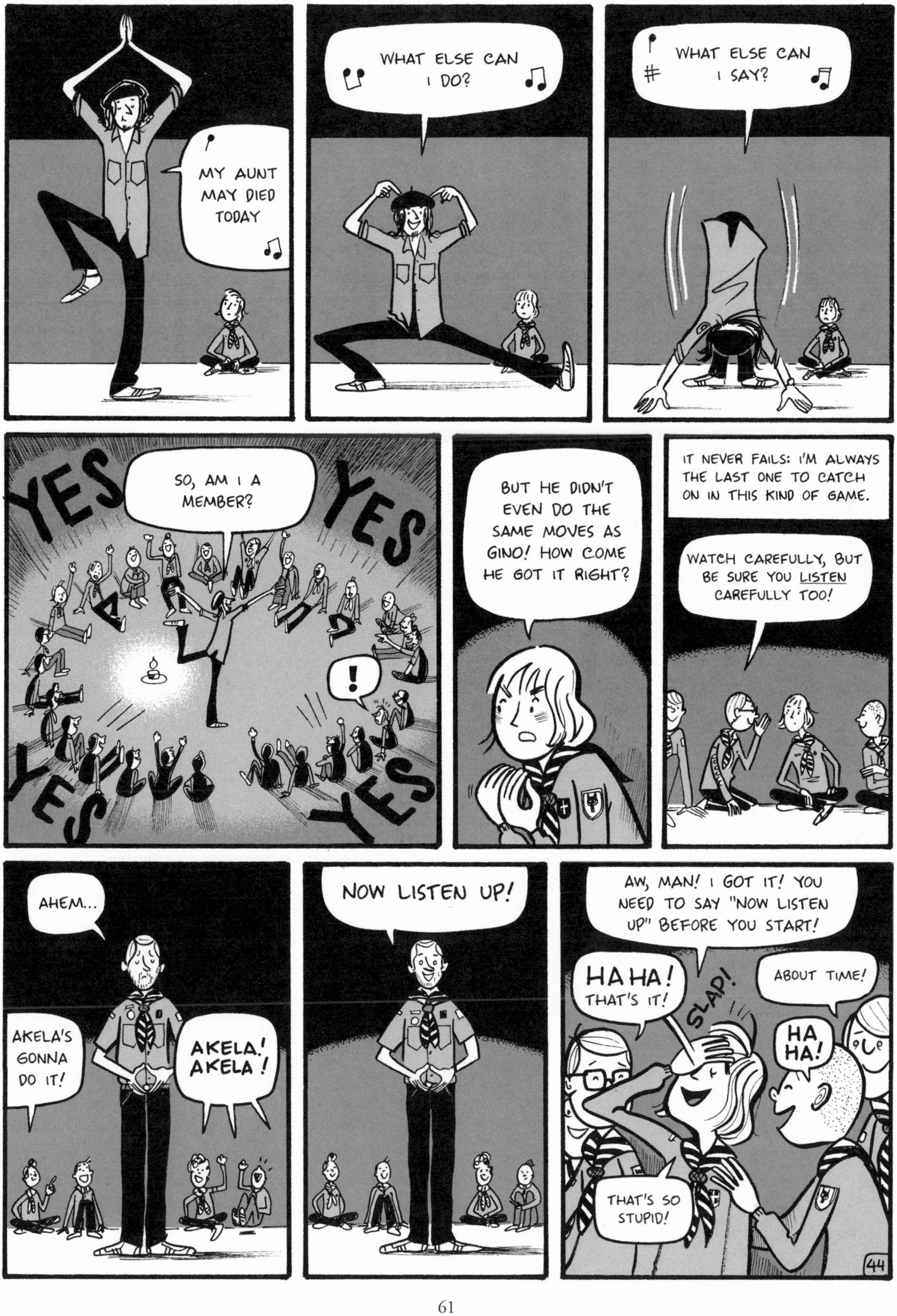
MY AUNT MAY DIED TODAY
WHAT ELSE CAN I DO?
WHAT ELSE CAN I SAY?
SO, AM I A MEMBER?
YES
YES
YES
YES
!
BUT HE DIDN'T EVEN DO THE SAME MOVES AS GINO! HOW COME HE GOT IT RIGHT?
IT NEVER FAILS: I'M ALWAYS THE LAST ONE TO CATCH ON IN THIS KIND OF GAME.
WATCH CAREFULLY, BUT BE SURE YOU LISTEN CAREFULLY TOO!
AHEM...
AKELA'S GONNA DO IT!
AKELA! AKELA!
NOW LISTEN UP!
AW, MAN! I GOT IT! YOU NEED TO SAY "NOW LISTEN UP" BEFORE YOU START!
HA HA! THAT'S IT!
SLAP!
ABOUT TIME!
HA HA!
THAT'S SO STUPID!
44

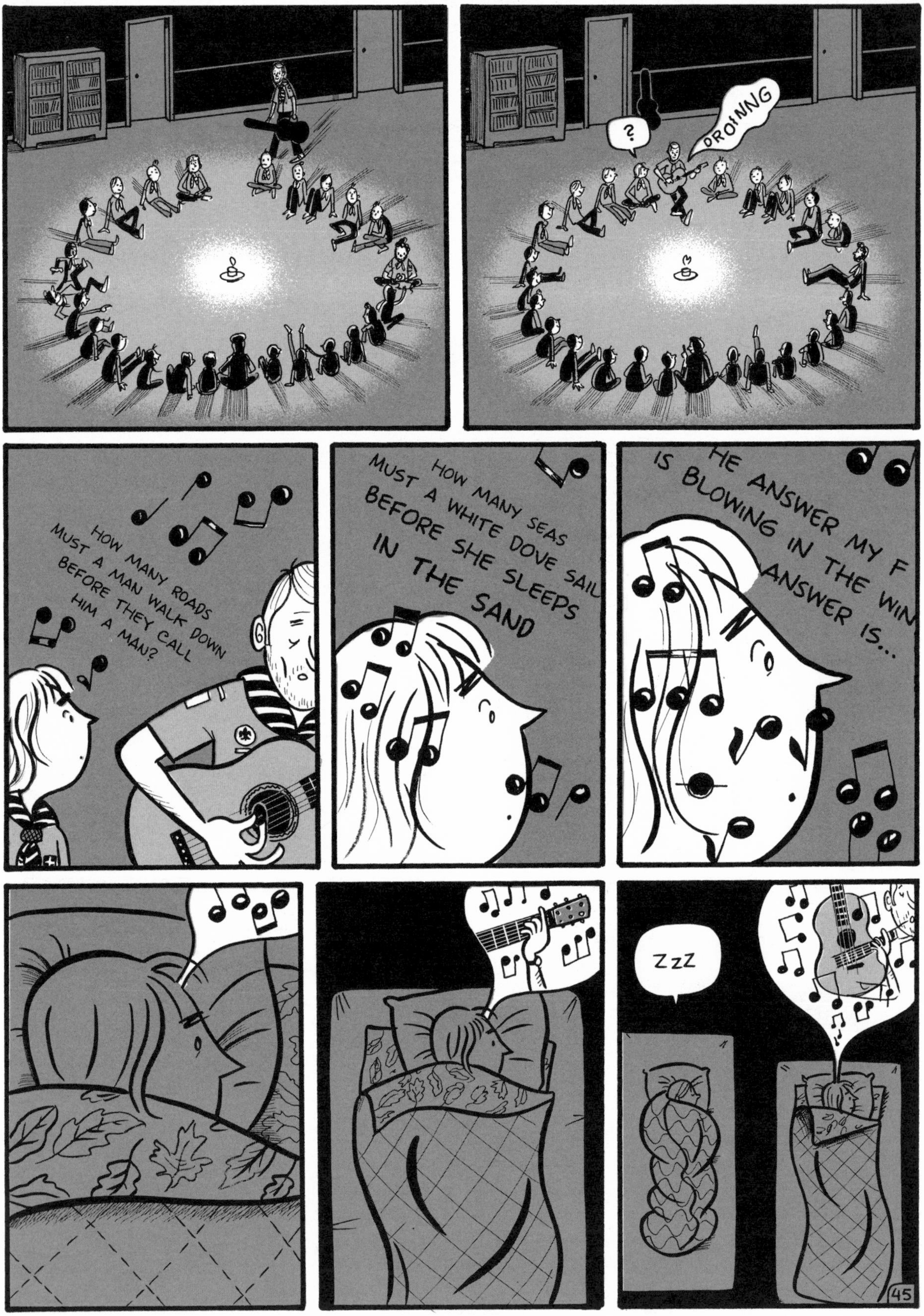
?
DROING
HOW MANY ROADS MUST A MAN WALK DOWN BEFORE THEY CALL HIM A MAN?
HOW MANY SEAS MUST A WHITE DOVE SAIL BEFORE SHE SLEEPS IN THE SAND
HE ANSWER MY F IS BLOWING IN THE WIN ANSWER IS...
ZzZ
45

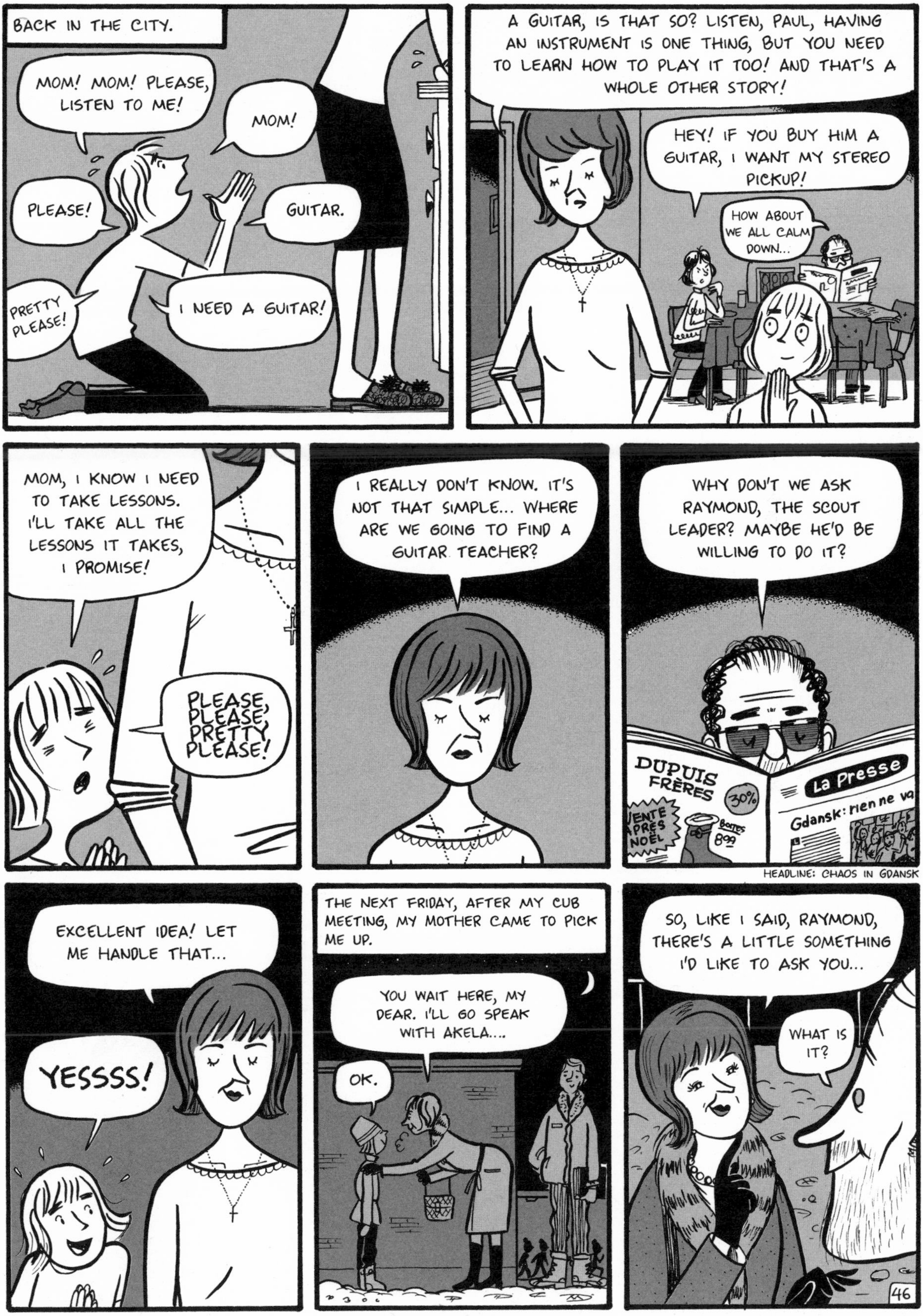
BACK IN THE CITY.
MOM! MOM! PLEASE, LISTEN TO ME!
MOM!
PLEASE!
GUITAR.
PRETTY PLEASE!
I NEED A GUITAR!
A GUITAR, IS THAT SO? LISTEN, PAUL, HAVING AN INSTRUMENT IS ONE THING, BUT YOU NEED TO LEARN HOW TO PLAY IT TOO! AND THAT'S A WHOLE OTHER STORY!
HEY! IF YOU BUY HIM A GUITAR, I WANT MY STEREO PICKUP!
HOW ABOUT WE ALL CALM DOWN...
MOM, I KNOW I NEED TO TAKE LESSONS. I'LL TAKE ALL THE LESSONS IT TAKES, I PROMISE!
PLEASE, PLEASE, PRETTY PLEASE!
I REALLY DON'T KNOW. IT'S NOT THAT SIMPLE... WHERE ARE WE GOING TO FIND A GUITAR TEACHER?
WHY DON'T WE ASK RAYMOND, THE SCOUT LEADER? MAYBE HE'D BE WILLING TO DO IT?
DUPUIS FRÈRES
30%
VENTE APRÈS NOËL
8.99
La Presse
Gdansk: rien ne va
HEADLINE: CHAOS IN GDANSK
EXCELLENT IDEA! LET ME HANDLE THAT...
YESSSS!
THE NEXT FRIDAY, AFTER MY CUB MEETING, MY MOTHER CAME TO PICK ME UP.
YOU WAIT HERE, MY DEAR. I'LL GO SPEAK WITH AKELA....
OK.
SO, LIKE I SAID, RAYMOND, THERE'S A LITTLE SOMETHING I'D LIKE TO ASK YOU...
WHAT IS IT?
46

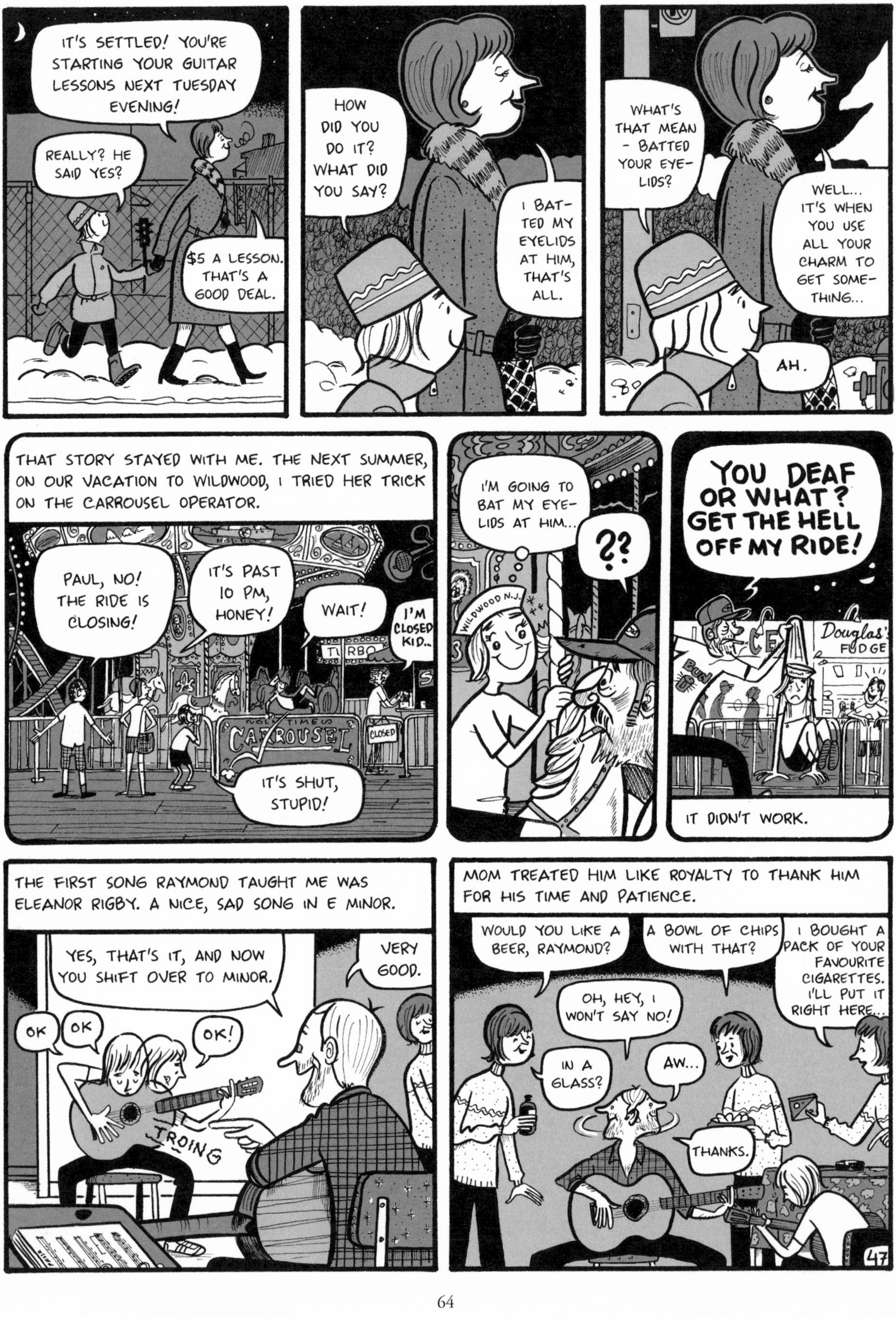
IT'S SETTLED! YOU'RE STARTING YOUR GUITAR LESSONS NEXT TUESDAY EVENING!
REALLY? HE SAID YES?
$5 A LESSON. THAT'S A GOOD DEAL.
HOW DID YOU DO IT? WHAT DID YOU SAY?
I BATTED MY EYELIDS AT HIM, THAT'S ALL.
WHAT'S THAT MEAN - BATTED YOUR EYELIDS?
WELL... IT'S WHEN YOU USE ALL YOUR CHARM TO GET SOMETHING...
AH.
THAT STORY STAYED WITH ME. THE NEXT SUMMER, ON OUR VACATION TO WILDWOOD, I TRIED HER TRICK ON THE CARROUSEL OPERATOR.
PAUL, NO! THE RIDE IS CLOSING!
IT'S PAST 10 PM, HONEY!
WAIT!
I'M CLOSED KID...
TURBO
CARROUSEL
CLOSED
IT'S SHUT, STUPID!
I'M GOING TO BAT MY EYELIDS AT HIM...
WILDWOOD N.J.
??
YOU DEAF OR WHAT? GET THE HELL OFF MY RIDE!
Douglas' FUDGE
IT DIDN'T WORK.
THE FIRST SONG RAYMOND TAUGHT ME WAS ELEANOR RIGBY. A NICE, SAD SONG IN E MINOR.
YES, THAT'S IT, AND NOW YOU SHIFT OVER TO MINOR.
VERY GOOD.
OK
OK
OK!
TROING
MOM TREATED HIM LIKE ROYALTY TO THANK HIM FOR HIS TIME AND PATIENCE.
WOULD YOU LIKE A BEER, RAYMOND?
A BOWL OF CHIPS WITH THAT?
I BOUGHT A PACK OF YOUR FAVOURITE CIGARETTES. I'LL PUT IT RIGHT HERE...
OH, HEY, I WON'T SAY NO!
IN A GLASS?
AW...
THANKS.
47

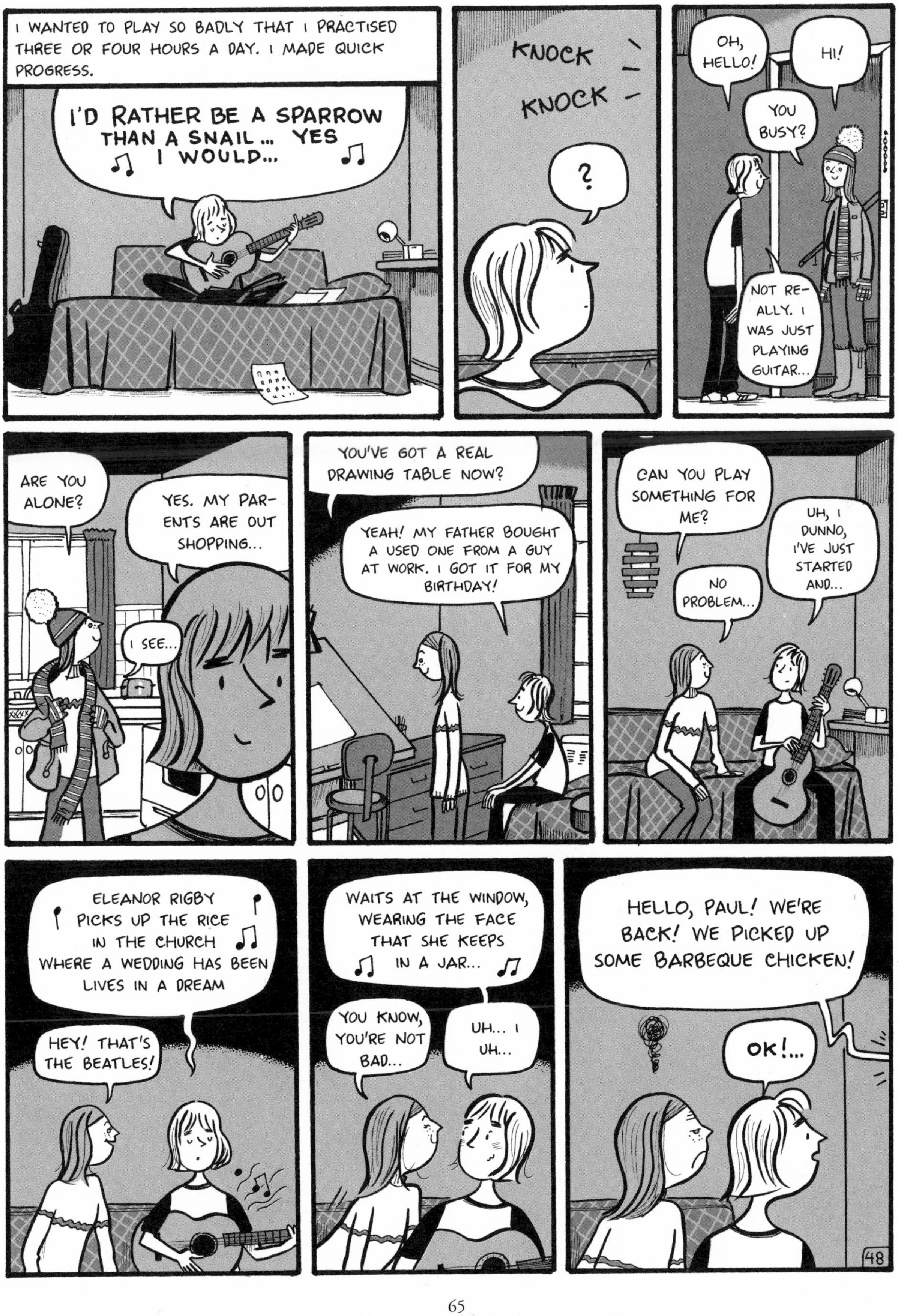
I WANTED TO PLAY SO BADLY THAT I PRACTISED THREE OR FOUR HOURS A DAY. I MADE QUICK PROGRESS.
I'D RATHER BE A SPARROW THAN A SNAIL... YES I WOULD...
KNOCK
KNOCK
?
OH, HELLO!
HI!
YOU BUSY?
NOT REALLY. I WAS JUST PLAYING GUITAR...
ARE YOU ALONE?
YES. MY PARENTS ARE OUT SHOPPING...
I SEE...
YOU'VE GOT A REAL DRAWING TABLE NOW?
YEAH! MY FATHER BOUGHT A USED ONE FROM A GUY AT WORK. I GOT IT FOR MY BIRTHDAY!
CAN YOU PLAY SOMETHING FOR ME?
UH, I DUNNO, I'VE JUST STARTED AND...
NO PROBLEM...
ELEANOR RIGBY PICKS UP THE RICE IN THE CHURCH WHERE A WEDDING HAS BEEN LIVES IN A DREAM
HEY! THAT'S THE BEATLES!
WAITS AT THE WINDOW, WEARING THE FACE THAT SHE KEEPS IN A JAR...
YOU KNOW, YOU'RE NOT BAD...
UH... I UH...
HELLO, PAUL! WE'RE BACK! WE PICKED UP SOME BARBEQUE CHICKEN!
OK!...
48

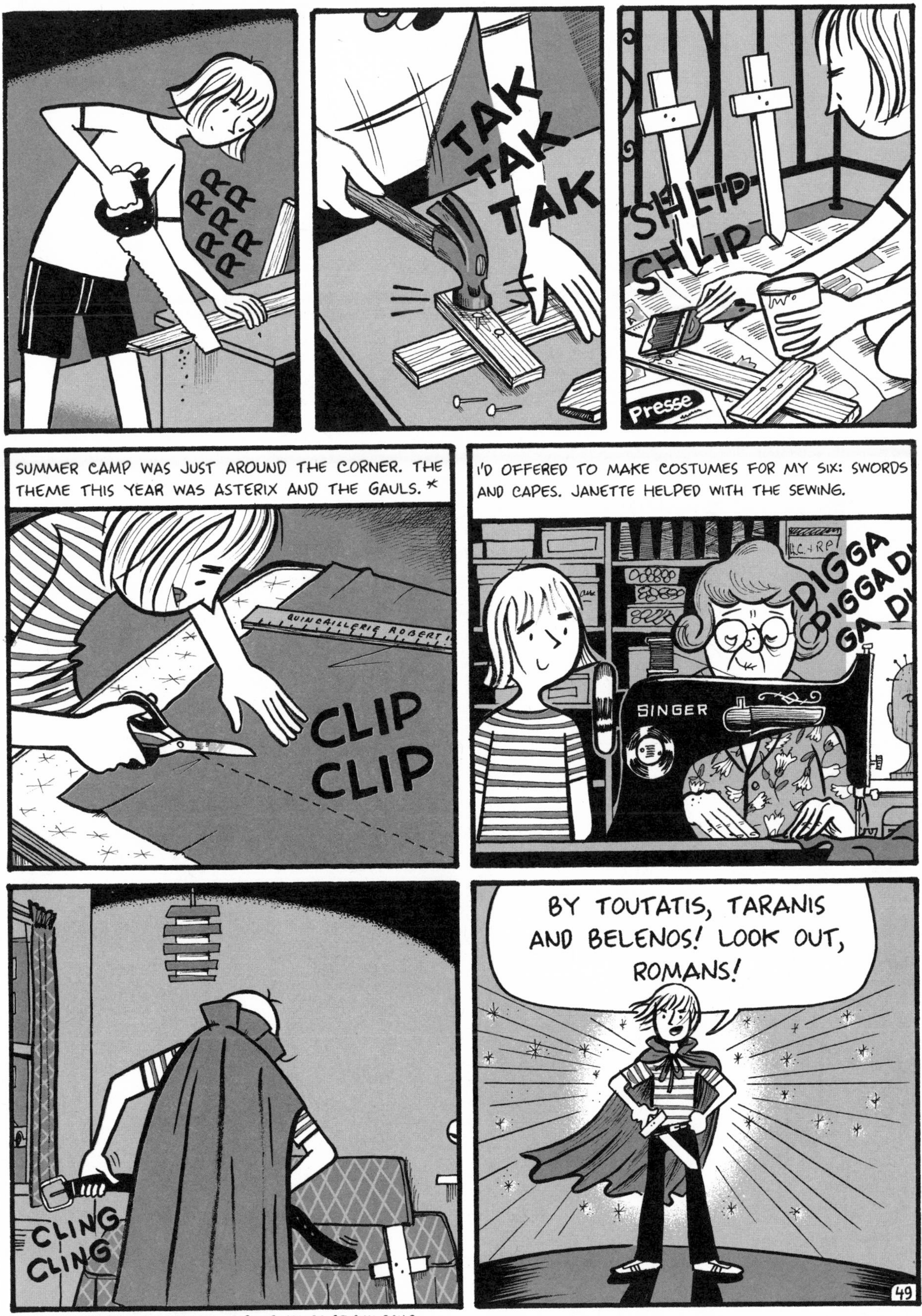
RR RRR RR
TAK TAK TAK
SHLIP SHLIP
Presse
SUMMER CAMP WAS JUST AROUND THE CORNER. THE THEME THIS YEAR WAS ASTERIX AND THE GAULS.*
QUINCAILLERIE ROBERT
CLIP CLIP
I'D OFFERED TO MAKE COSTUMES FOR MY SIX: SWORDS AND CAPES. JANETTE HELPED WITH THE SEWING.
SINGER
DIGGA DIGGA GA
CLING CLING
BY TOUTATIS, TARANIS AND BELENOS! LOOK OUT, ROMANS!
49

* *THE ADVENTURES OF ASTERIX.* THIS POPULAR FRANCO-BELGIAN COMIC SERIES, ORIGINALLY WRITTEN BY RENÉ GOSCINNY AND DRAWN BY ALBERT UDERZO, FOLLOWS THE EXPLOITS OF A VILLAGE OF INDOMITABLE GAULS AS THEY RESIST ROMAN OCCUPATION.

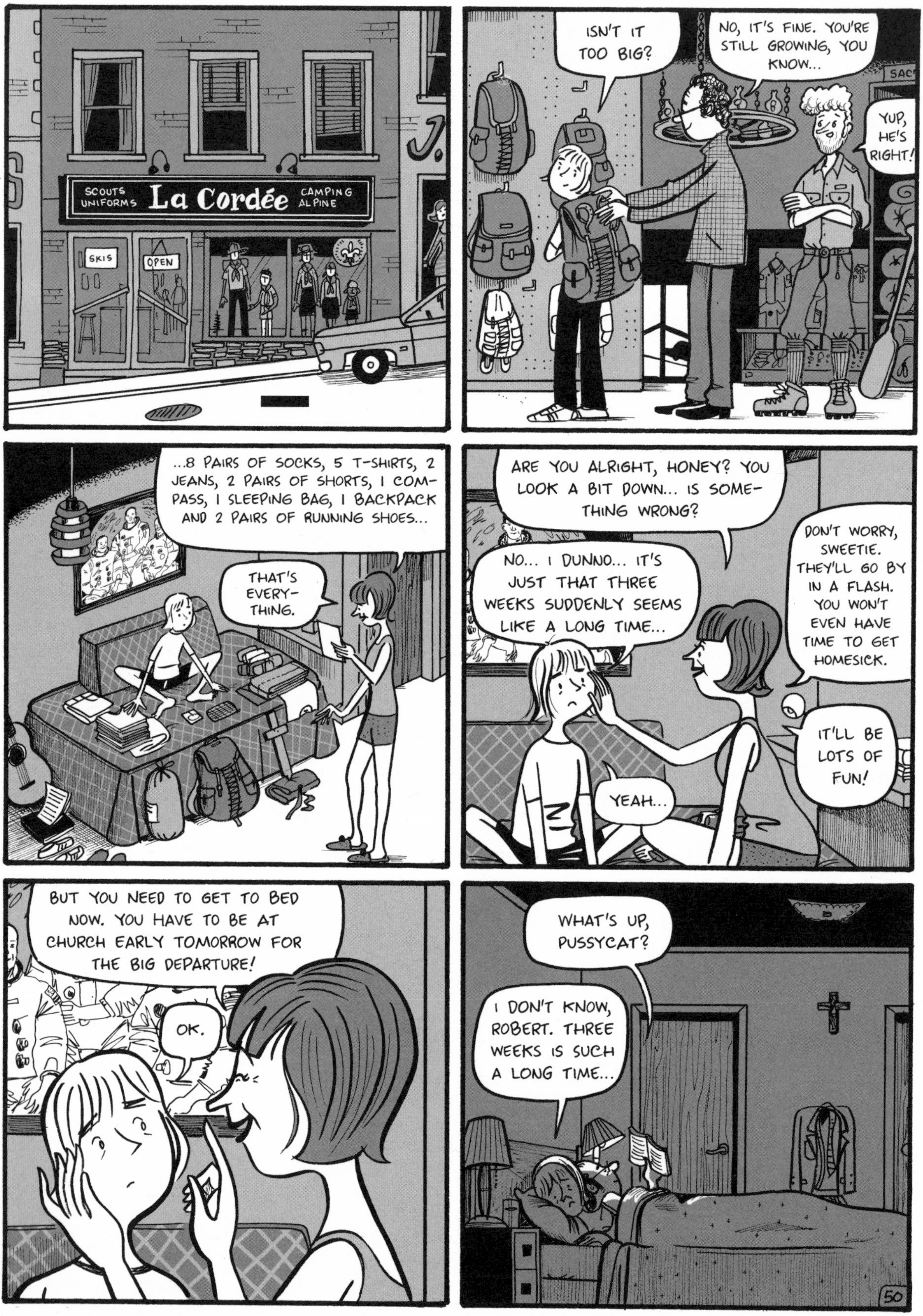
SCOUTS UNIFORMS
La Cordée
CAMPING ALPINE
SKIS
OPEN
ISN'T IT TOO BIG?
NO, IT'S FINE. YOU'RE STILL GROWING, YOU KNOW...
YUP, HE'S RIGHT!
...8 PAIRS OF SOCKS, 5 T-SHIRTS, 2 JEANS, 2 PAIRS OF SHORTS, 1 COMPASS, 1 SLEEPING BAG, 1 BACKPACK AND 2 PAIRS OF RUNNING SHOES...
THAT'S EVERYTHING.
ARE YOU ALRIGHT, HONEY? YOU LOOK A BIT DOWN... IS SOMETHING WRONG?
NO... I DUNNO... IT'S JUST THAT THREE WEEKS SUDDENLY SEEMS LIKE A LONG TIME...
DON'T WORRY, SWEETIE. THEY'LL GO BY IN A FLASH. YOU WON'T EVEN HAVE TIME TO GET HOMESICK.
IT'LL BE LOTS OF FUN!
YEAH...
BUT YOU NEED TO GET TO BED NOW. YOU HAVE TO BE AT CHURCH EARLY TOMORROW FOR THE BIG DEPARTURE!
OK.
WHAT'S UP, PUSSYCAT?
I DON'T KNOW, ROBERT. THREE WEEKS IS SUCH A LONG TIME...
50

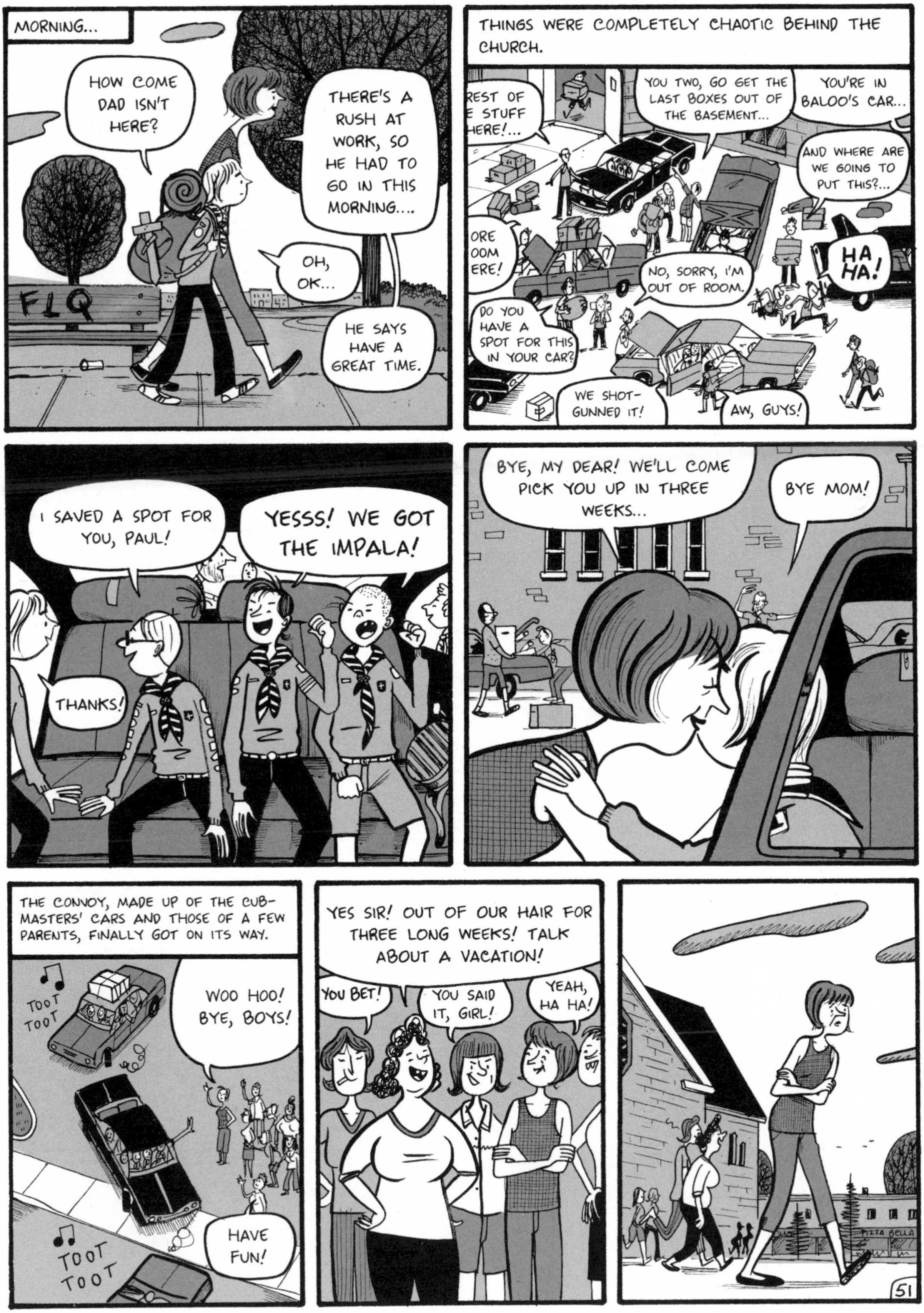

MORNING...
HOW COME DAD ISN'T HERE?
THERE'S A RUSH AT WORK, SO HE HAD TO GO IN THIS MORNING....
OH, OK...
HE SAYS HAVE A GREAT TIME.
FLQ
THINGS WERE COMPLETELY CHAOTIC BEHIND THE CHURCH.
REST OF E STUFF HERE!...
YOU TWO, GO GET THE LAST BOXES OUT OF THE BASEMENT...
YOU'RE IN BALOO'S CAR...
AND WHERE ARE WE GOING TO PUT THIS?...
ORE OOM ERE!
HA HA!
NO, SORRY, I'M OUT OF ROOM.
DO YOU HAVE A SPOT FOR THIS IN YOUR CAR?
WE SHOT-GUNNED IT!
AW, GUYS!
I SAVED A SPOT FOR YOU, PAUL!
YESSS! WE GOT THE IMPALA!
THANKS!
BYE, MY DEAR! WE'LL COME PICK YOU UP IN THREE WEEKS...
BYE MOM!
THE CONVOY, MADE UP OF THE CUB-MASTERS' CARS AND THOSE OF A FEW PARENTS, FINALLY GOT ON ITS WAY.
TOOT TOOT
WOO HOO! BYE, BOYS!
TOOT TOOT
HAVE FUN!
YES SIR! OUT OF OUR HAIR FOR THREE LONG WEEKS! TALK ABOUT A VACATION!
YOU BET!
YOU SAID IT, GIRL!
YEAH, HA HA!
PIZZA BELLA
51

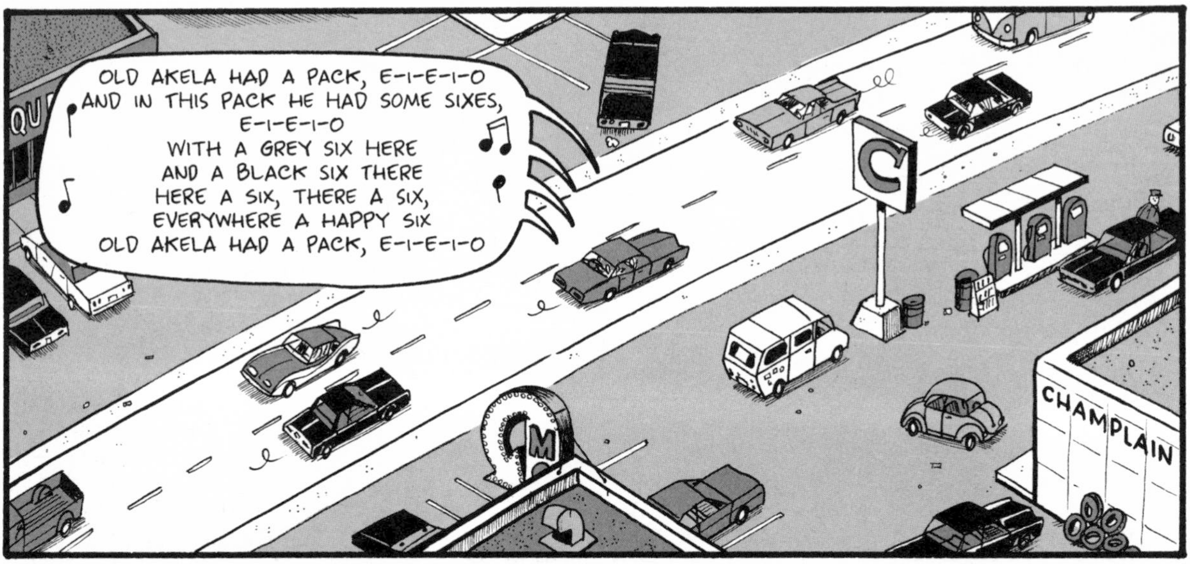
OLD AKELA HAD A PACK, E-I-E-I-O AND IN THIS PACK HE HAD SOME SIXES, E-I-E-I-O WITH A GREY SIX HERE AND A BLACK SIX THERE HERE A SIX, THERE A SIX, EVERYWHERE A HAPPY SIX OLD AKELA HAD A PACK, E-I-E-I-O
CHAMPLAIN

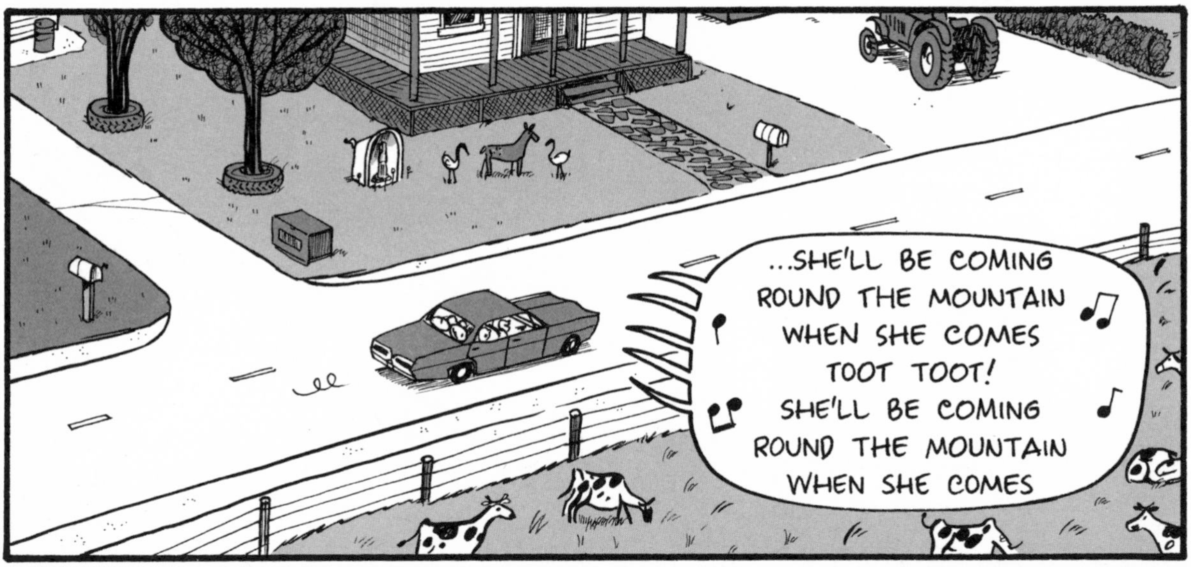
...SHE'LL BE COMING ROUND THE MOUNTAIN WHEN SHE COMES TOOT TOOT! SHE'LL BE COMING ROUND THE MOUNTAIN WHEN SHE COMES

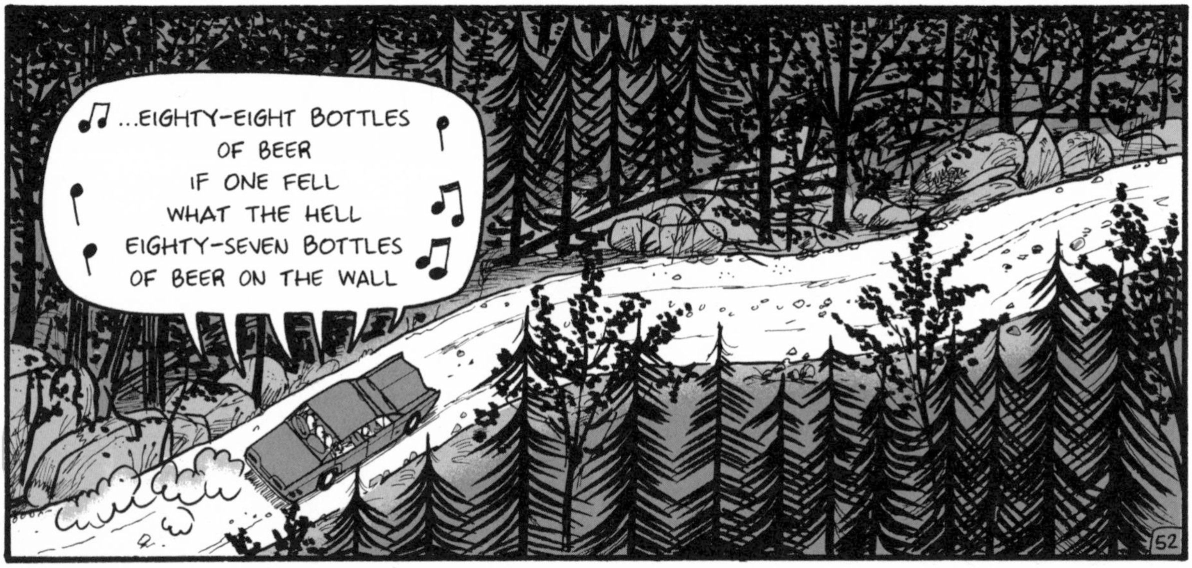
...EIGHTY-EIGHT BOTTLES OF BEER IF ONE FELL WHAT THE HELL EIGHTY-SEVEN BOTTLES OF BEER ON THE WALL
52

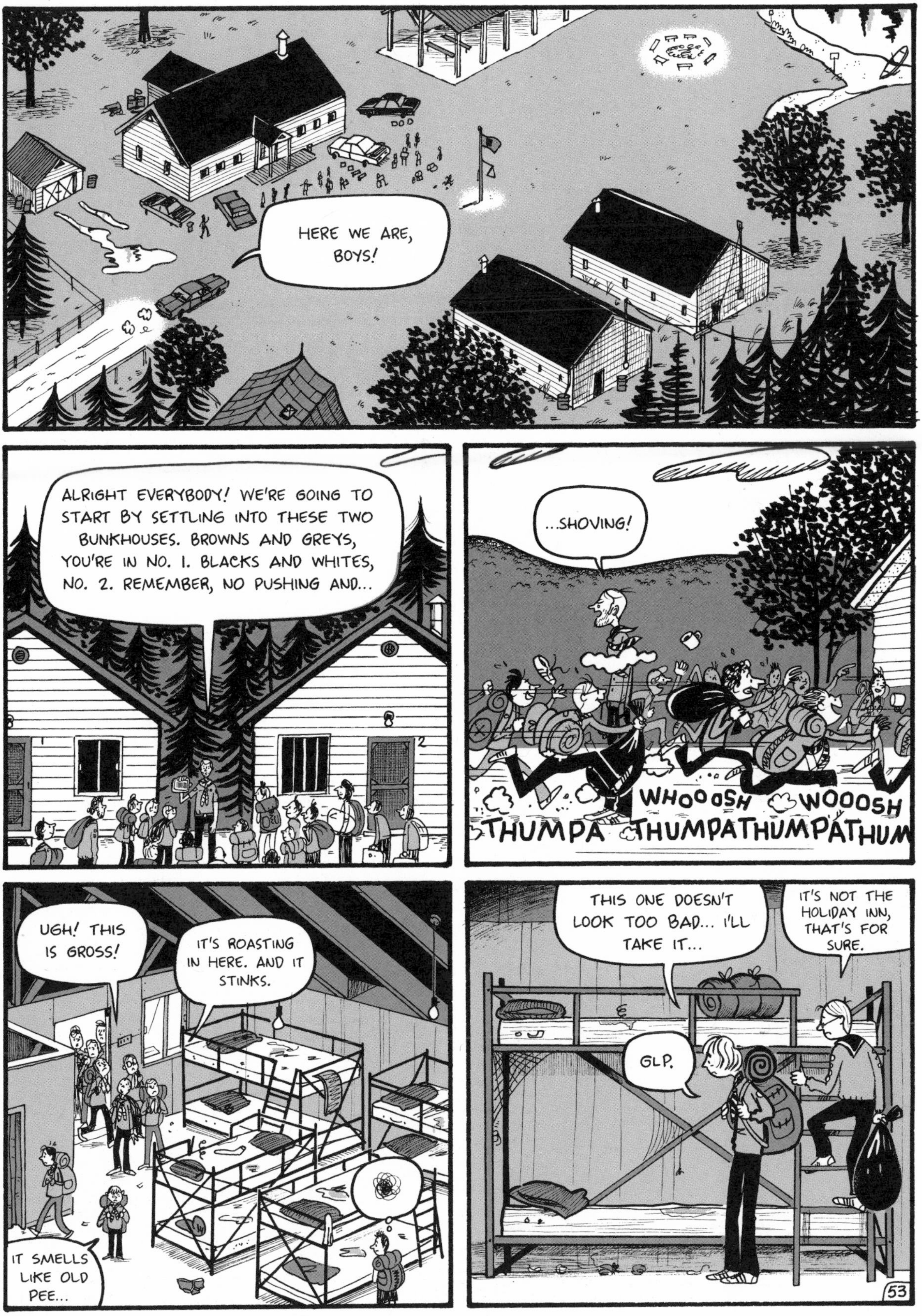
HERE WE ARE, BOYS!
ALRIGHT EVERYBODY! WE'RE GOING TO START BY SETTLING INTO THESE TWO BUNKHOUSES. BROWNS AND GREYS, YOU'RE IN NO. 1. BLACKS AND WHITES, NO. 2. REMEMBER, NO PUSHING AND...
...SHOVING!
WHOOOSH WOOOSH
THUMPA THUMPATHUMPATHUM
UGH! THIS IS GROSS!
IT'S ROASTING IN HERE. AND IT STINKS.
IT SMELLS LIKE OLD PEE...
THIS ONE DOESN'T LOOK TOO BAD... I'LL TAKE IT...
IT'S NOT THE HOLIDAY INN, THAT'S FOR SURE.
GLP.
53

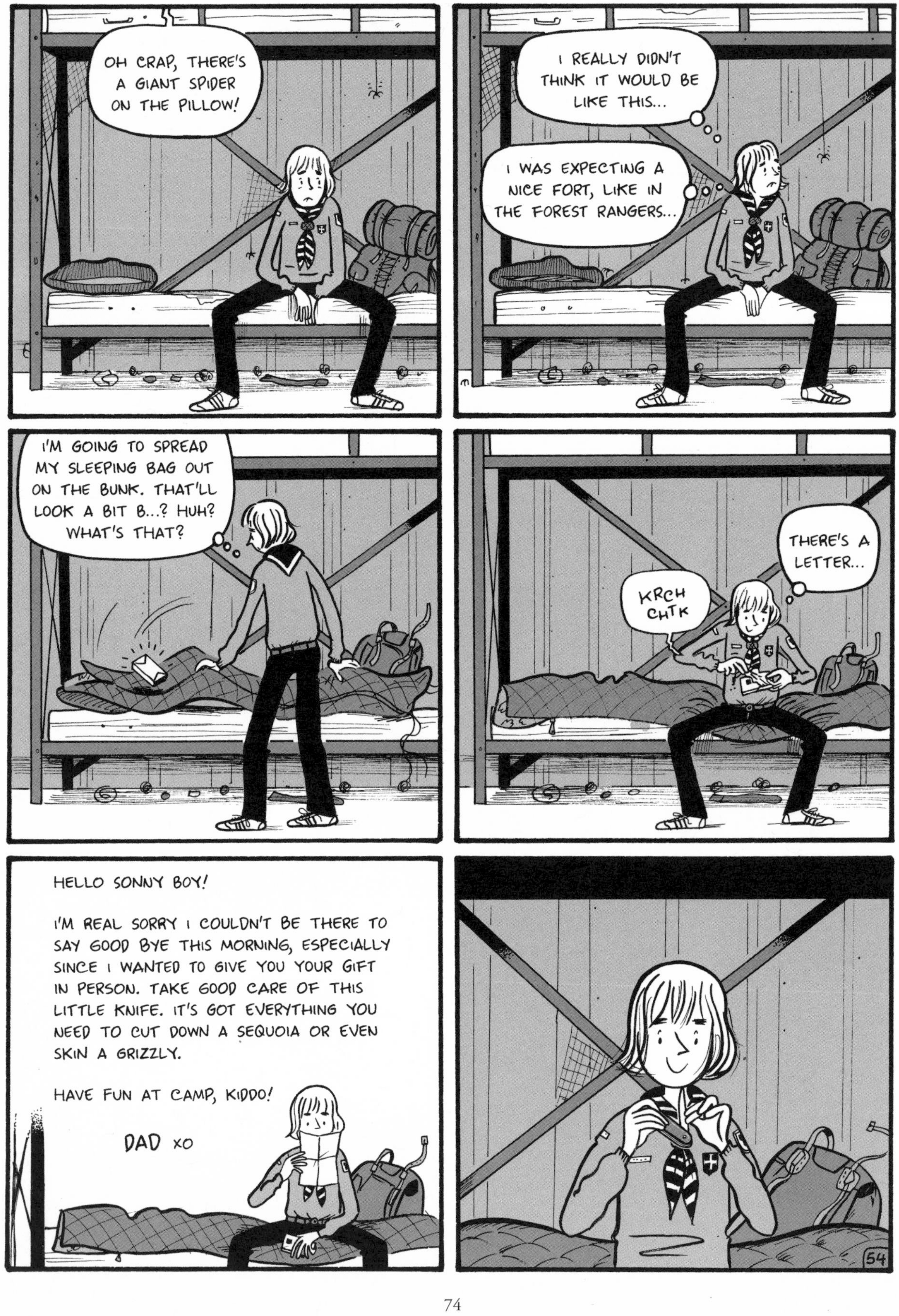
OH CRAP, THERE'S A GIANT SPIDER ON THE PILLOW!
I REALLY DIDN'T THINK IT WOULD BE LIKE THIS...
I WAS EXPECTING A NICE FORT, LIKE IN THE FOREST RANGERS...
I'M GOING TO SPREAD MY SLEEPING BAG OUT ON THE BUNK. THAT'LL LOOK A BIT B...? HUH? WHAT'S THAT?
KRCH CHTK
THERE'S A LETTER...
HELLO SONNY BOY!
I'M REAL SORRY I COULDN'T BE THERE TO SAY GOOD BYE THIS MORNING, ESPECIALLY SINCE I WANTED TO GIVE YOU YOUR GIFT IN PERSON. TAKE GOOD CARE OF THIS LITTLE KNIFE. IT'S GOT EVERYTHING YOU NEED TO CUT DOWN A SEQUOIA OR EVEN SKIN A GRIZZLY.
HAVE FUN AT CAMP, KIDDO!
DAD XO
54

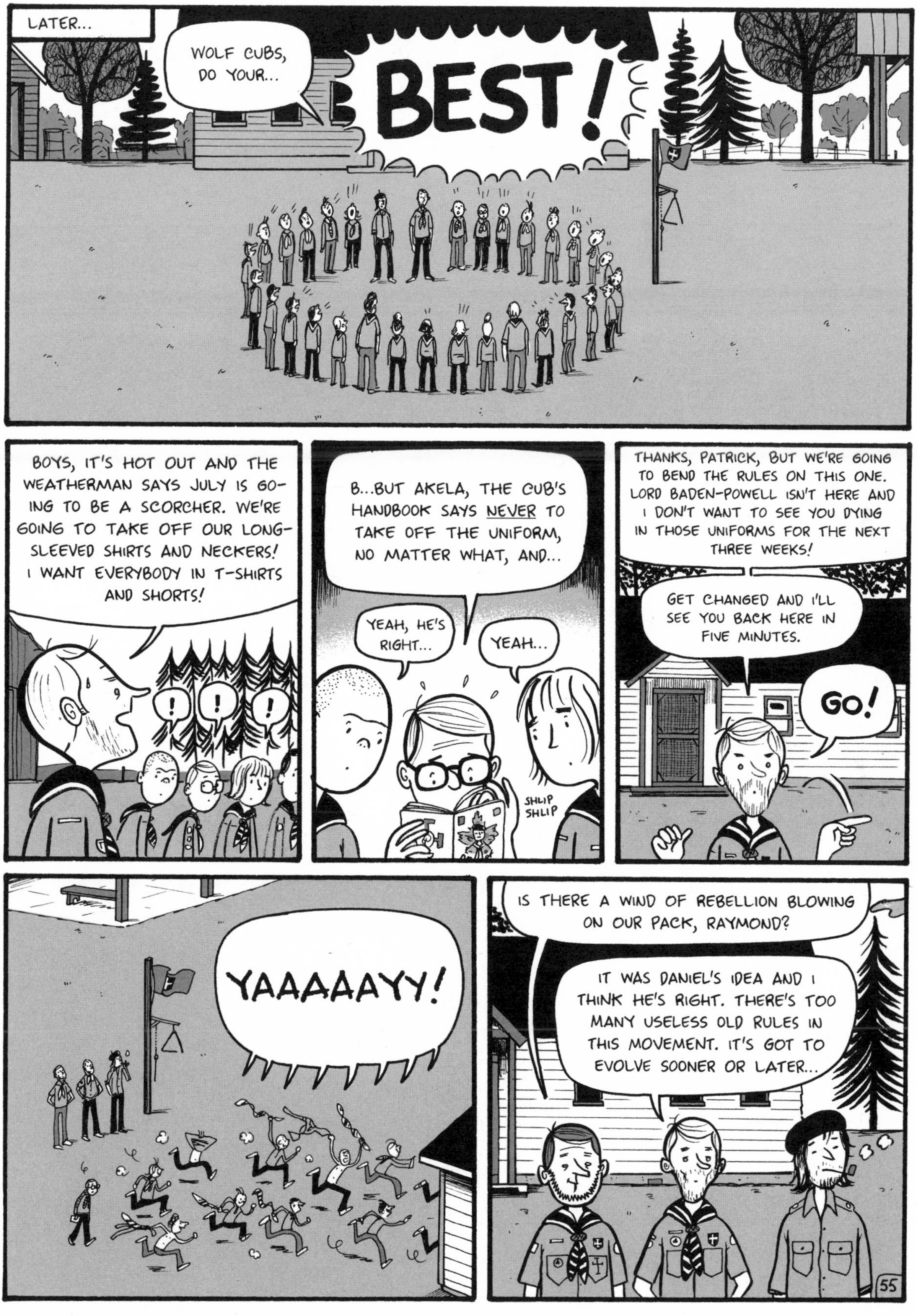
LATER...
WOLF CUBS, DO YOUR...
BEST!
BOYS, IT'S HOT OUT AND THE WEATHERMAN SAYS JULY IS GOING TO BE A SCORCHER. WE'RE GOING TO TAKE OFF OUR LONG-SLEEVED SHIRTS AND NECKERS! I WANT EVERYBODY IN T-SHIRTS AND SHORTS!
!
!
!
B...BUT AKELA, THE CUB'S HANDBOOK SAYS NEVER TO TAKE OFF THE UNIFORM, NO MATTER WHAT, AND...
YEAH, HE'S RIGHT...
YEAH...
SHLIP SHLIP
THANKS, PATRICK, BUT WE'RE GOING TO BEND THE RULES ON THIS ONE. LORD BADEN-POWELL ISN'T HERE AND I DON'T WANT TO SEE YOU DYING IN THOSE UNIFORMS FOR THE NEXT THREE WEEKS!
GET CHANGED AND I'LL SEE YOU BACK HERE IN FIVE MINUTES.
GO!
YAAAAAYY!
IS THERE A WIND OF REBELLION BLOWING ON OUR PACK, RAYMOND?
IT WAS DANIEL'S IDEA AND I THINK HE'S RIGHT. THERE'S TOO MANY USELESS OLD RULES IN THIS MOVEMENT. IT'S GOT TO EVOLVE SOONER OR LATER...
55

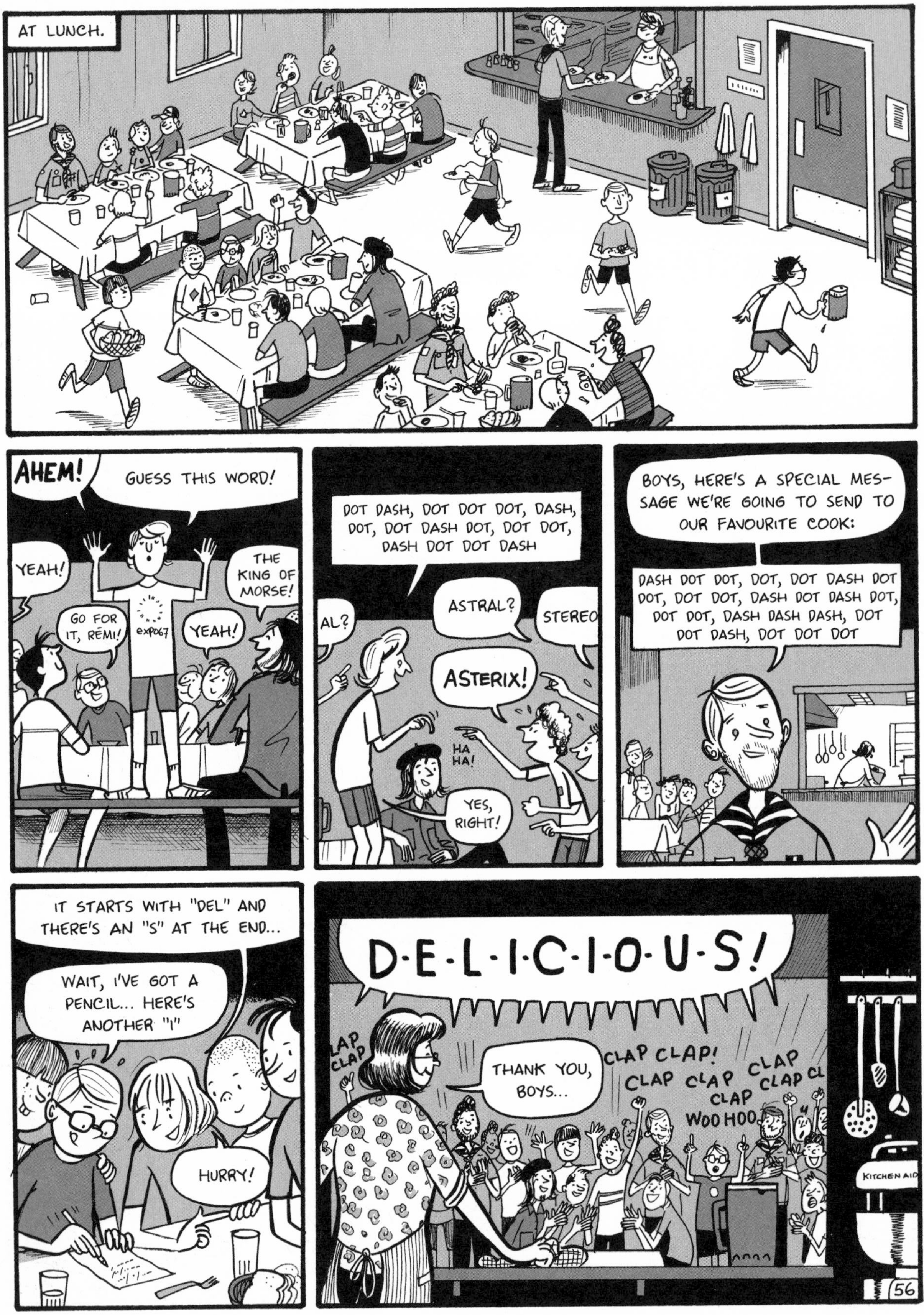

AT LUNCH.
AHEM!
GUESS THIS WORD!
YEAH!
THE KING OF MORSE!
GO FOR IT, RÉMI!
EXPO67
YEAH!
DOT DASH, DOT DOT DOT, DASH, DOT, DOT DASH DOT, DOT DOT, DASH DOT DOT DASH
AL?
ASTRAL?
STEREO
ASTERIX!
HA HA!
YES, RIGHT!
BOYS, HERE'S A SPECIAL MESSAGE WE'RE GOING TO SEND TO OUR FAVOURITE COOK:
DASH DOT DOT, DOT, DOT DASH DOT DOT, DOT DOT, DASH DOT DASH DOT, DOT DOT, DASH DASH DASH, DOT DOT DASH, DOT DOT DOT
IT STARTS WITH "DEL" AND THERE'S AN "S" AT THE END...
WAIT, I'VE GOT A PENCIL... HERE'S ANOTHER "I"
HURRY!
D-E-L-I-C-I-O-U-S!
CLAP CLAP
THANK YOU, BOYS...
CLAP CLAP! CLAP CLAP CLAP CLAP CLAP CLAP
WOO HOO
KITCHENAID
56

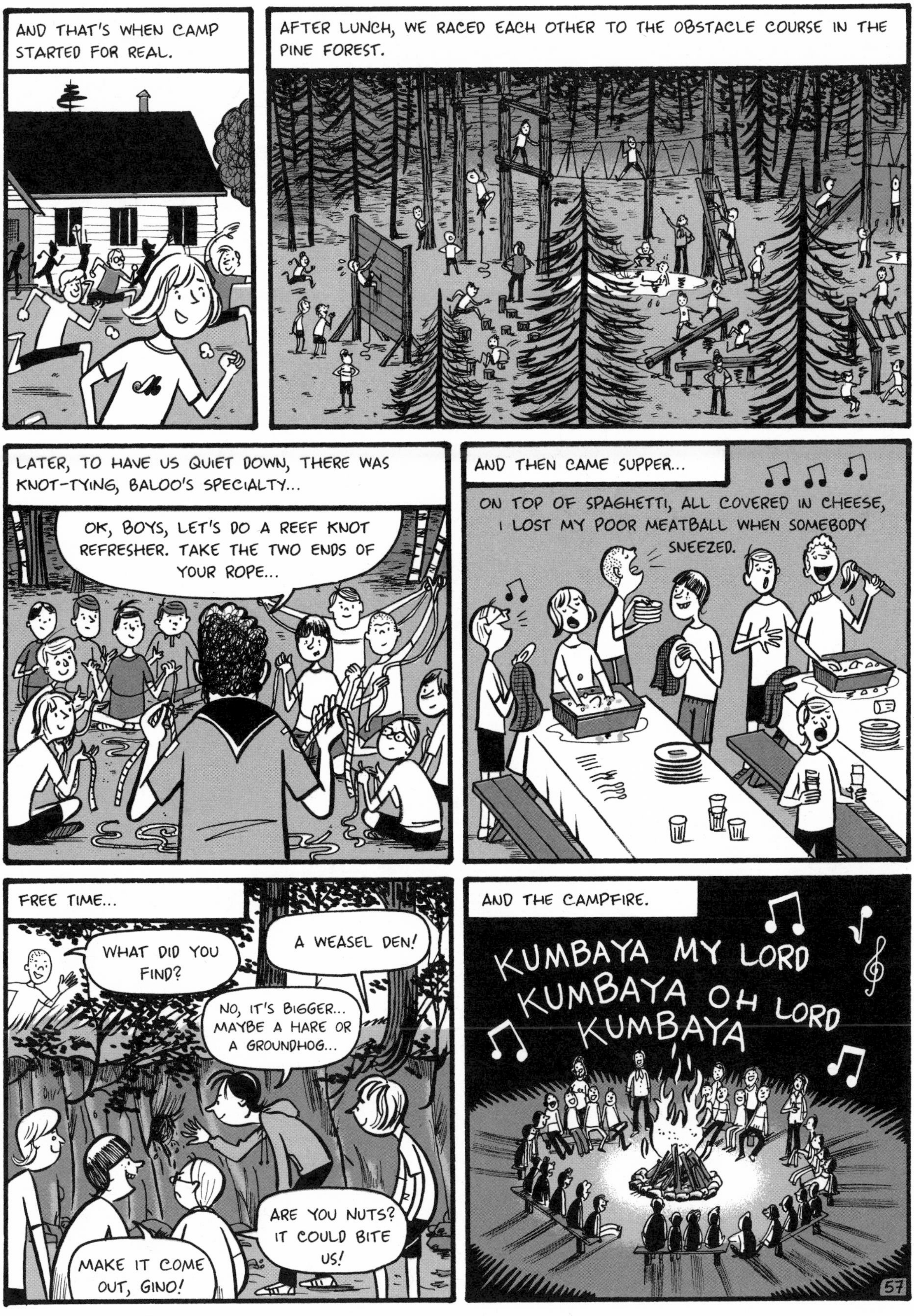
AND THAT'S WHEN CAMP STARTED FOR REAL.
AFTER LUNCH, WE RACED EACH OTHER TO THE OBSTACLE COURSE IN THE PINE FOREST.
LATER, TO HAVE US QUIET DOWN, THERE WAS KNOT-TYING, BALOO'S SPECIALTY...
OK, BOYS, LET'S DO A REEF KNOT REFRESHER. TAKE THE TWO ENDS OF YOUR ROPE...
AND THEN CAME SUPPER...
ON TOP OF SPAGHETTI, ALL COVERED IN CHEESE, I LOST MY POOR MEATBALL WHEN SOMEBODY SNEEZED.
FREE TIME...
WHAT DID YOU FIND?
A WEASEL DEN!
NO, IT'S BIGGER... MAYBE A HARE OR A GROUNDHOG...
ARE YOU NUTS? IT COULD BITE US!
MAKE IT COME OUT, GINO!
AND THE CAMPFIRE.
KUMBAYA MY LORD
KUMBAYA OH LORD
KUMBAYA
57

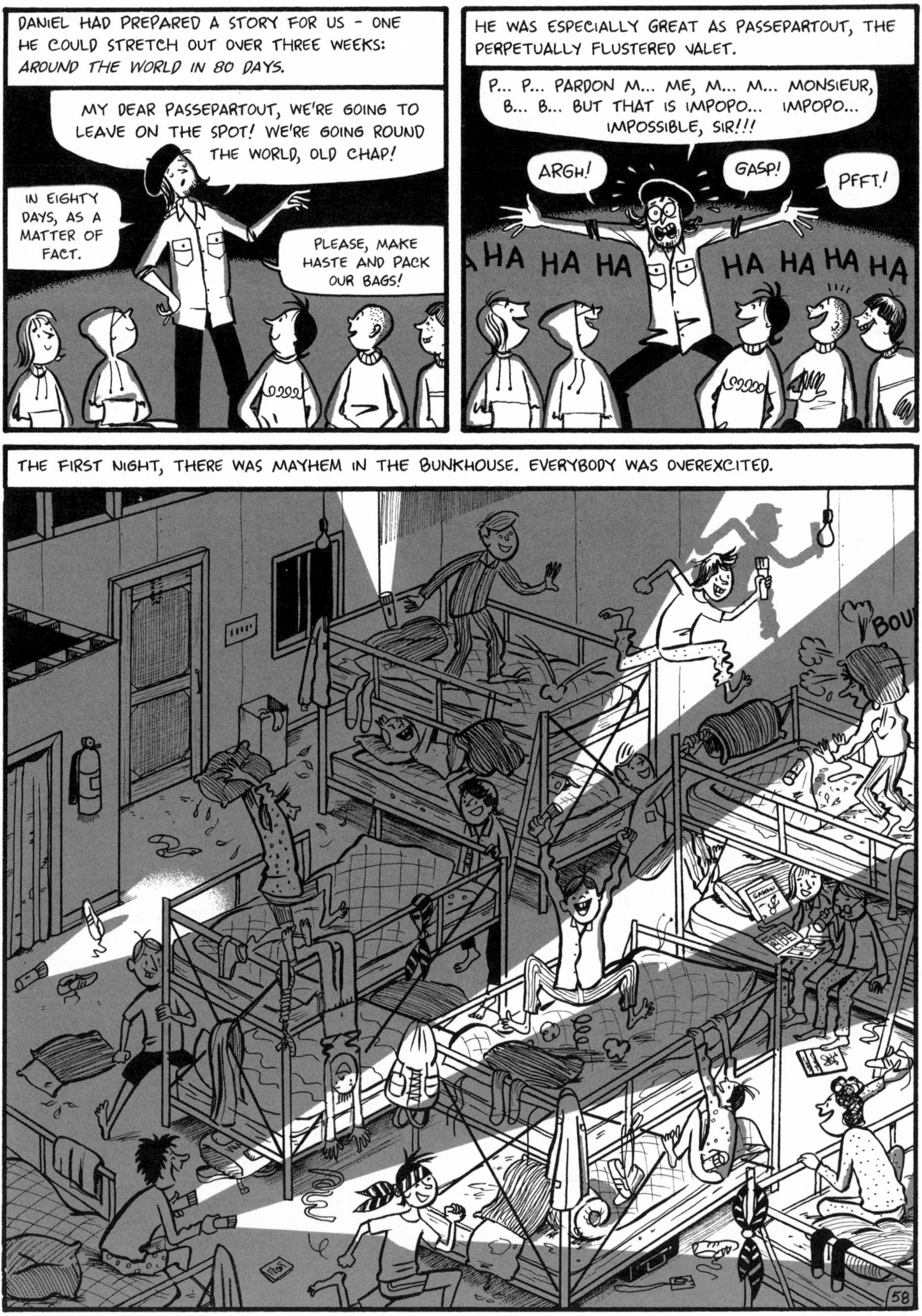
DANIEL HAD PREPARED A STORY FOR US - ONE HE COULD STRETCH OUT OVER THREE WEEKS: *AROUND THE WORLD IN 80 DAYS.*
MY DEAR PASSEPARTOUT, WE'RE GOING TO LEAVE ON THE SPOT! WE'RE GOING ROUND THE WORLD, OLD CHAP!
IN EIGHTY DAYS, AS A MATTER OF FACT.
PLEASE, MAKE HASTE AND PACK OUR BAGS!
HE WAS ESPECIALLY GREAT AS PASSEPARTOUT, THE PERPETUALLY FLUSTERED VALET.
P... P... PARDON M... ME, M... M... MONSIEUR, B... B... BUT THAT IS IMPOPO... IMPOPO... IMPOSSIBLE, SIR!!!
ARGH!
GASP!
PFFT!
HA HA HA HA
HA HA HA HA HA
THE FIRST NIGHT, THERE WAS MAYHEM IN THE BUNKHOUSE. EVERYBODY WAS OVEREXCITED.
BOU
58

WHAT'S GOING ON HERE? ARE YOU OUT OF YOUR MINDS?

IT'S PAST ELEVEN!

CLIC

IT'S THE GREYS, BALOO! THEY'RE THE ONES WHO STARTED THROWING PILLOWS AROUND!

YEAH!

THAT'S NOT TRUE!

I DON'T WANT TO HEAR ABOUT IT. LIGHTS OUT MEANS LIGHTS OUT! YOU HIT THE SACK AND YOU QUIET DOWN!

QUIET! KNOW WHAT THAT MEANS?

BUT BALOO, THEY'RE THE ONES WHO...

GINO AND SYLVAIN! YOU'RE SIXERS, BOTH OF YOU! DO YOU THINK YOU'RE SETTING A GOOD EXAMPLE FOR THE OTHERS?

NO...

NO...

I HOPE I DON'T NEED TO COME BACK. IF I CATCH YOU ACTING UP AGAIN, I'M CONFISCATING ALL YOUR FLASHLIGHTS FOR A WEEK!

GET TO BED! WE START EARLY TO-MORROW!

SLAM

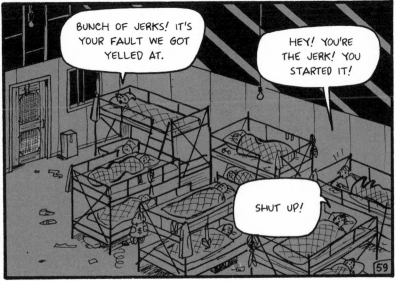

BUNCH OF JERKS! IT'S YOUR FAULT WE GOT YELLED AT.

HEY! YOU'RE THE JERK! YOU STARTED IT!

SHUT UP!

59

79

Jean-Claude

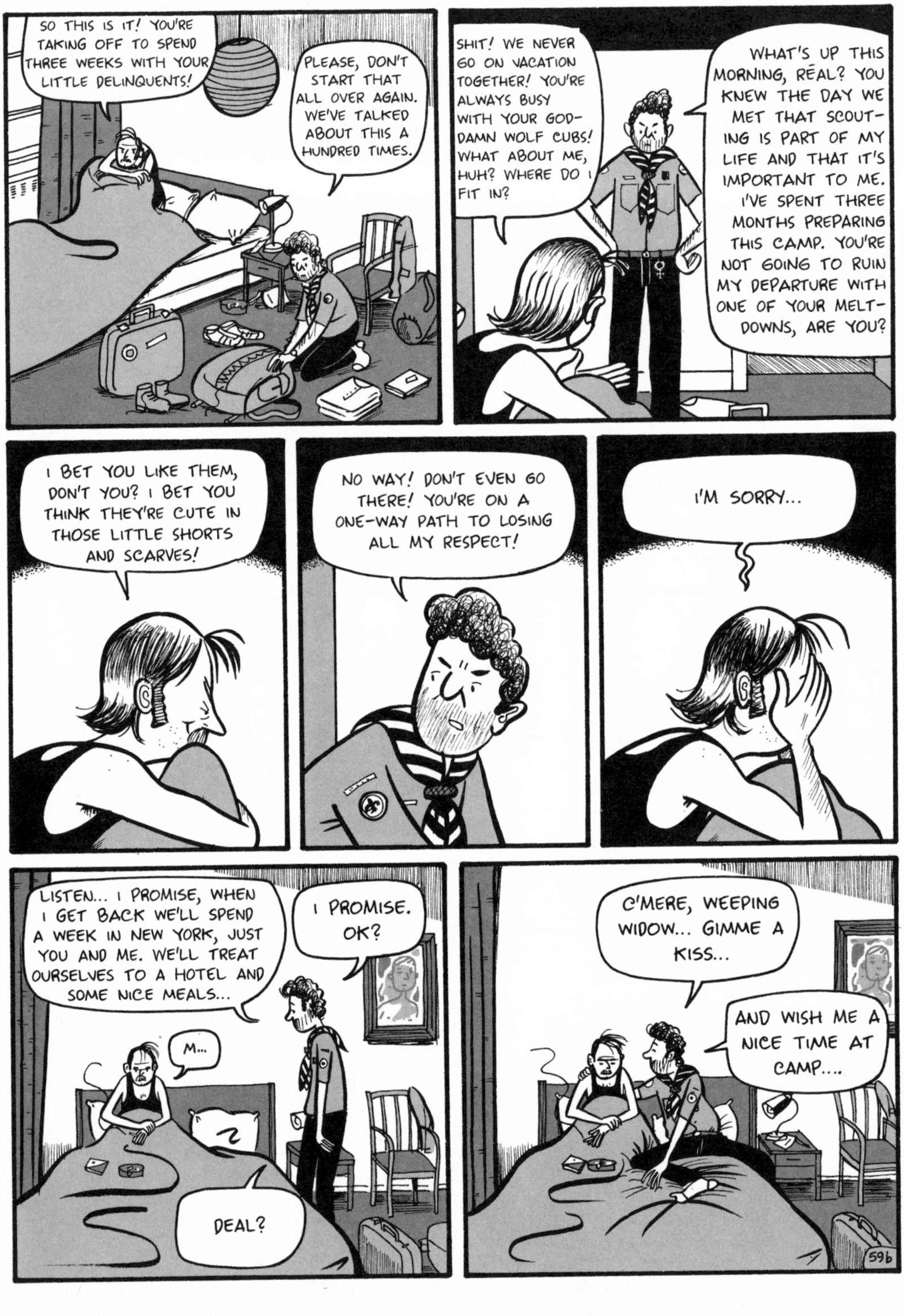
SO THIS IS IT! YOU'RE TAKING OFF TO SPEND THREE WEEKS WITH YOUR LITTLE DELINQUENTS!
PLEASE, DON'T START THAT ALL OVER AGAIN. WE'VE TALKED ABOUT THIS A HUNDRED TIMES.
SHIT! WE NEVER GO ON VACATION TOGETHER! YOU'RE ALWAYS BUSY WITH YOUR GOD-DAMN WOLF CUBS! WHAT ABOUT ME, HUH? WHERE DO I FIT IN?
WHAT'S UP THIS MORNING, RÉAL? YOU KNEW THE DAY WE MET THAT SCOUT-ING IS PART OF MY LIFE AND THAT IT'S IMPORTANT TO ME. I'VE SPENT THREE MONTHS PREPARING THIS CAMP. YOU'RE NOT GOING TO RUIN MY DEPARTURE WITH ONE OF YOUR MELT-DOWNS, ARE YOU?
I BET YOU LIKE THEM, DON'T YOU? I BET YOU THINK THEY'RE CUTE IN THOSE LITTLE SHORTS AND SCARVES!
NO WAY! DON'T EVEN GO THERE! YOU'RE ON A ONE-WAY PATH TO LOSING ALL MY RESPECT!
I'M SORRY...
LISTEN... I PROMISE, WHEN I GET BACK WE'LL SPEND A WEEK IN NEW YORK, JUST YOU AND ME. WE'LL TREAT OURSELVES TO A HOTEL AND SOME NICE MEALS...
I PROMISE. OK?
M...
DEAL?
C'MERE, WEEPING WIDOW... GIMME A KISS...
AND WISH ME A NICE TIME AT CAMP....
59b

BRAAA!

EVERYBODY OUTSIDE, BY BELANOS!

ALRIGHT, GAULS, WE'RE GONNA DO A FEW EXERCISES TO WAKE UP!

NO WAY!

AWW!

MBL MLN GLMB...

THESE ROMANS ARE CRAZY...

WHAT TIME IS IT ANYWAY?

WE'LL START WITH TWENTY JUMPING JACKS! 1, 2, 3...

HA HA! C'MON GUYS! THE REAL GAUL WARRIORS WERE BACK FROM THE HUNT BY NOW!

6, 7, 8...

AND NOW, TEN PUSH-UPS! KEEP IT UP!

2, 3...

PFF!

ARF!

ARGH!

HIT THE PALMS OF YOUR HANDS WITH YOUR KNEES, 1, 2, 3...

HIGHER!

SLAP SLAP

SLAP SLAP

TARAA

EVERYBODY IN THE LAKE! AS FAST AS YOU CAN!

MOVE IT! HUT! HUT! HUT!

HAHA!

CHAAARGE!

60

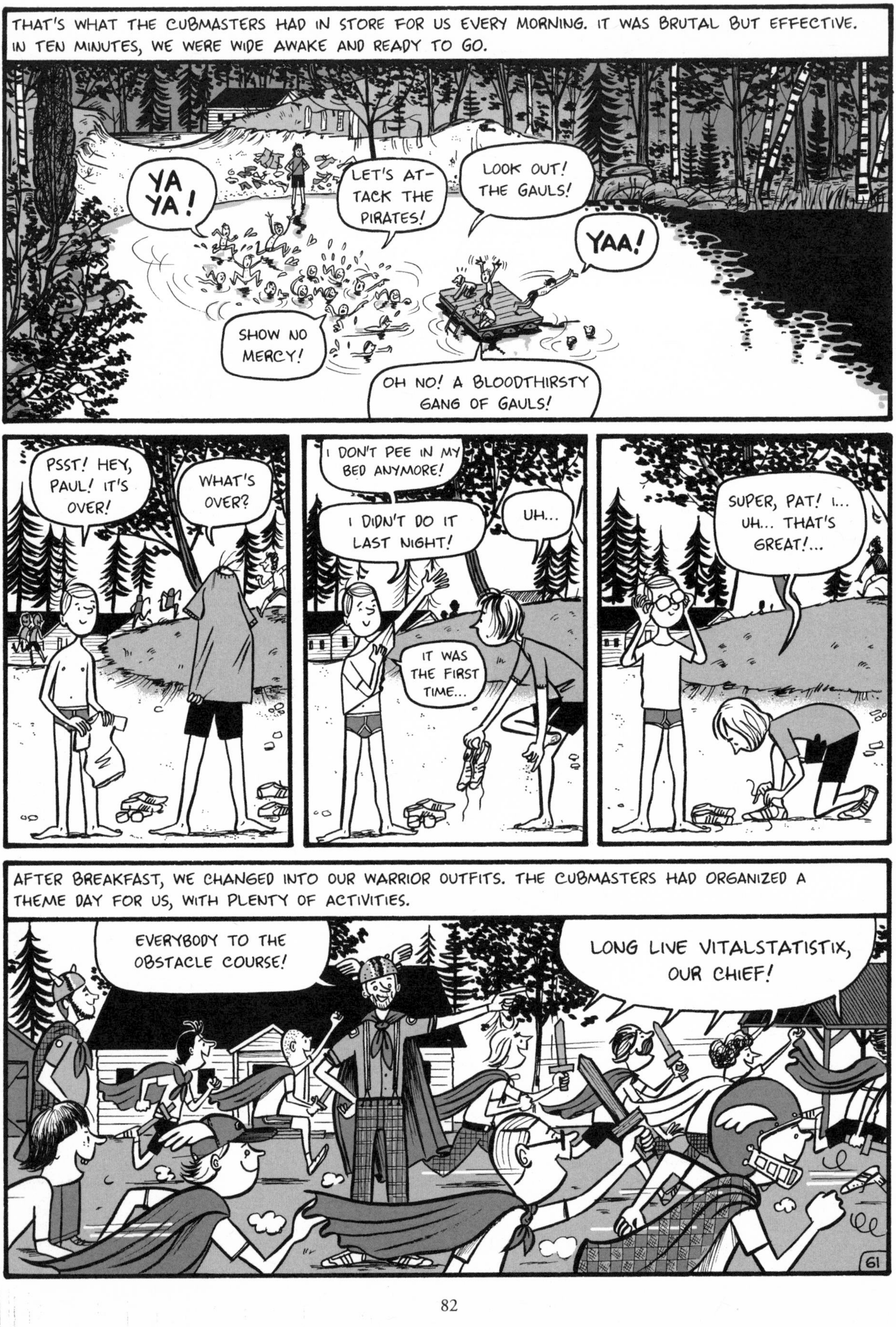
THAT'S WHAT THE CUBMASTERS HAD IN STORE FOR US EVERY MORNING. IT WAS BRUTAL BUT EFFECTIVE. IN TEN MINUTES, WE WERE WIDE AWAKE AND READY TO GO.
YA YA!
LET'S AT-TACK THE PIRATES!
LOOK OUT! THE GAULS!
YAA!
SHOW NO MERCY!
OH NO! A BLOODTHIRSTY GANG OF GAULS!
PSST! HEY, PAUL! IT'S OVER!
WHAT'S OVER?
I DON'T PEE IN MY BED ANYMORE!
I DIDN'T DO IT LAST NIGHT!
UH...
IT WAS THE FIRST TIME...
SUPER, PAT! I... UH... THAT'S GREAT!...
AFTER BREAKFAST, WE CHANGED INTO OUR WARRIOR OUTFITS. THE CUBMASTERS HAD ORGANIZED A THEME DAY FOR US, WITH PLENTY OF ACTIVITIES.
EVERYBODY TO THE OBSTACLE COURSE!
LONG LIVE VITALSTATISTIX, OUR CHIEF!
61

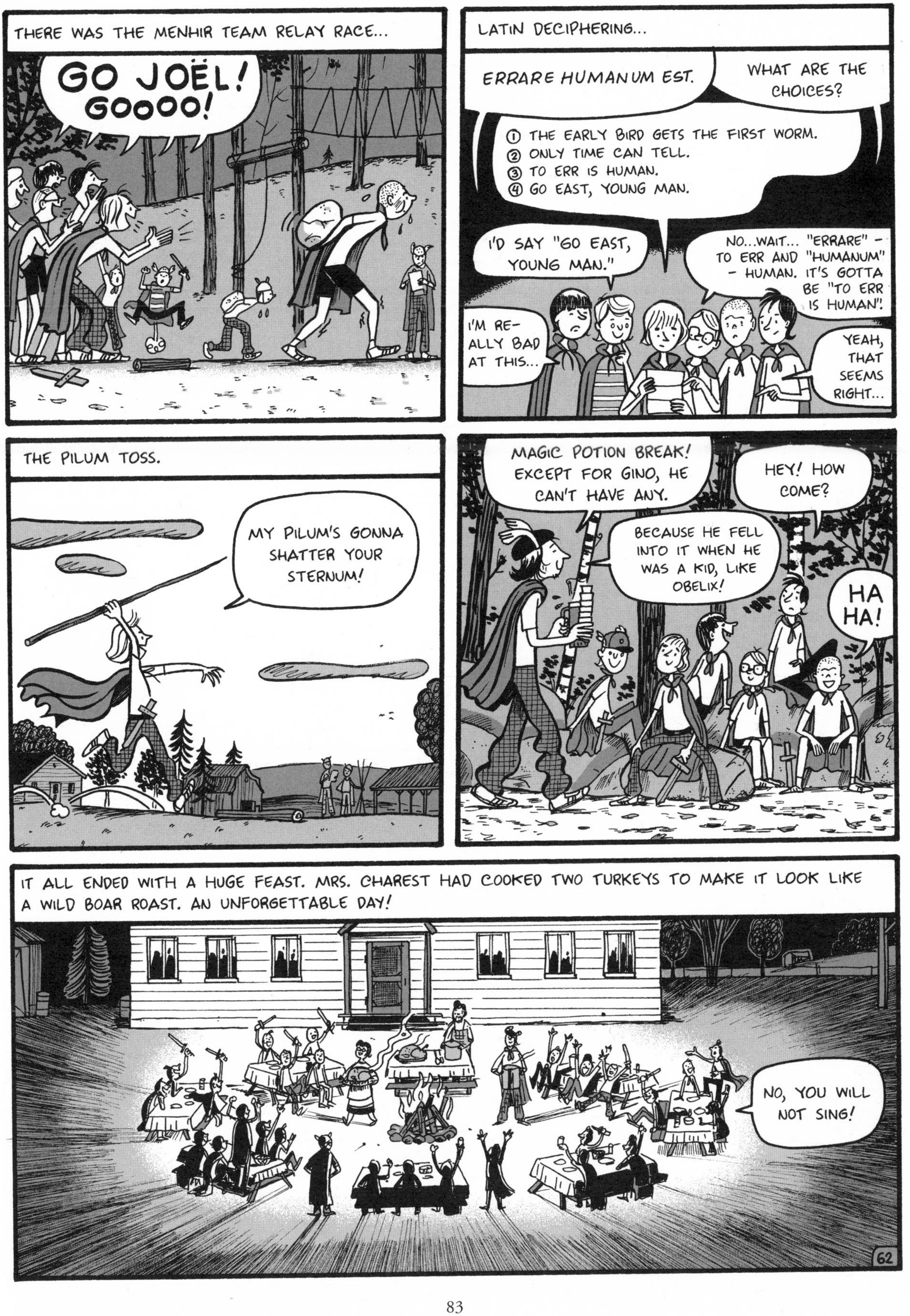
THERE WAS THE MENHIR TEAM RELAY RACE...
GO JOËL! GOOOO!
LATIN DECIPHERING...
ERRARE HUMANUM EST.
WHAT ARE THE CHOICES?
① THE EARLY BIRD GETS THE FIRST WORM.
② ONLY TIME CAN TELL.
③ TO ERR IS HUMAN.
④ GO EAST, YOUNG MAN.
I'D SAY "GO EAST, YOUNG MAN."
NO...WAIT... "ERRARE" - TO ERR AND "HUMANUM" - HUMAN. IT'S GOTTA BE "TO ERR IS HUMAN".
I'M REALLY BAD AT THIS...
YEAH, THAT SEEMS RIGHT...
THE PILUM TOSS.
MY PILUM'S GONNA SHATTER YOUR STERNUM!
MAGIC POTION BREAK! EXCEPT FOR GINO, HE CAN'T HAVE ANY.
HEY! HOW COME?
BECAUSE HE FELL INTO IT WHEN HE WAS A KID, LIKE OBELIX!
HA HA!
IT ALL ENDED WITH A HUGE FEAST. MRS. CHAREST HAD COOKED TWO TURKEYS TO MAKE IT LOOK LIKE A WILD BOAR ROAST. AN UNFORGETTABLE DAY!
NO, YOU WILL NOT SING!
62

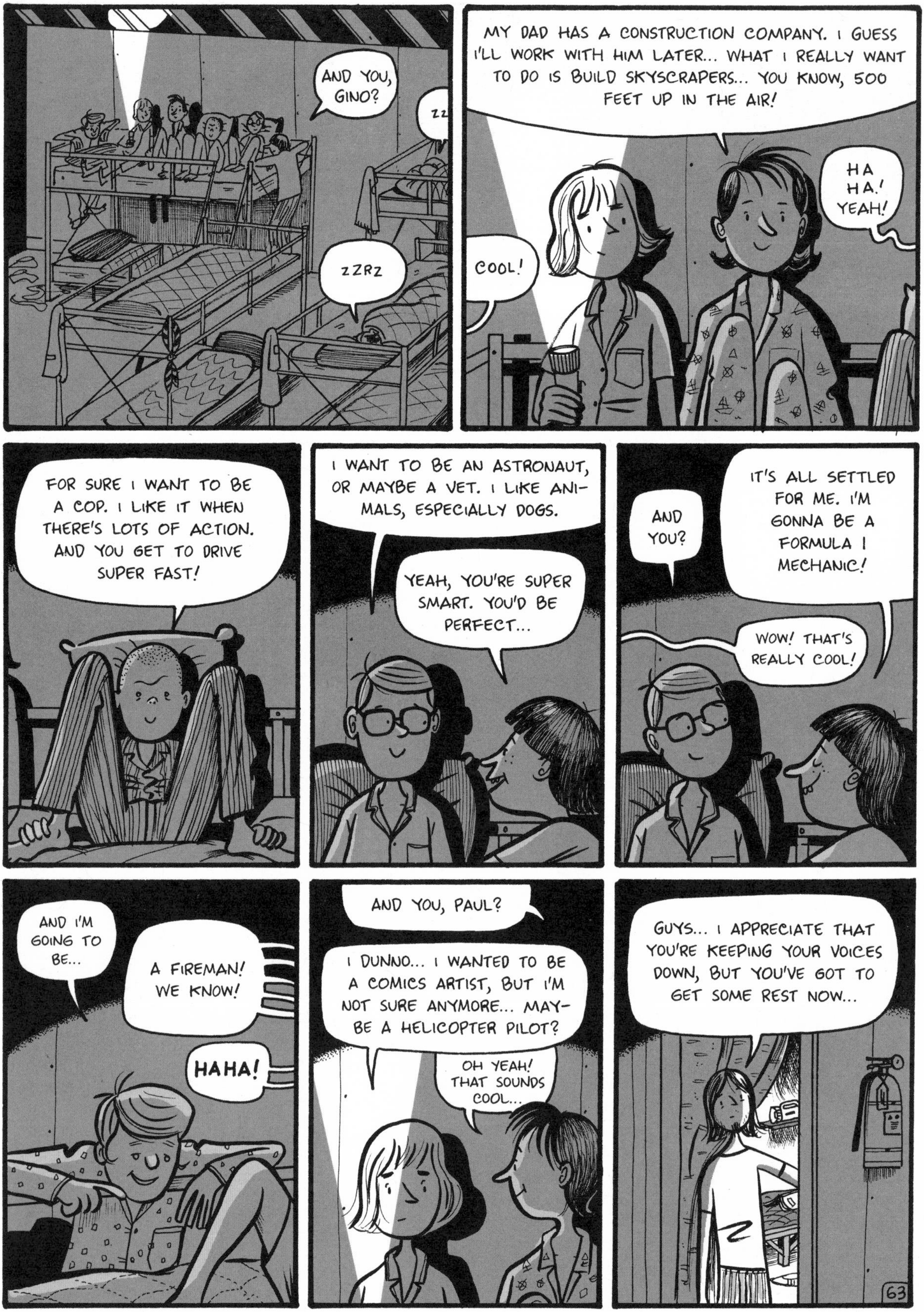
AND YOU, GINO?
ZZ
ZZRZ
MY DAD HAS A CONSTRUCTION COMPANY. I GUESS I'LL WORK WITH HIM LATER... WHAT I REALLY WANT TO DO IS BUILD SKYSCRAPERS... YOU KNOW, 500 FEET UP IN THE AIR!
COOL!
HA HA! YEAH!
FOR SURE I WANT TO BE A COP. I LIKE IT WHEN THERE'S LOTS OF ACTION. AND YOU GET TO DRIVE SUPER FAST!
I WANT TO BE AN ASTRONAUT, OR MAYBE A VET. I LIKE ANI-MALS, ESPECIALLY DOGS.
YEAH, YOU'RE SUPER SMART. YOU'D BE PERFECT...
AND YOU?
IT'S ALL SETTLED FOR ME. I'M GONNA BE A FORMULA 1 MECHANIC!
WOW! THAT'S REALLY COOL!
AND I'M GOING TO BE...
A FIREMAN! WE KNOW!
HAHA!
AND YOU, PAUL?
I DUNNO... I WANTED TO BE A COMICS ARTIST, BUT I'M NOT SURE ANYMORE... MAY-BE A HELICOPTER PILOT?
OH YEAH! THAT SOUNDS COOL...
GUYS... I APPRECIATE THAT YOU'RE KEEPING YOUR VOICES DOWN, BUT YOU'VE GOT TO GET SOME REST NOW...
63

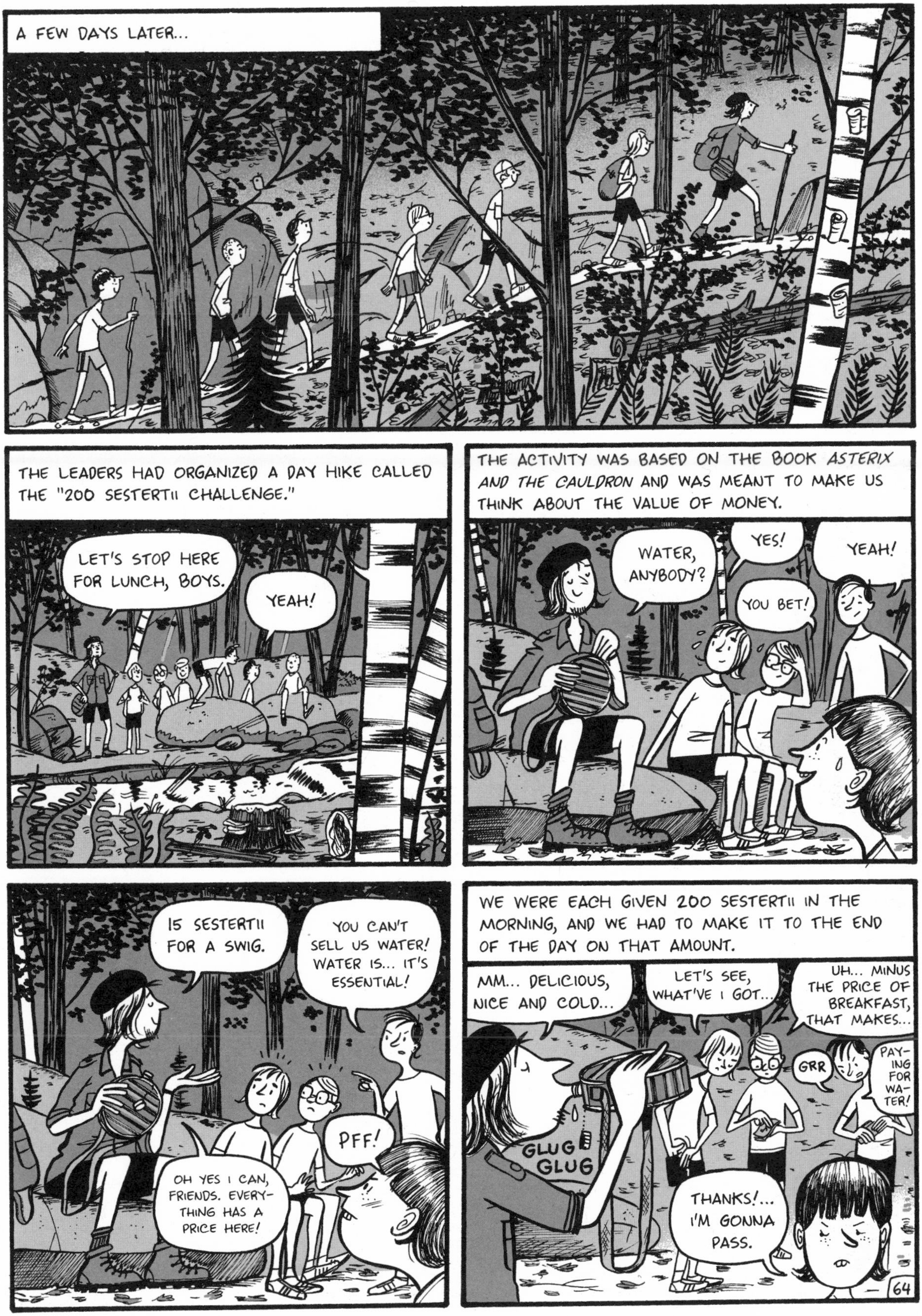
A FEW DAYS LATER...
THE LEADERS HAD ORGANIZED A DAY HIKE CALLED THE "200 SESTERTII CHALLENGE."
LET'S STOP HERE FOR LUNCH, BOYS.
YEAH!
THE ACTIVITY WAS BASED ON THE BOOK *ASTERIX AND THE CAULDRON* AND WAS MEANT TO MAKE US THINK ABOUT THE VALUE OF MONEY.
WATER, ANYBODY?
YES!
YEAH!
YOU BET!
15 SESTERTII FOR A SWIG.
YOU CAN'T SELL US WATER! WATER IS... IT'S ESSENTIAL!
PFF!
OH YES I CAN, FRIENDS. EVERYTHING HAS A PRICE HERE!
WE WERE EACH GIVEN 200 SESTERTII IN THE MORNING, AND WE HAD TO MAKE IT TO THE END OF THE DAY ON THAT AMOUNT.
MM... DELICIOUS, NICE AND COLD...
LET'S SEE, WHAT'VE I GOT...
UH... MINUS THE PRICE OF BREAKFAST, THAT MAKES...
GRR
PAYING FOR WATER!
GLUG GLUG
THANKS!... I'M GONNA PASS.
64

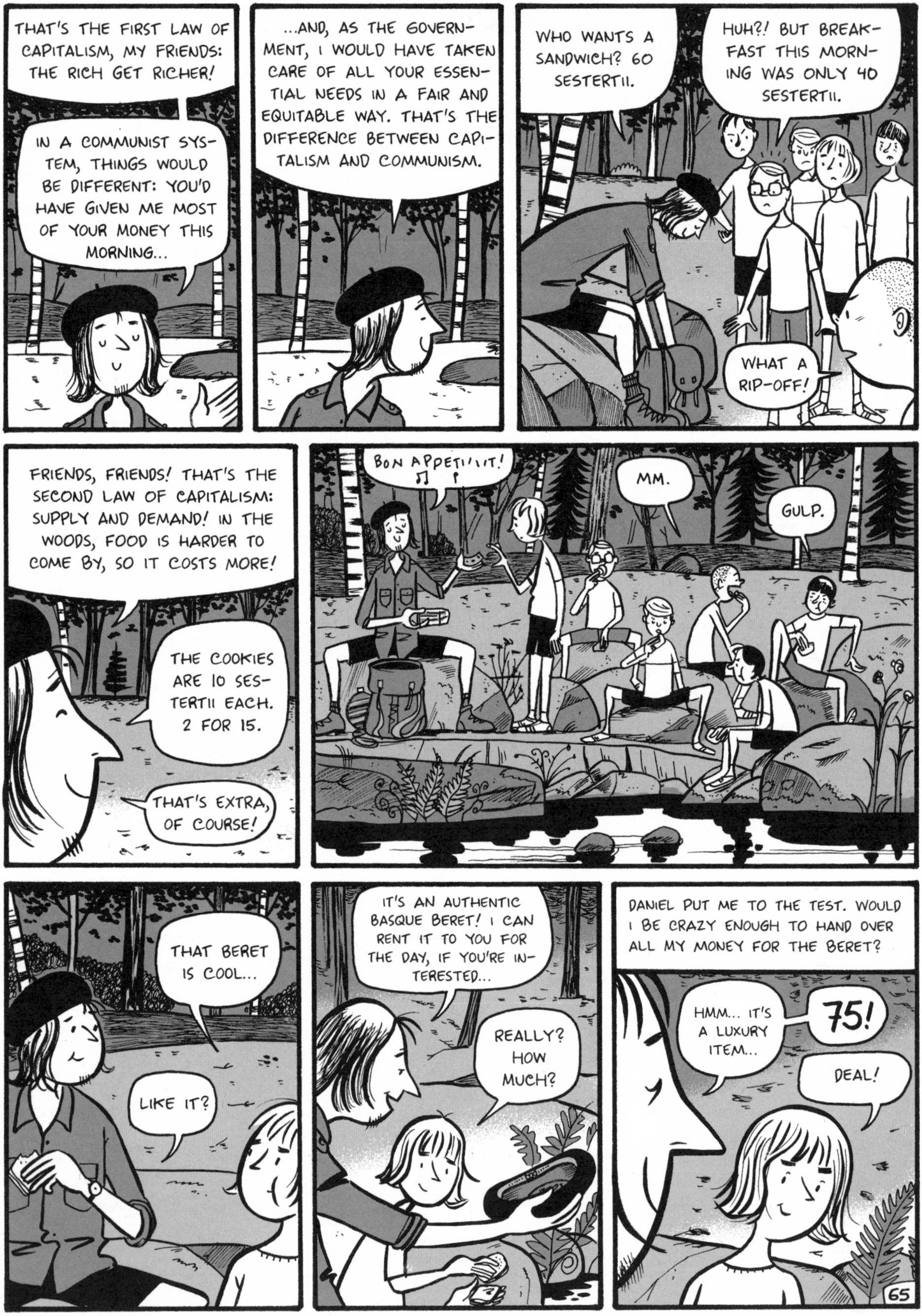
THAT'S THE FIRST LAW OF CAPITALISM, MY FRIENDS: THE RICH GET RICHER!
IN A COMMUNIST SYSTEM, THINGS WOULD BE DIFFERENT: YOU'D HAVE GIVEN ME MOST OF YOUR MONEY THIS MORNING...
...AND, AS THE GOVERNMENT, I WOULD HAVE TAKEN CARE OF ALL YOUR ESSENTIAL NEEDS IN A FAIR AND EQUITABLE WAY. THAT'S THE DIFFERENCE BETWEEN CAPITALISM AND COMMUNISM.
WHO WANTS A SANDWICH? 60 SESTERTII.
HUH?! BUT BREAKFAST THIS MORNING WAS ONLY 40 SESTERTII.
WHAT A RIP-OFF!
FRIENDS, FRIENDS! THAT'S THE SECOND LAW OF CAPITALISM: SUPPLY AND DEMAND! IN THE WOODS, FOOD IS HARDER TO COME BY, SO IT COSTS MORE!
THE COOKIES ARE 10 SESTERTII EACH. 2 FOR 15.
THAT'S EXTRA, OF COURSE!
BON APPETIIIIIT!
MM.
GULP.
THAT BERET IS COOL...
LIKE IT?
IT'S AN AUTHENTIC BASQUE BERET! I CAN RENT IT TO YOU FOR THE DAY, IF YOU'RE INTERESTED...
REALLY? HOW MUCH?
DANIEL PUT ME TO THE TEST. WOULD I BE CRAZY ENOUGH TO HAND OVER ALL MY MONEY FOR THE BERET?
HMM... IT'S A LUXURY ITEM...
75!
DEAL!
65

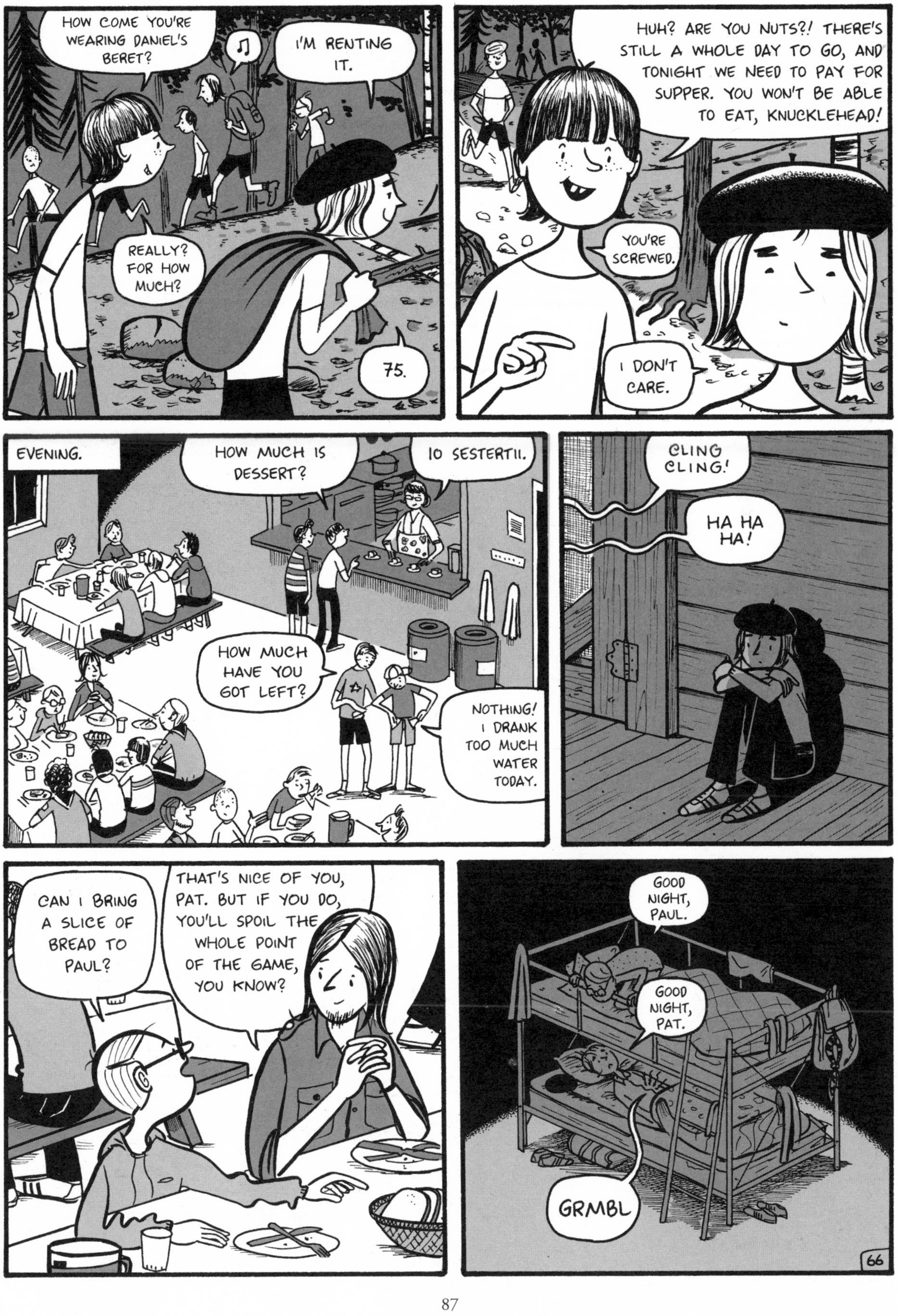
HOW COME YOU'RE WEARING DANIEL'S BERET?
♫
I'M RENTING IT.
REALLY? FOR HOW MUCH?
75.
HUH? ARE YOU NUTS?! THERE'S STILL A WHOLE DAY TO GO, AND TONIGHT WE NEED TO PAY FOR SUPPER. YOU WON'T BE ABLE TO EAT, KNUCKLEHEAD!
YOU'RE SCREWED.
I DON'T CARE.
EVENING.
HOW MUCH IS DESSERT?
10 SESTERTII.
HOW MUCH HAVE YOU GOT LEFT?
NOTHING! I DRANK TOO MUCH WATER TODAY.
CLING CLING!
HA HA HA!
CAN I BRING A SLICE OF BREAD TO PAUL?
THAT'S NICE OF YOU, PAT. BUT IF YOU DO, YOU'LL SPOIL THE WHOLE POINT OF THE GAME, YOU KNOW?
GOOD NIGHT, PAUL.
GOOD NIGHT, PAT.
GRMBL
66

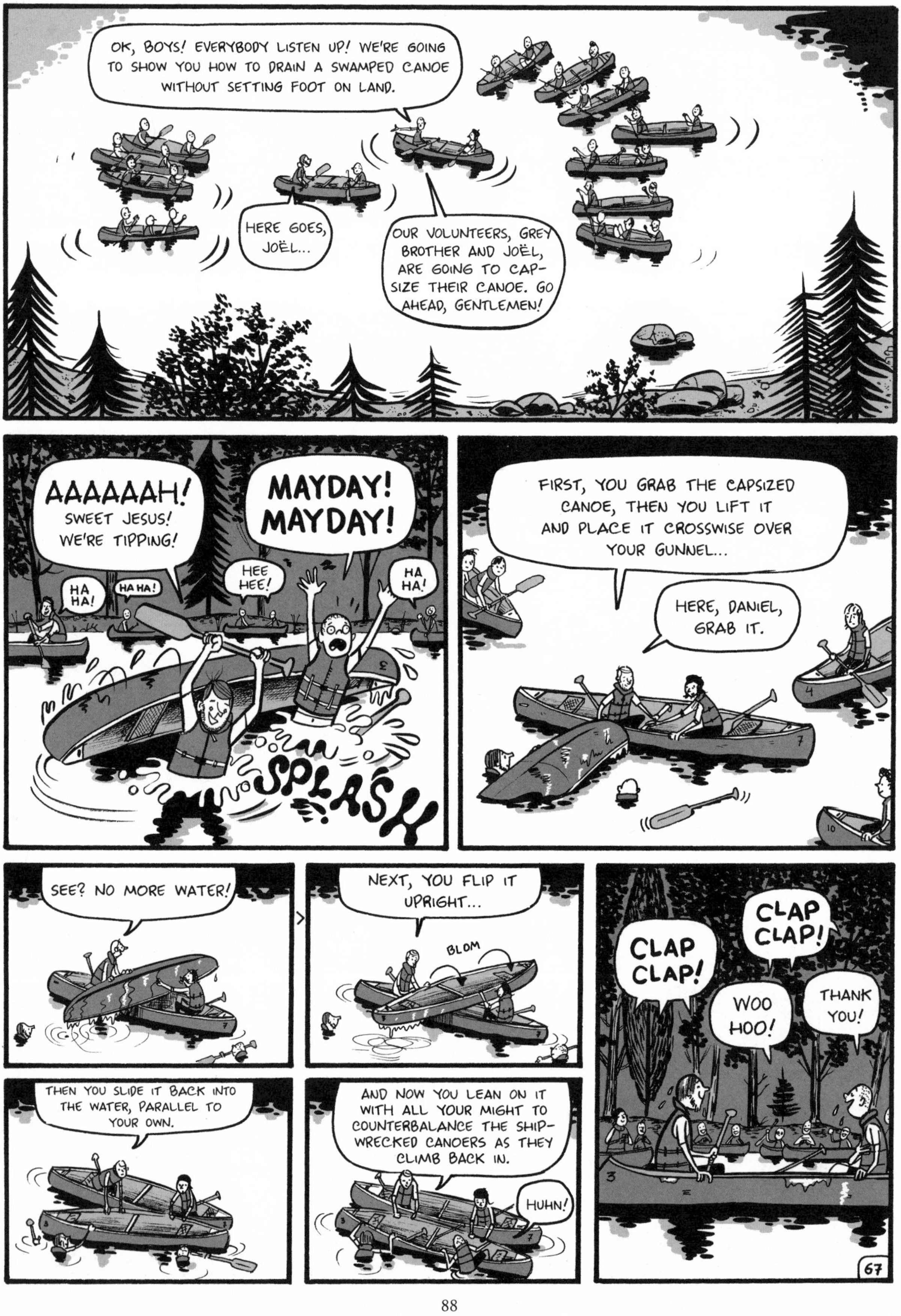
OK, BOYS! EVERYBODY LISTEN UP! WE'RE GOING TO SHOW YOU HOW TO DRAIN A SWAMPED CANOE WITHOUT SETTING FOOT ON LAND.
HERE GOES, JOËL...
OUR VOLUNTEERS, GREY BROTHER AND JOËL, ARE GOING TO CAPSIZE THEIR CANOE. GO AHEAD, GENTLEMEN!
AAAAAAH! SWEET JESUS! WE'RE TIPPING!
MAYDAY! MAYDAY!
HA HA!
HA HA!
HEE HEE!
HA HA!
SPLASH
FIRST, YOU GRAB THE CAPSIZED CANOE, THEN YOU LIFT IT AND PLACE IT CROSSWISE OVER YOUR GUNNEL...
HERE, DANIEL, GRAB IT.
SEE? NO MORE WATER!
NEXT, YOU FLIP IT UPRIGHT...
BLOM
THEN YOU SLIDE IT BACK INTO THE WATER, PARALLEL TO YOUR OWN.
AND NOW YOU LEAN ON IT WITH ALL YOUR MIGHT TO COUNTERBALANCE THE SHIPWRECKED CANOERS AS THEY CLIMB BACK IN.
HUHN!
CLAP CLAP!
CLAP CLAP!
WOO HOO!
THANK YOU!
67

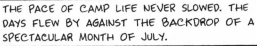

THE PACE OF CAMP LIFE NEVER SLOWED. THE DAYS FLEW BY AGAINST THE BACKDROP OF A SPECTACULAR MONTH OF JULY.

NO, SOMETHING'S NOT RIGHT... WE'RE MOVING AWAY FROM THE LAKE...

HOLD ON... ARE WE FOLLOWING THE RIGHT PATH OR ARE WE GOING NORTH?

I THINK WE SHOULD TURN BACK...

THERE'S VULTURES OVERHEAD, GUYS!...

AND SUDDENLY, JUST WHEN THEY THOUGHT THEY WERE SAFE, FIX EMERGED FROM THE DARK, LOOKING STRAIGHT AT THEM!

WHAT DO YOU THINK, MRS. CHAREST? DOES IT LOOK LIKE TONSILLITIS?

AG!

COULD BE, BUT WE NEED TO TAKE HIM TO A CLINIC TO BE SURE...

SEE, IN NORMAL MODE, THE MIRROR IS DOWN, BUT AS SOON AS YOU HIT THE SHUTTER RELEASE, IT GOES UP AND THE IMAGE IS PRINTED ONTO THE FILM.

WHOEVER DREAMED THAT UP WAS A GENIUS.

KLAK

THIS IS WHAT'S CALLED THE FOUR-HAND SEAT. IT'S THE BEST WAY FOR TWO PEOPLE TO CARRY AN INJURED PERSON WITHOUT A STRETCHER.

AAARGH! LET ME DIE, SOLDIERS, AND SAVE YOUR OWN SKINS!

THAT'S IT!

UGH! DISGUSTING! WHAT IS IT?

YOU'VE GOT TO GUESS, MARC. DON'T WORRY, EVERYTHING IS EDIBLE!

A... ARE YOU SURE?...

WE'VE MADE OUR OWN LITTLE SPECIAL BLENDS, THAT'S ALL!

68

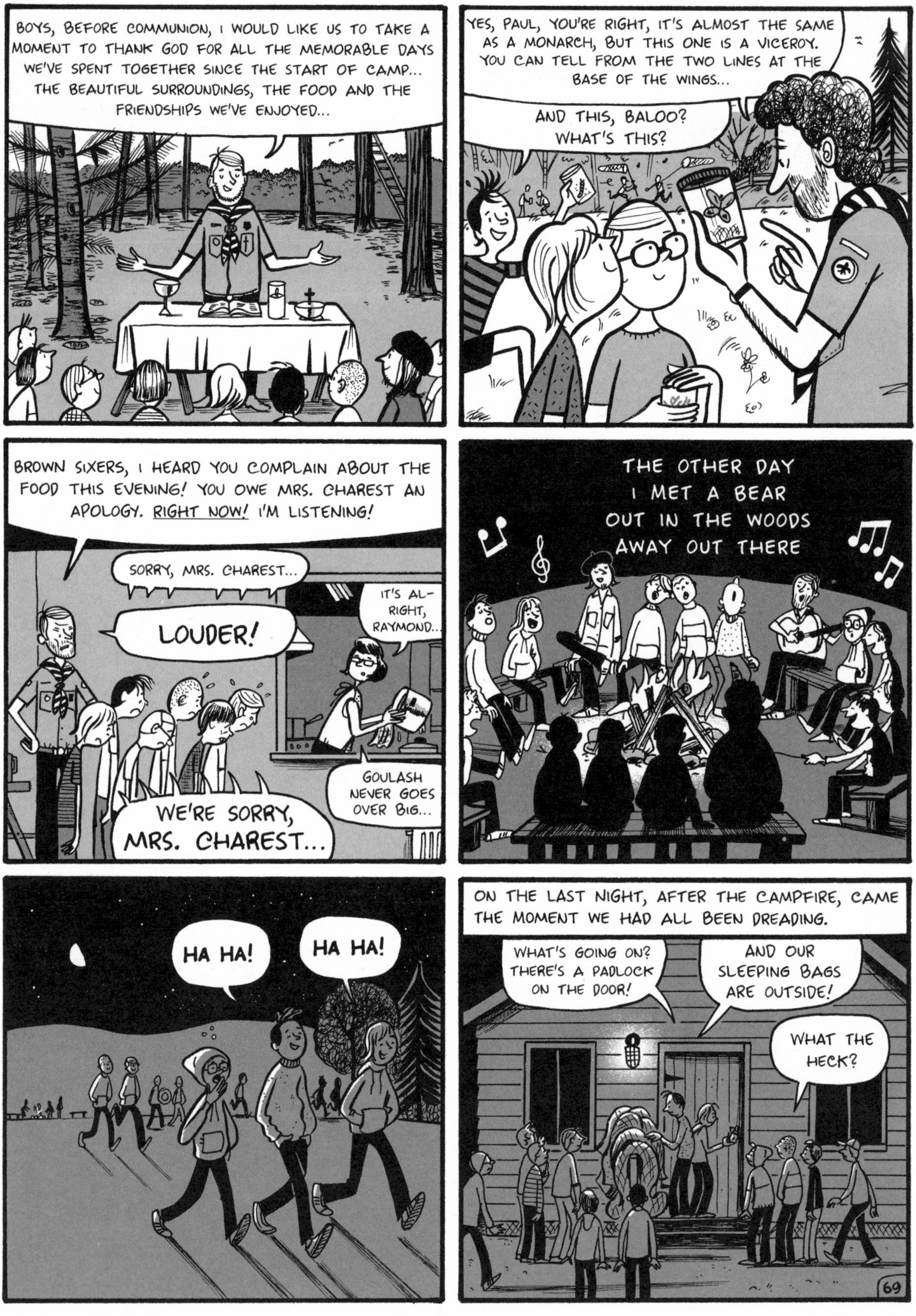
BOYS, BEFORE COMMUNION, I WOULD LIKE US TO TAKE A MOMENT TO THANK GOD FOR ALL THE MEMORABLE DAYS WE'VE SPENT TOGETHER SINCE THE START OF CAMP... THE BEAUTIFUL SURROUNDINGS, THE FOOD AND THE FRIENDSHIPS WE'VE ENJOYED...
YES, PAUL, YOU'RE RIGHT, IT'S ALMOST THE SAME AS A MONARCH, BUT THIS ONE IS A VICEROY. YOU CAN TELL FROM THE TWO LINES AT THE BASE OF THE WINGS...
AND THIS, BALOO? WHAT'S THIS?
BROWN SIXERS, I HEARD YOU COMPLAIN ABOUT THE FOOD THIS EVENING! YOU OWE MRS. CHAREST AN APOLOGY. RIGHT NOW! I'M LISTENING!
SORRY, MRS. CHAREST...
LOUDER!
IT'S ALRIGHT, RAYMOND...
WE'RE SORRY, MRS. CHAREST...
GOULASH NEVER GOES OVER BIG...
THE OTHER DAY I MET A BEAR OUT IN THE WOODS AWAY OUT THERE
HA HA!
HA HA!
ON THE LAST NIGHT, AFTER THE CAMPFIRE, CAME THE MOMENT WE HAD ALL BEEN DREADING.
WHAT'S GOING ON? THERE'S A PADLOCK ON THE DOOR!
AND OUR SLEEPING BAGS ARE OUTSIDE!
WHAT THE HECK?
69

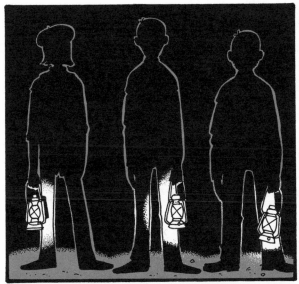

WE'VE OFTEN TALKED ABOUT IT AT OUR MEETINGS, BOYS. REMEMBER?

TONIGHT'S THE BIG NIGHT.

TAKE YOUR SLEEPING BAGS AND FOLLOW US.

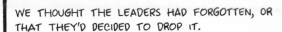
WE THOUGHT THE LEADERS HAD FORGOTTEN, OR THAT THEY'D DECIDED TO DROP IT.

IN FACT, THEY'D BEEN WAITING FOR US TO GET USED TO CAMP LIFE, AND FOR A WARM NIGHT WITH A CLEAR SKY LIKE THIS ONE.

GINO, THIS IS YOUR SPOT...

OK...

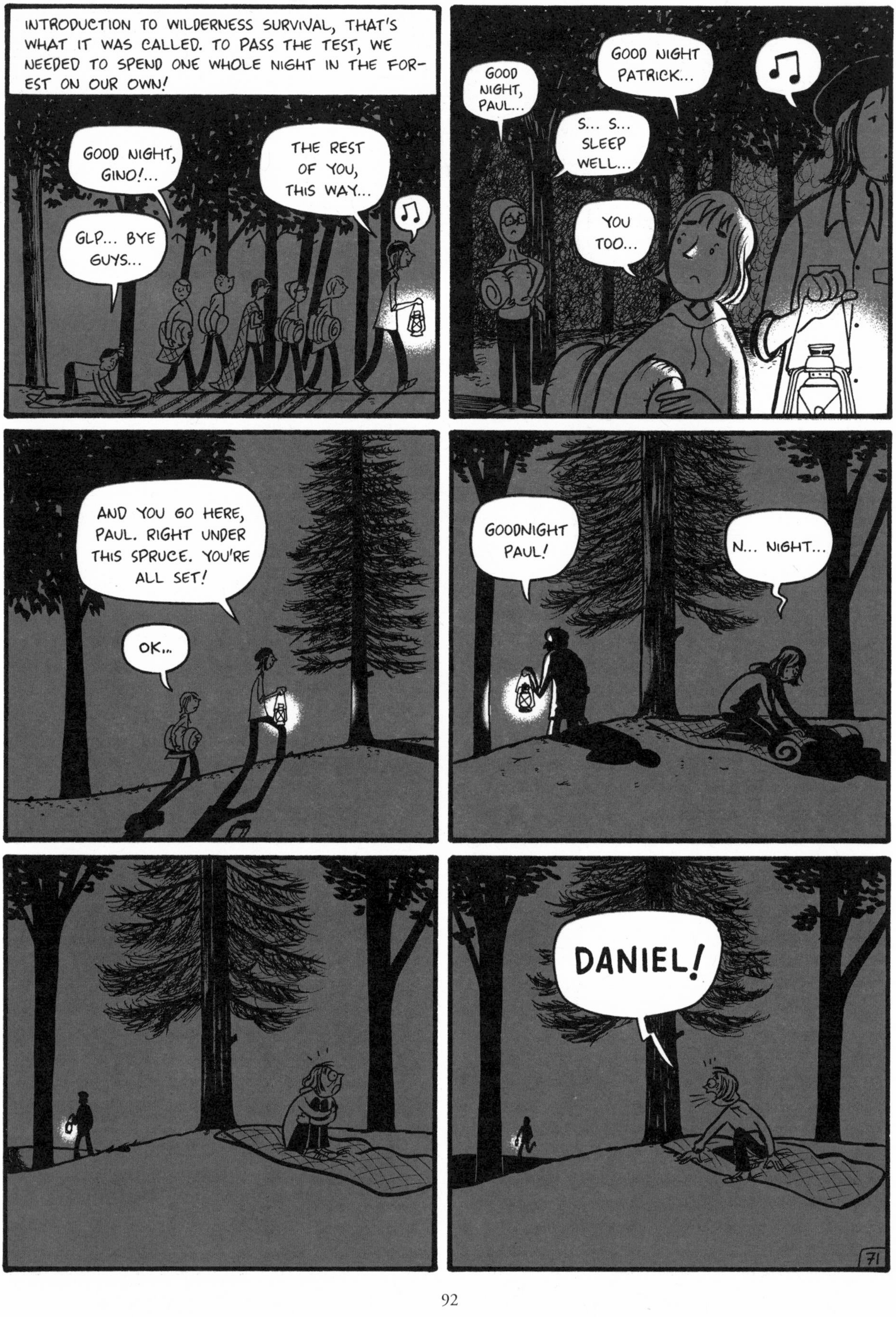
INTRODUCTION TO WILDERNESS SURVIVAL, THAT'S WHAT IT WAS CALLED. TO PASS THE TEST, WE NEEDED TO SPEND ONE WHOLE NIGHT IN THE FOREST ON OUR OWN!
GOOD NIGHT, GINO!...
GLP... BYE GUYS...
THE REST OF YOU, THIS WAY...
♫
GOOD NIGHT, PAUL...
GOOD NIGHT PATRICK...
S... S... SLEEP WELL...
YOU TOO...
♫
AND YOU GO HERE, PAUL. RIGHT UNDER THIS SPRUCE. YOU'RE ALL SET!
OK...
GOODNIGHT PAUL!
N... NIGHT...
DANIEL!
71

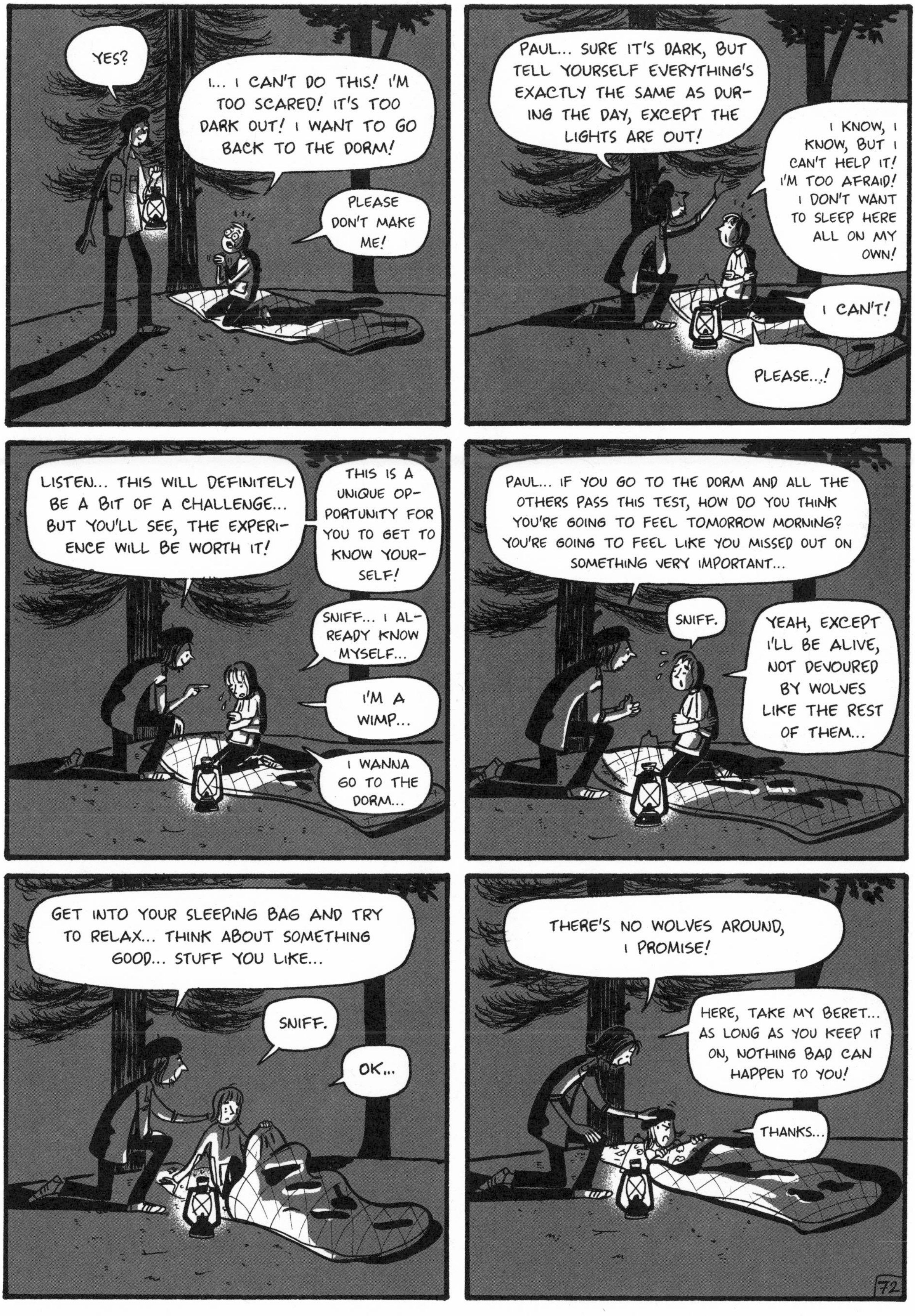
YES?
I... I CAN'T DO THIS! I'M TOO SCARED! IT'S TOO DARK OUT! I WANT TO GO BACK TO THE DORM!
PLEASE DON'T MAKE ME!
PAUL... SURE IT'S DARK, BUT TELL YOURSELF EVERYTHING'S EXACTLY THE SAME AS DURING THE DAY, EXCEPT THE LIGHTS ARE OUT!
I KNOW, I KNOW, BUT I CAN'T HELP IT! I'M TOO AFRAID! I DON'T WANT TO SLEEP HERE ALL ON MY OWN!
I CAN'T!
PLEASE...!
LISTEN... THIS WILL DEFINITELY BE A BIT OF A CHALLENGE... BUT YOU'LL SEE, THE EXPERIENCE WILL BE WORTH IT!
THIS IS A UNIQUE OPPORTUNITY FOR YOU TO GET TO KNOW YOURSELF!
SNIFF... I ALREADY KNOW MYSELF...
I'M A WIMP...
I WANNA GO TO THE DORM...
PAUL... IF YOU GO TO THE DORM AND ALL THE OTHERS PASS THIS TEST, HOW DO YOU THINK YOU'RE GOING TO FEEL TOMORROW MORNING? YOU'RE GOING TO FEEL LIKE YOU MISSED OUT ON SOMETHING VERY IMPORTANT...
SNIFF.
YEAH, EXCEPT I'LL BE ALIVE, NOT DEVOURED BY WOLVES LIKE THE REST OF THEM...
GET INTO YOUR SLEEPING BAG AND TRY TO RELAX... THINK ABOUT SOMETHING GOOD... STUFF YOU LIKE...
SNIFF.
OK...
THERE'S NO WOLVES AROUND, I PROMISE!
HERE, TAKE MY BERET... AS LONG AS YOU KEEP IT ON, NOTHING BAD CAN HAPPEN TO YOU!
THANKS...
72

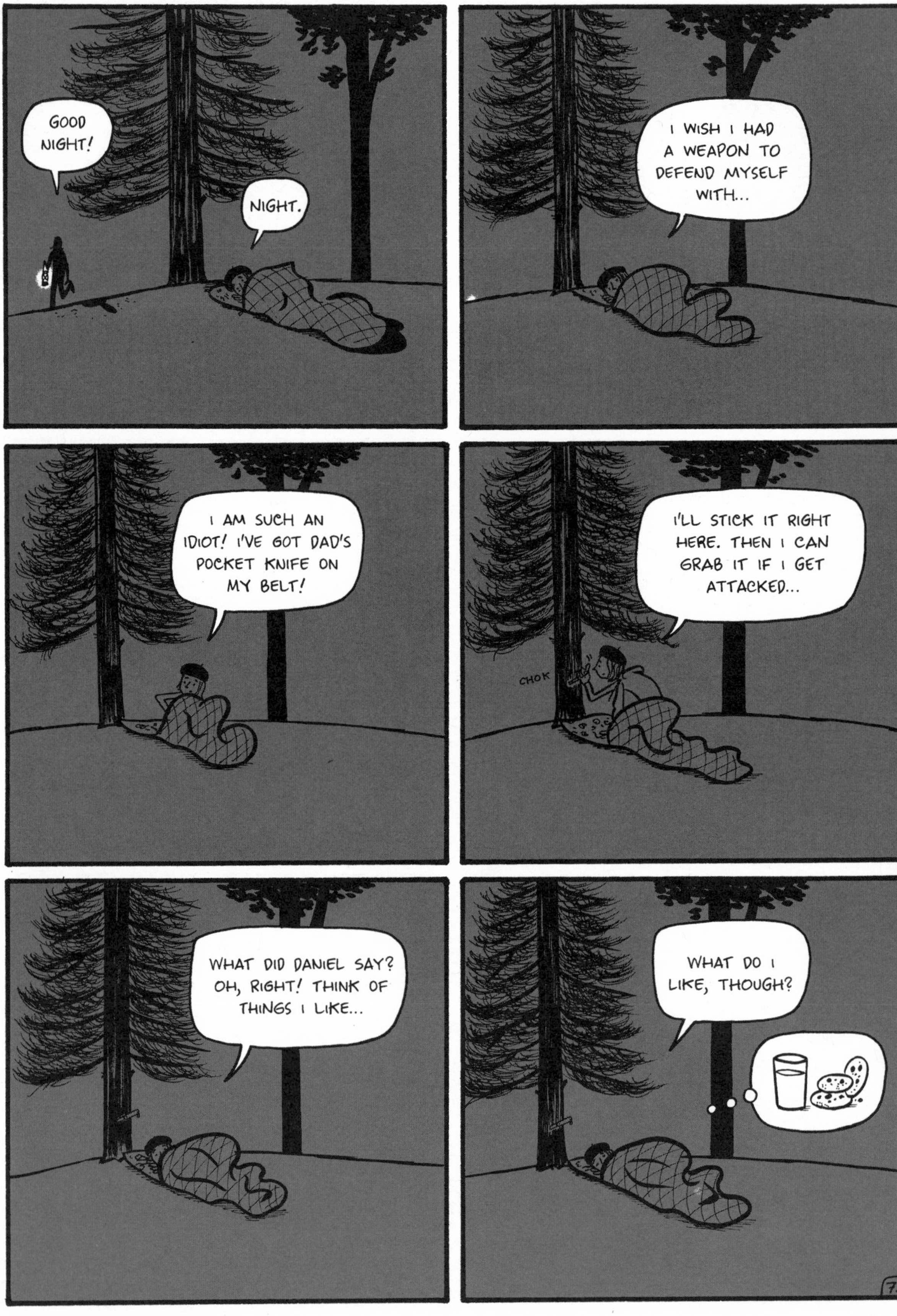
GOOD NIGHT!
NIGHT.
I WISH I HAD A WEAPON TO DEFEND MYSELF WITH...
I AM SUCH AN IDIOT! I'VE GOT DAD'S POCKET KNIFE ON MY BELT!
I'LL STICK IT RIGHT HERE. THEN I CAN GRAB IT IF I GET ATTACKED...
CHOK
WHAT DID DANIEL SAY? OH, RIGHT! THINK OF THINGS I LIKE...
WHAT DO I LIKE, THOUGH?
73

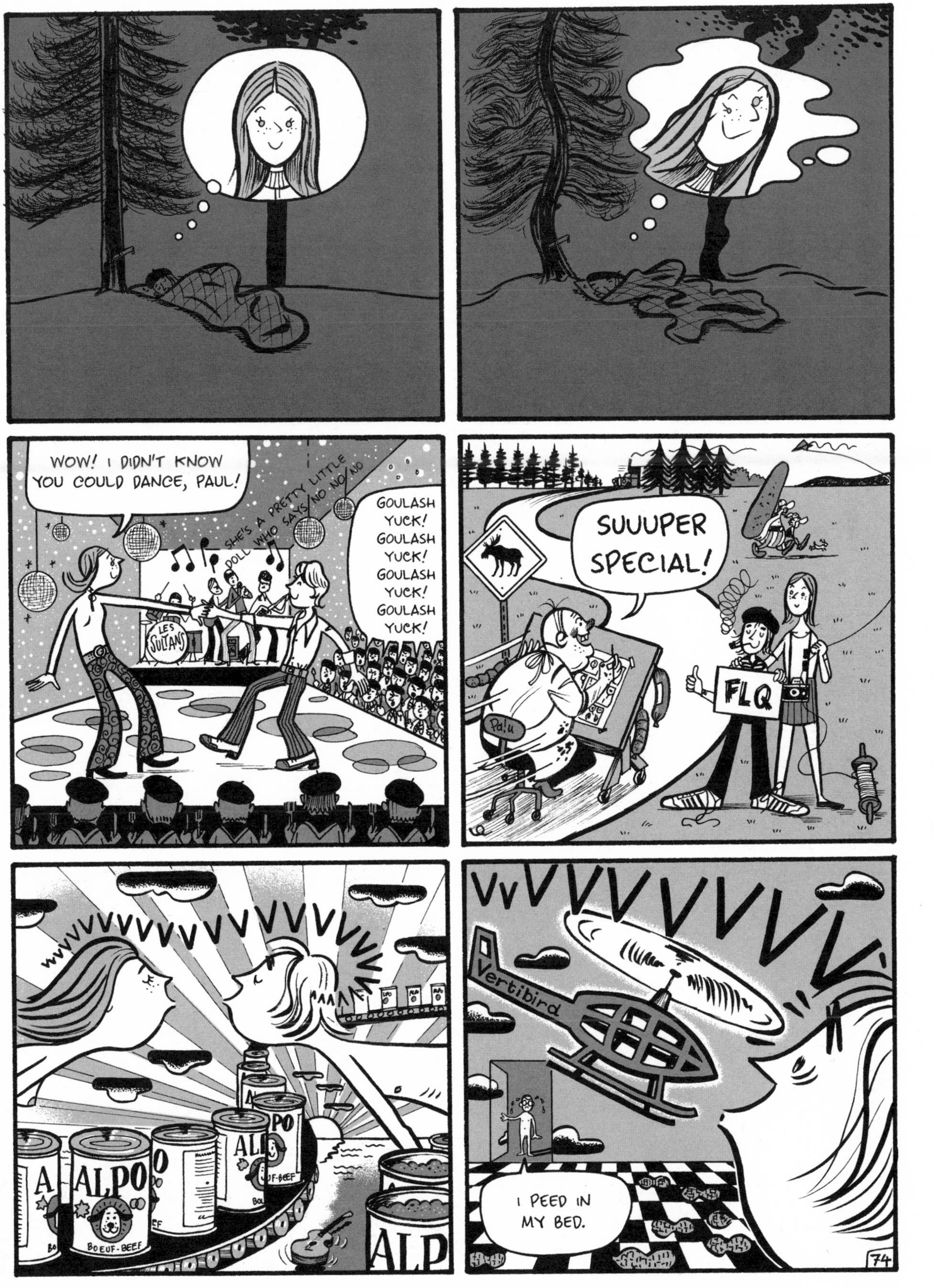

WOW! I DIDN'T KNOW YOU COULD DANCE, PAUL!
SHE'S A PRETTY LITTLE DOLL WHO SAYS NO NO NO
LES SULTANS
GOULASH YUCK! GOULASH YUCK! GOULASH YUCK! GOULASH YUCK!
SUUUPER SPECIAL!
Pa|u
FLQ
VvVVVVVVVVVVVVVVV
ALPO
BOEUF-BEEF
VvVVVVVVVVV
Vertibird
I PEED IN MY BED.
74

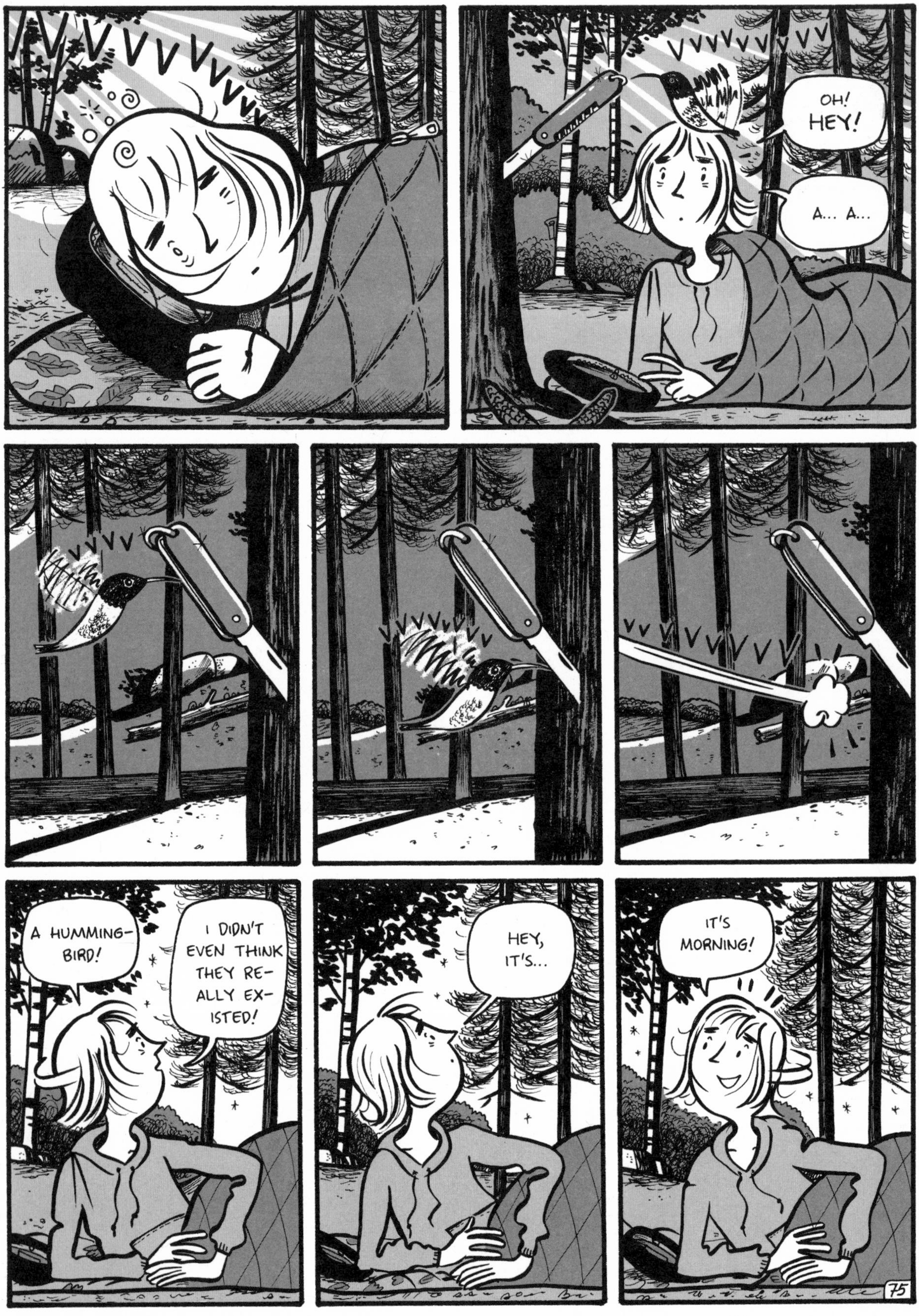
VVVVVVVVV
VVVVVVVVVV
OH! HEY!
A... A...
VVVV
VVVVVVVV
VVVVVVVVVVV
A HUMMING-BIRD!
I DIDN'T EVEN THINK THEY RE-ALLY EX-ISTED!
HEY, IT'S...
IT'S MORNING!
75

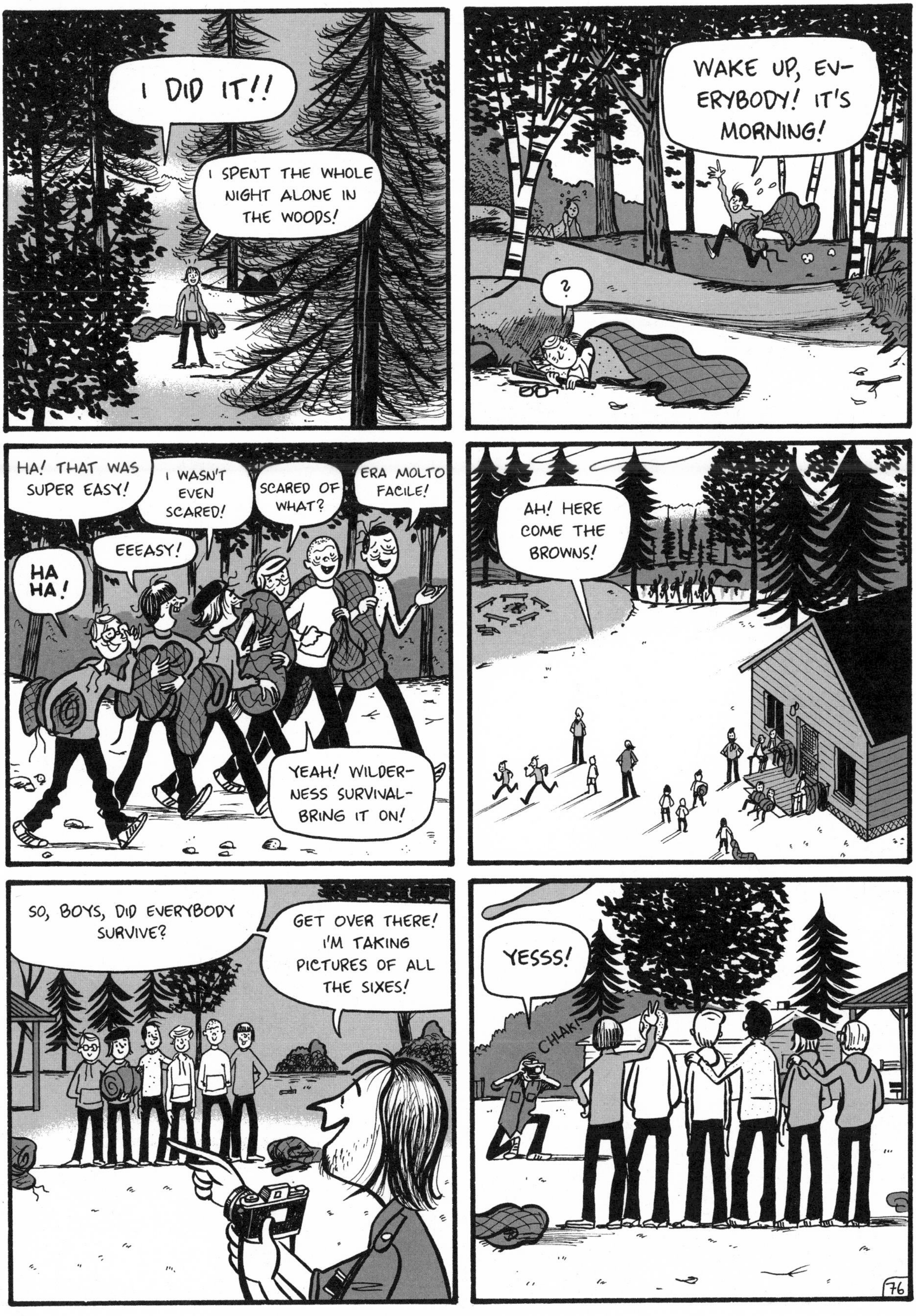
I DID IT!!
I SPENT THE WHOLE NIGHT ALONE IN THE WOODS!
WAKE UP, EV-ERYBODY! IT'S MORNING!
?
HA! THAT WAS SUPER EASY!
I WASN'T EVEN SCARED!
SCARED OF WHAT?
ERA MOLTO FACILE!
HA HA!
EEEASY!
YEAH! WILDER-NESS SURVIVAL-BRING IT ON!
AH! HERE COME THE BROWNS!
SO, BOYS, DID EVERYBODY SURVIVE?
GET OVER THERE! I'M TAKING PICTURES OF ALL THE SIXES!
YESSS!
CHLAK!
76

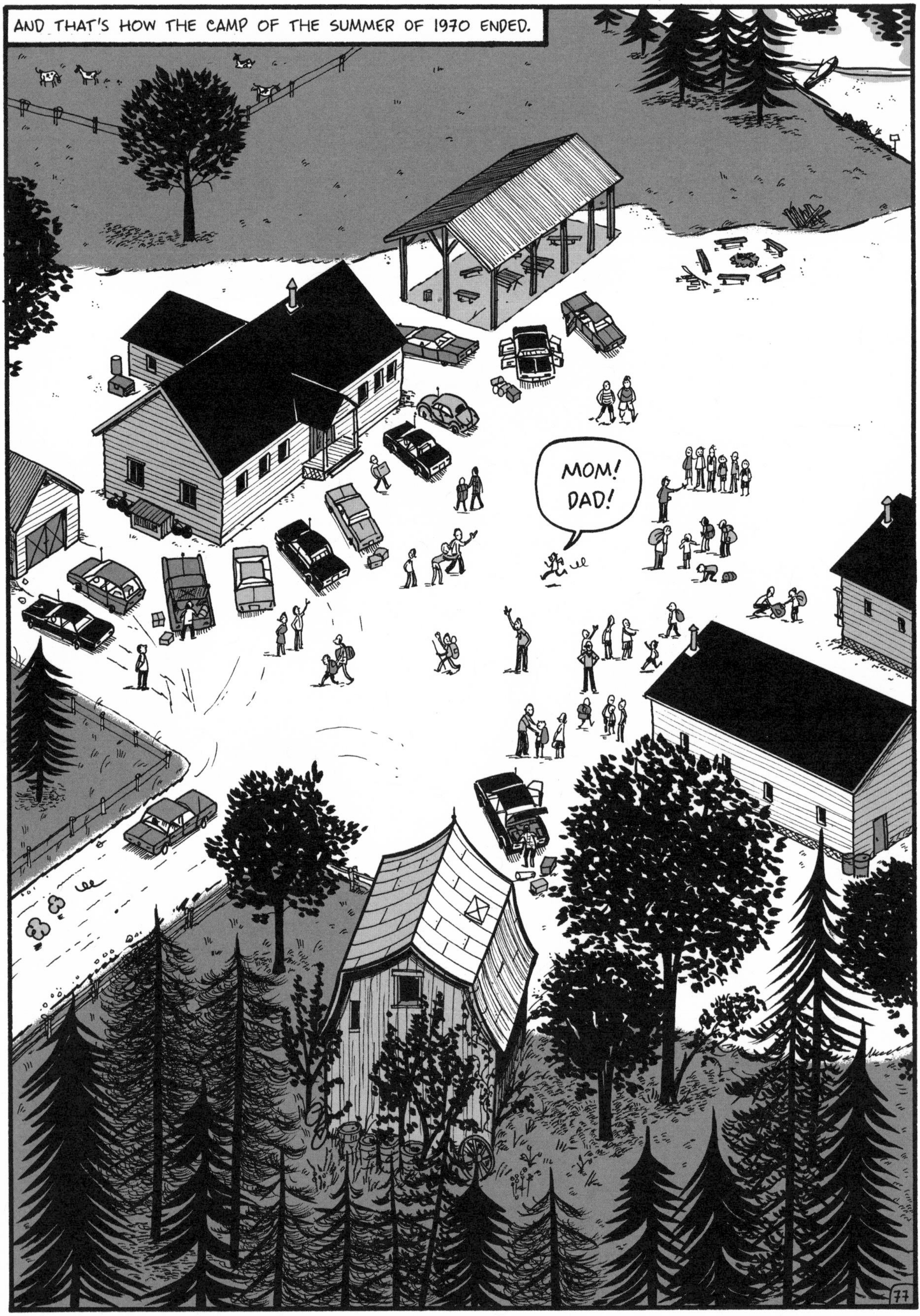
AND THAT'S HOW THE CAMP OF THE SUMMER OF 1970 ENDED.
MOM! DAD!
77

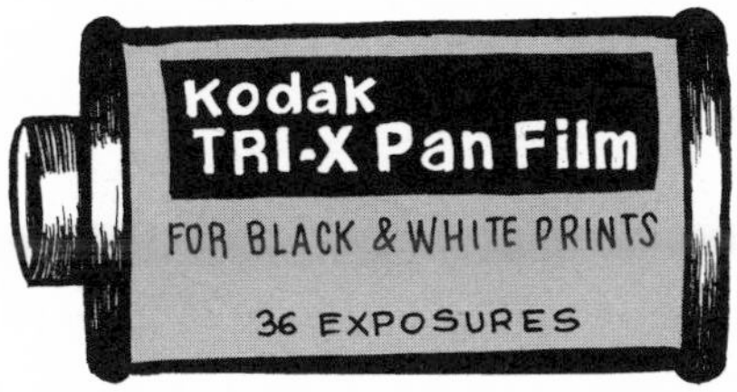
Kodak
TRI-X Pan Film
FOR BLACK & WHITE PRINTS
36 EXPOSURES

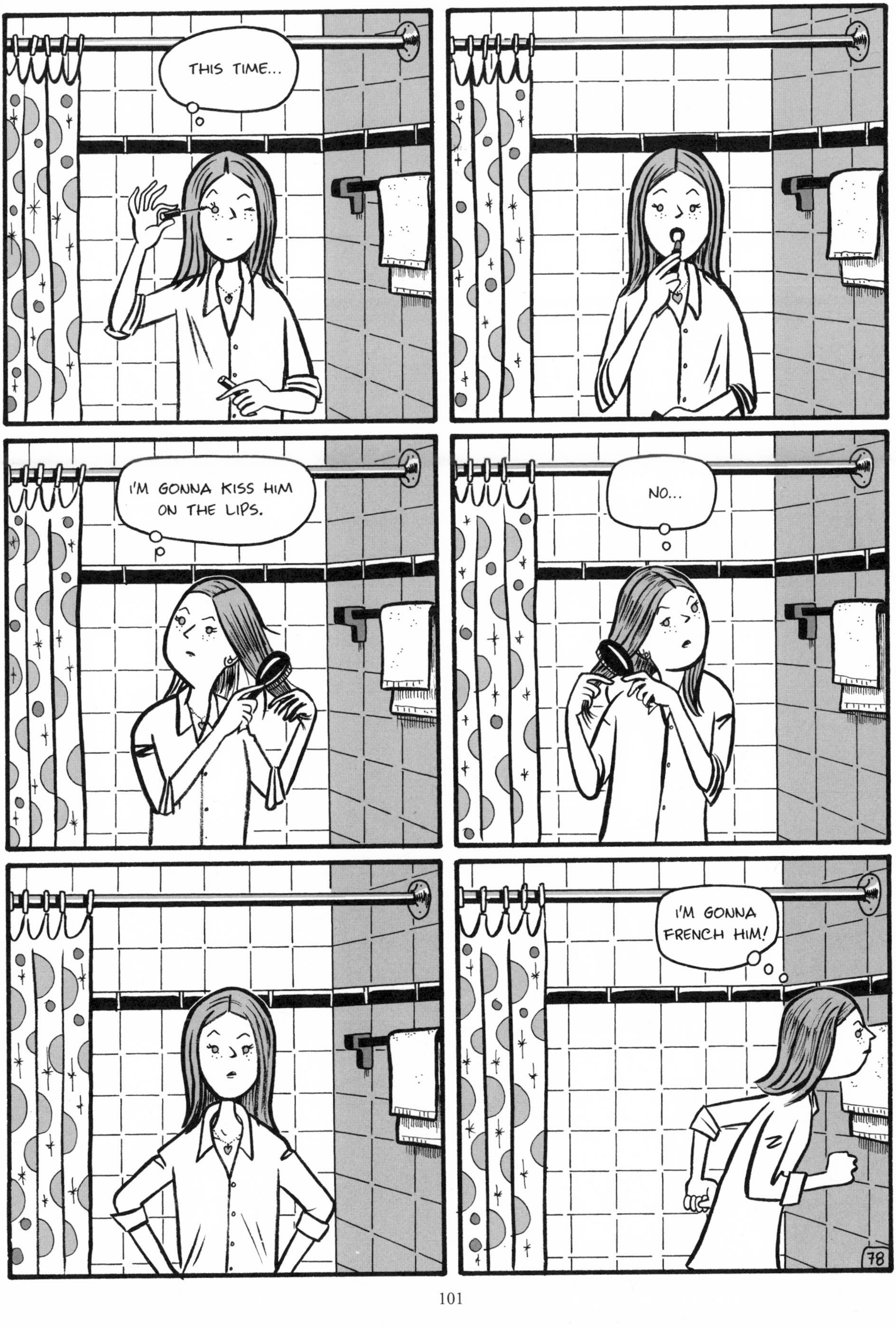
THIS TIME...
I'M GONNA KISS HIM ON THE LIPS.
NO...
I'M GONNA FRENCH HIM!
78

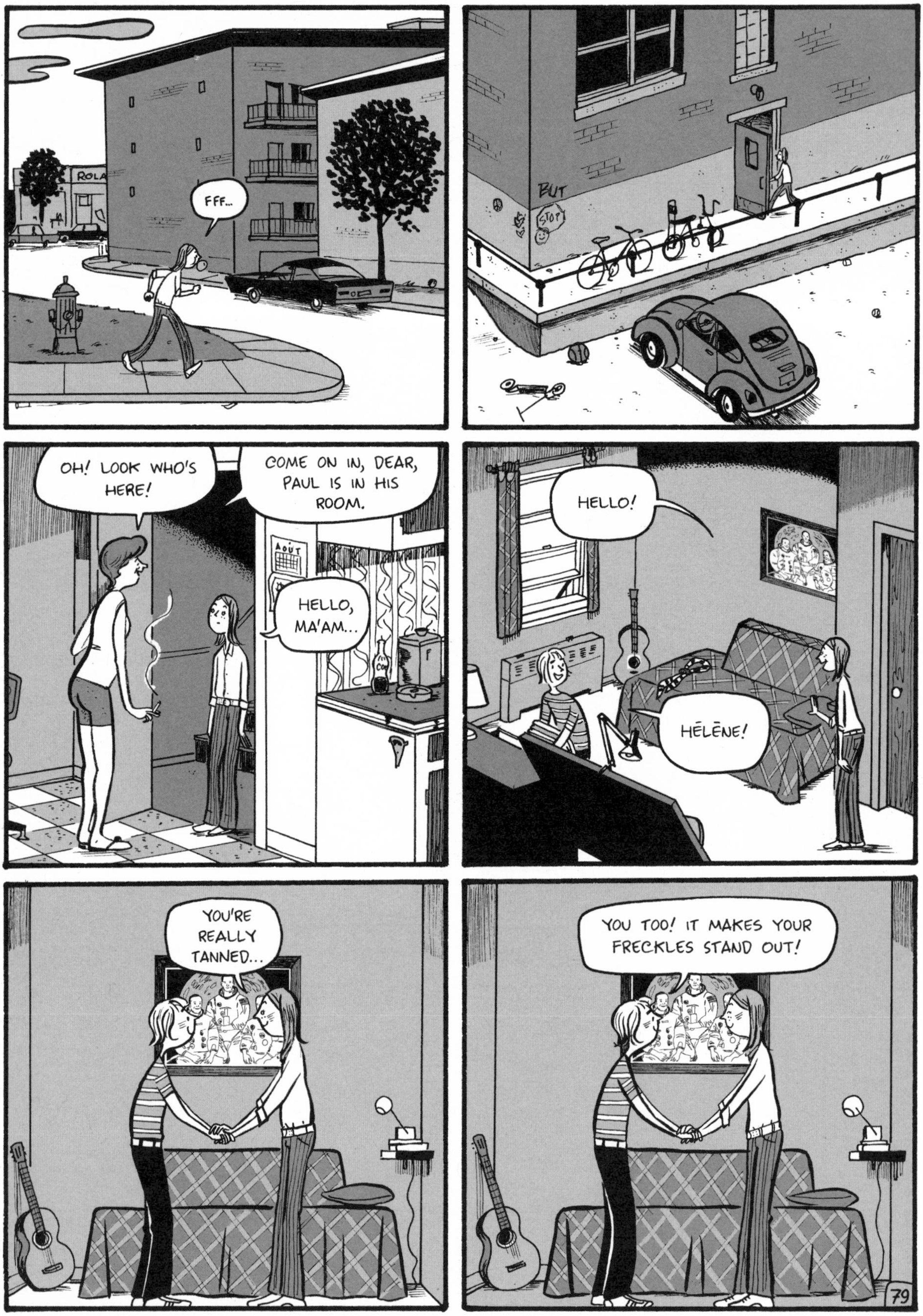
FFF...
BUT
STOP
OH! LOOK WHO'S HERE!
COME ON IN, DEAR, PAUL IS IN HIS ROOM.
AOÛT
HELLO, MA'AM...
HELLO!
HÉLÈNE!
YOU'RE REALLY TANNED...
YOU TOO! IT MAKES YOUR FRECKLES STAND OUT!
79

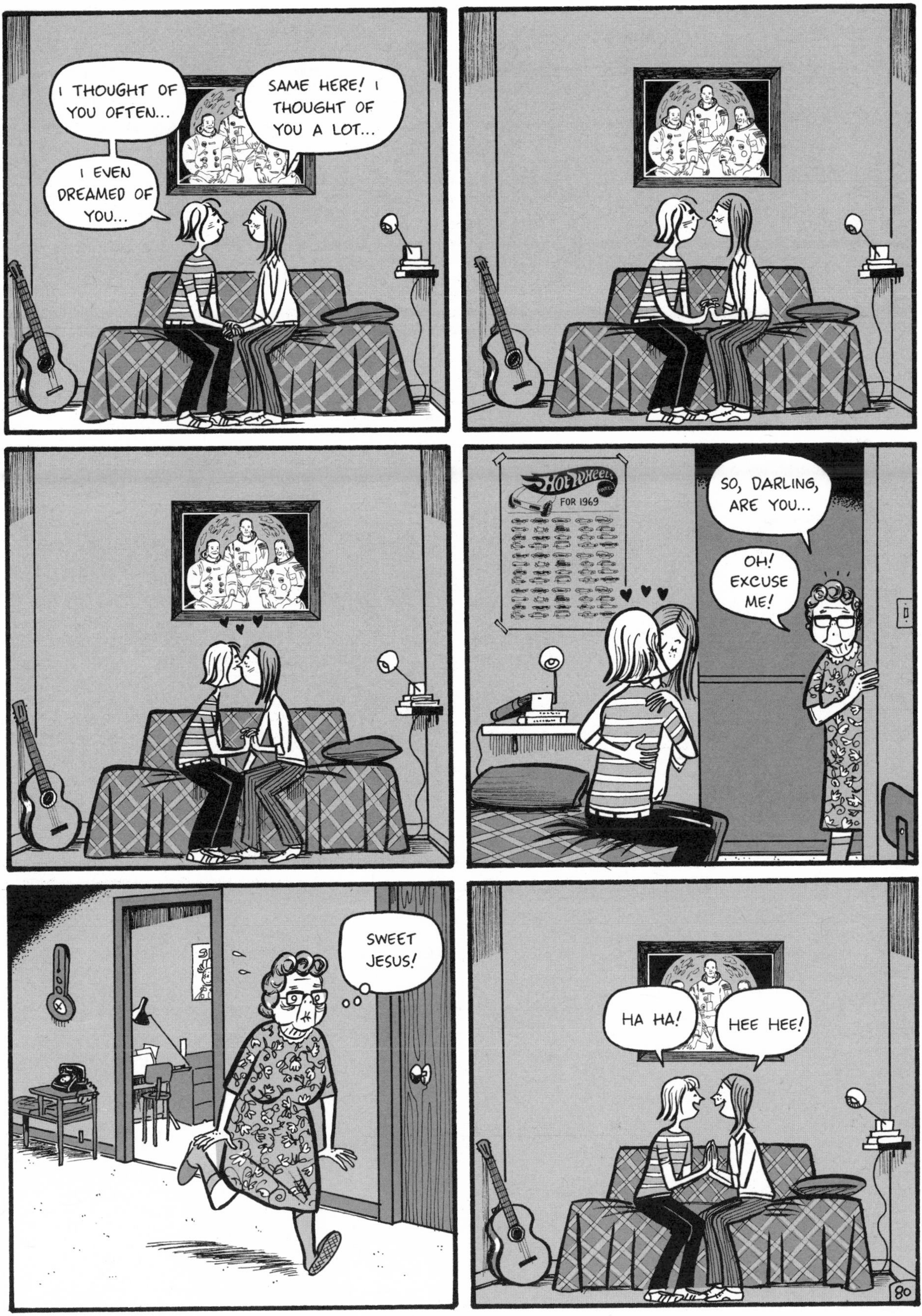
I THOUGHT OF YOU OFTEN...
I EVEN DREAMED OF YOU...
SAME HERE! I THOUGHT OF YOU A LOT...
HOT WHEELS FOR 1969
SO, DARLING, ARE YOU...
OH! EXCUSE ME!
SWEET JESUS!
HA HA!
HEE HEE!
80

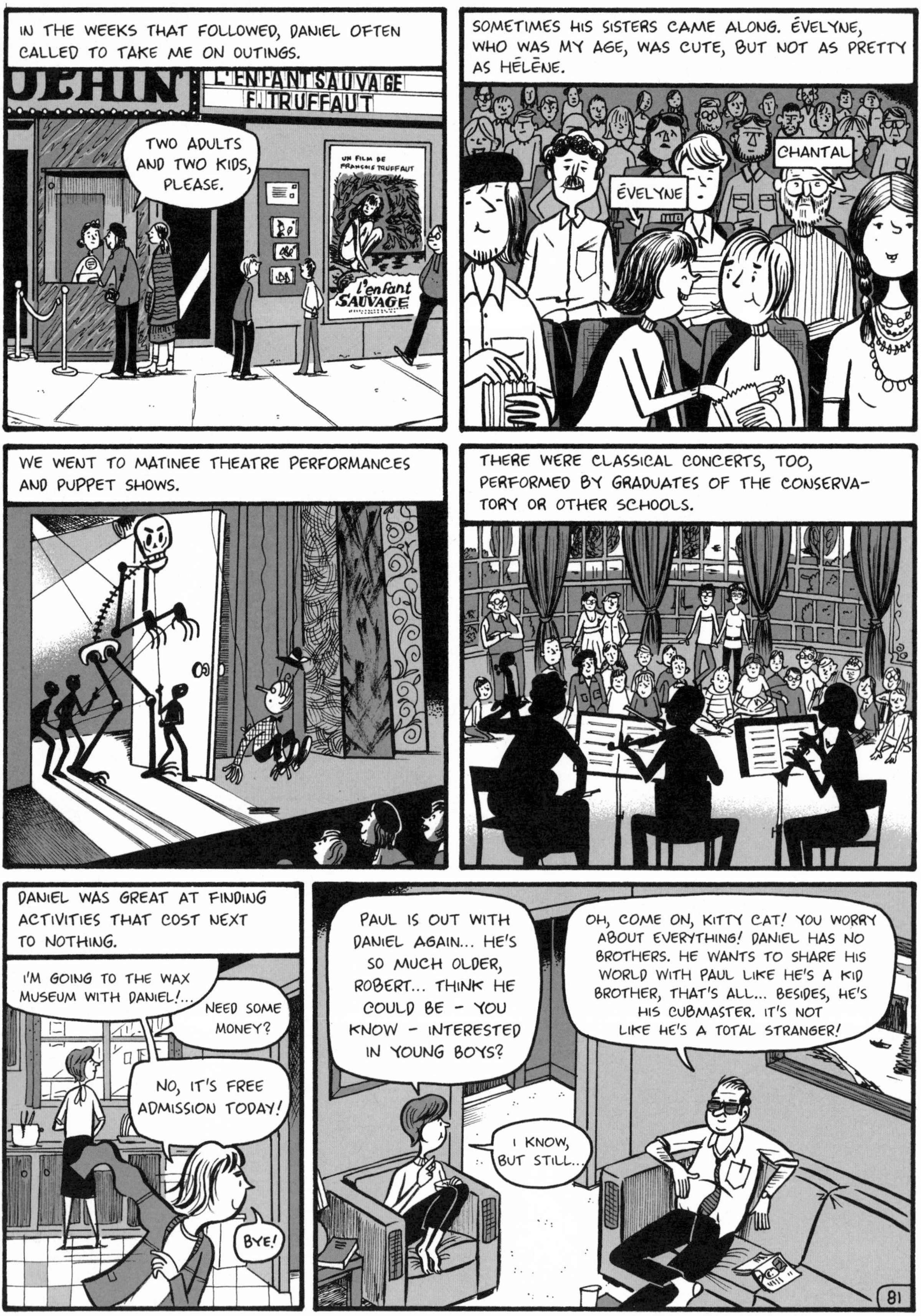

IN THE WEEKS THAT FOLLOWED, DANIEL OFTEN CALLED TO TAKE ME ON OUTINGS.
L'ENFANT SAUVAGE
F. TRUFFAUT
TWO ADULTS AND TWO KIDS, PLEASE.
UN FILM DE FRANÇOIS TRUFFAUT
l'enfant SAUVAGE
SOMETIMES HIS SISTERS CAME ALONG. ÉVELYNE, WHO WAS MY AGE, WAS CUTE, BUT NOT AS PRETTY AS HÉLÈNE.
CHANTAL
ÉVELYNE
WE WENT TO MATINEE THEATRE PERFORMANCES AND PUPPET SHOWS.
THERE WERE CLASSICAL CONCERTS, TOO, PERFORMED BY GRADUATES OF THE CONSERVATORY OR OTHER SCHOOLS.
DANIEL WAS GREAT AT FINDING ACTIVITIES THAT COST NEXT TO NOTHING.
I'M GOING TO THE WAX MUSEUM WITH DANIEL!...
NEED SOME MONEY?
NO, IT'S FREE ADMISSION TODAY!
BYE!
PAUL IS OUT WITH DANIEL AGAIN... HE'S SO MUCH OLDER, ROBERT... THINK HE COULD BE - YOU KNOW - INTERESTED IN YOUNG BOYS?
OH, COME ON, KITTY CAT! YOU WORRY ABOUT EVERYTHING! DANIEL HAS NO BROTHERS. HE WANTS TO SHARE HIS WORLD WITH PAUL LIKE HE'S A KID BROTHER, THAT'S ALL... BESIDES, HE'S HIS CUBMASTER. IT'S NOT LIKE HE'S A TOTAL STRANGER!
I KNOW, BUT STILL...
81

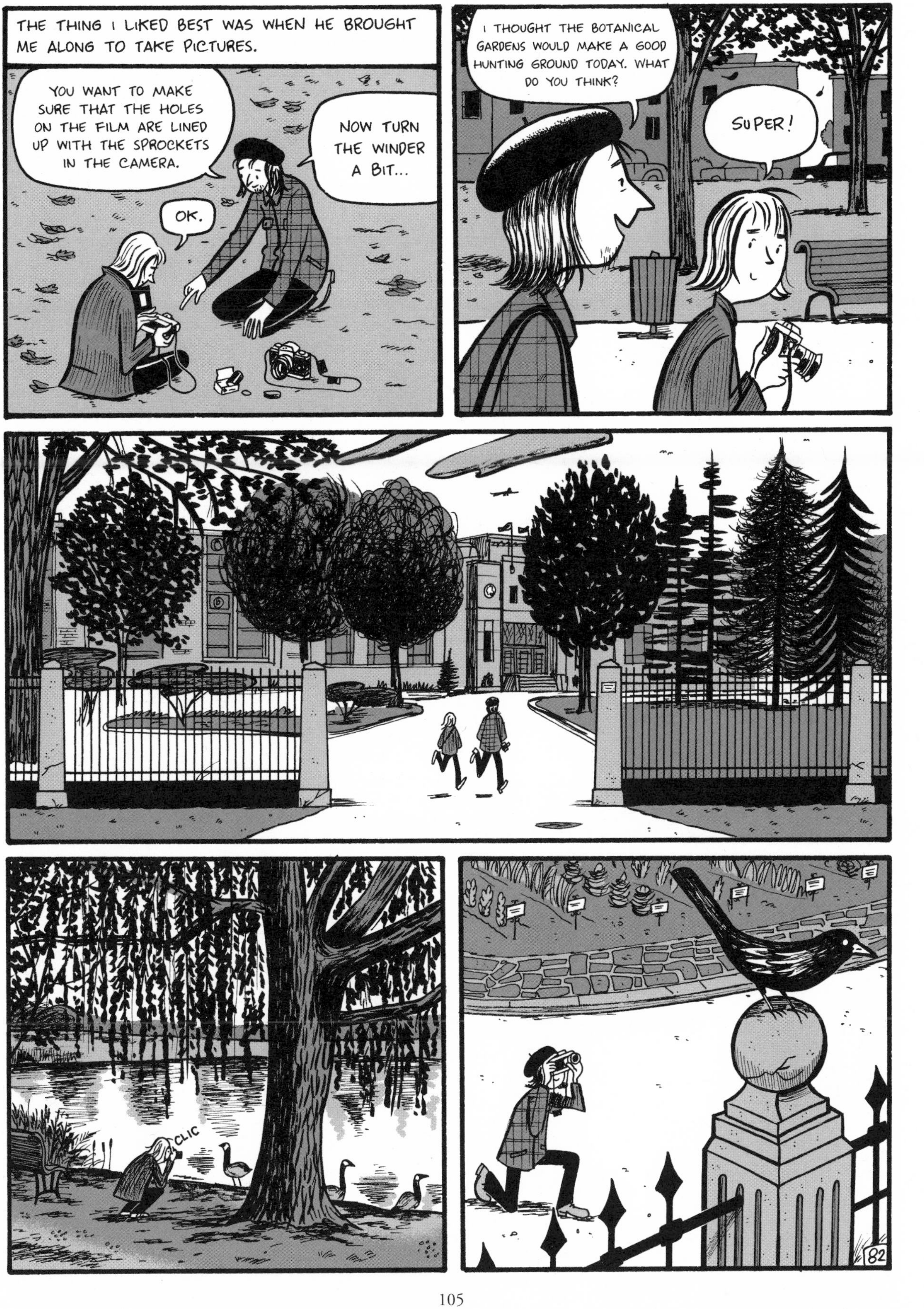
THE THING I LIKED BEST WAS WHEN HE BROUGHT ME ALONG TO TAKE PICTURES.
YOU WANT TO MAKE SURE THAT THE HOLES ON THE FILM ARE LINED UP WITH THE SPROCKETS IN THE CAMERA.
OK.
NOW TURN THE WINDER A BIT...
I THOUGHT THE BOTANICAL GARDENS WOULD MAKE A GOOD HUNTING GROUND TODAY. WHAT DO YOU THINK?
SUPER!
CLIC
82

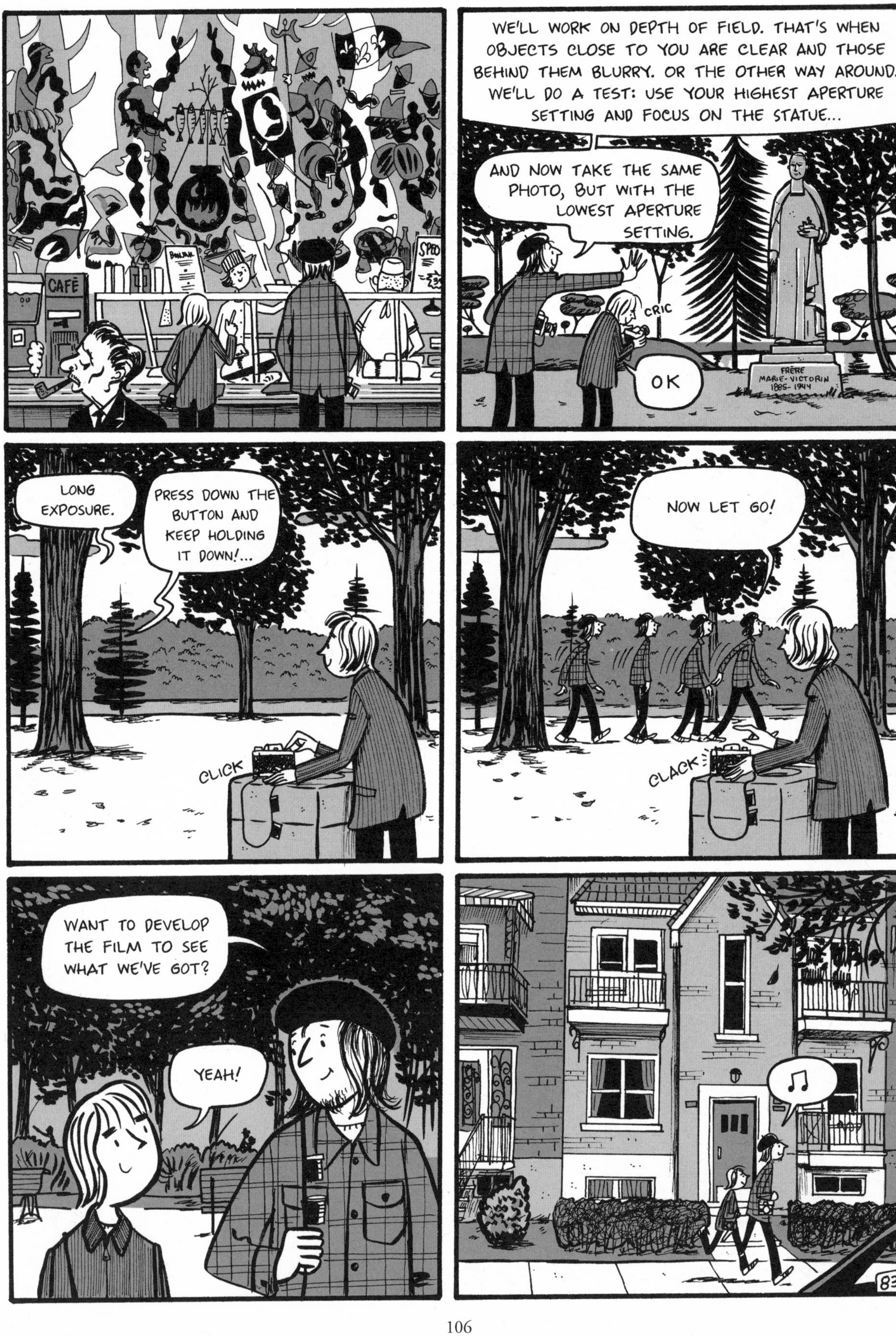
CAFÉ
WE'LL WORK ON DEPTH OF FIELD. THAT'S WHEN OBJECTS CLOSE TO YOU ARE CLEAR AND THOSE BEHIND THEM BLURRY. OR THE OTHER WAY AROUND. WE'LL DO A TEST: USE YOUR HIGHEST APERTURE SETTING AND FOCUS ON THE STATUE...
AND NOW TAKE THE SAME PHOTO, BUT WITH THE LOWEST APERTURE SETTING.
CRIC
OK
FRÈRE MARIE-VICTORIN 1885-1944
LONG EXPOSURE.
PRESS DOWN THE BUTTON AND KEEP HOLDING IT DOWN!...
CLICK
NOW LET GO!
CLACK
WANT TO DEVELOP THE FILM TO SEE WHAT WE'VE GOT?
YEAH!
83

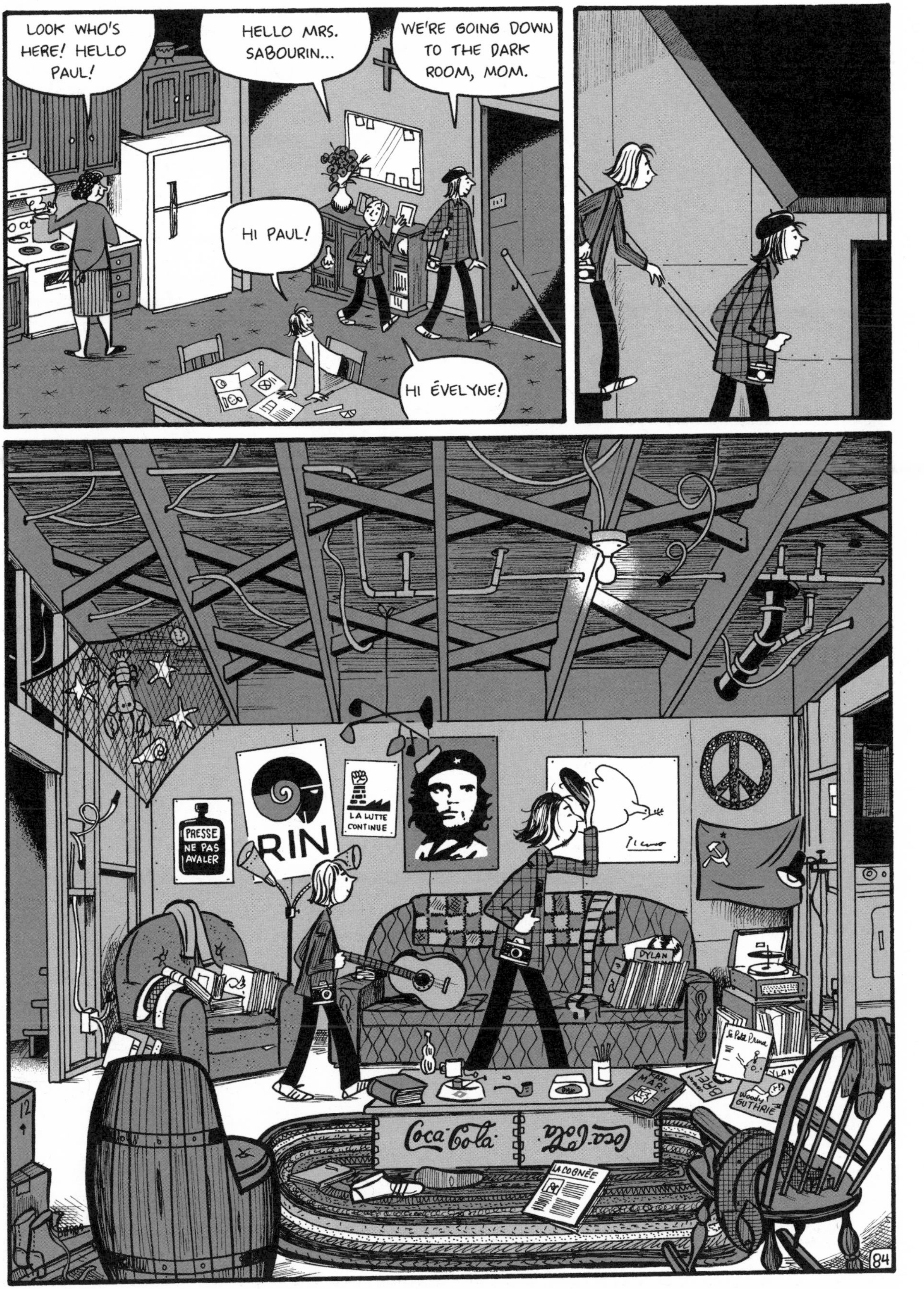
LOOK WHO'S HERE! HELLO PAUL!
HELLO MRS. SABOURIN...
WE'RE GOING DOWN TO THE DARK ROOM, MOM.
HI PAUL!
HI ÉVELYNE!
PRESSE NE PAS AVALER
RIN
LA LUTTE CONTINUE
DYLAN
KARL MARX
BREL
WOODY GUTHRIE
Coca-Cola
Coca-Cola
LA COGNÉE
84

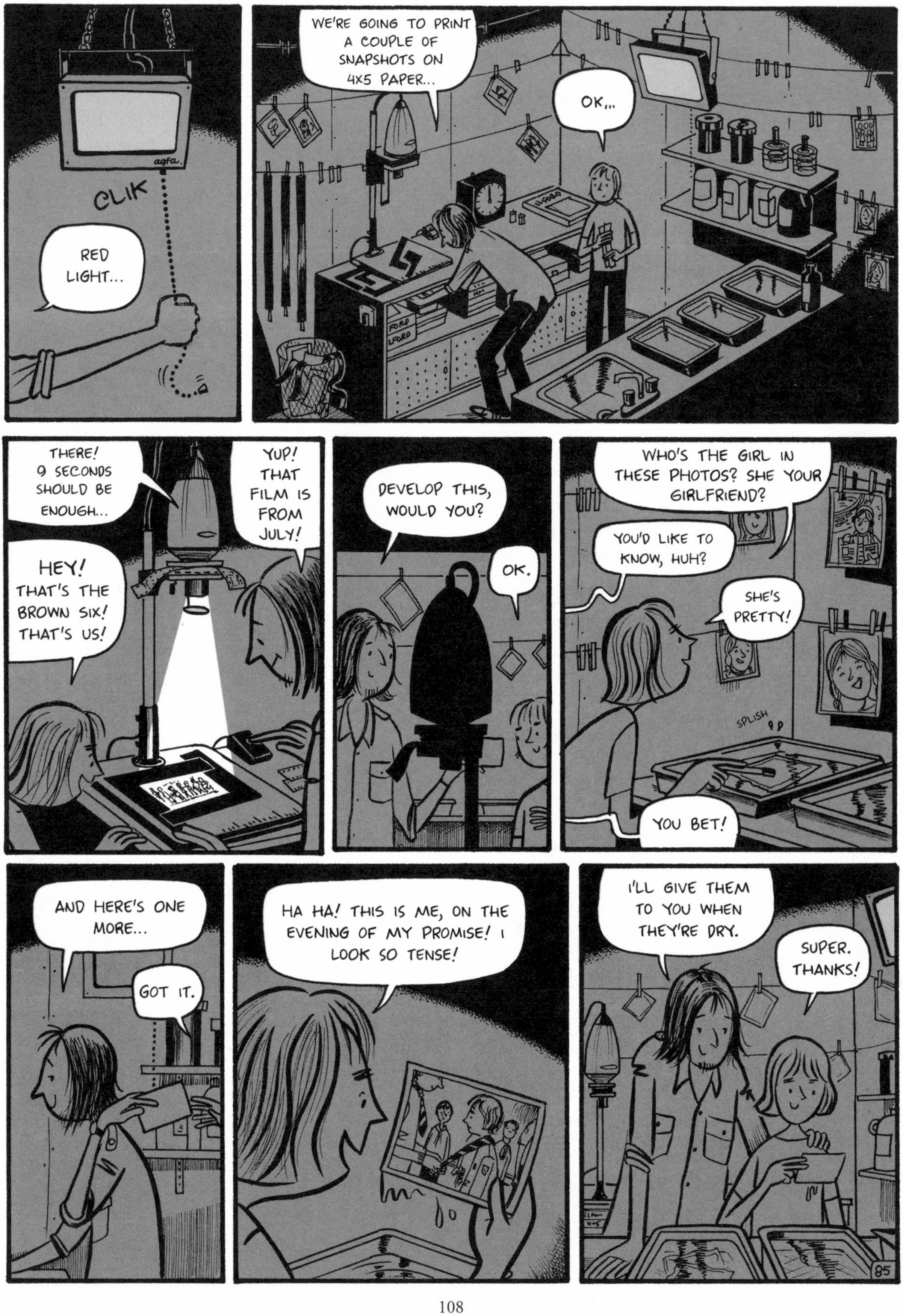

CLIK
RED LIGHT...
WE'RE GOING TO PRINT A COUPLE OF SNAPSHOTS ON 4X5 PAPER...
OK,..
THERE! 9 SECONDS SHOULD BE ENOUGH...
YUP! THAT FILM IS FROM JULY!
HEY! THAT'S THE BROWN SIX! THAT'S US!
DEVELOP THIS, WOULD YOU?
OK.
WHO'S THE GIRL IN THESE PHOTOS? SHE YOUR GIRLFRIEND?
YOU'D LIKE TO KNOW, HUH?
SHE'S PRETTY!
SPLISH
YOU BET!
AND HERE'S ONE MORE...
GOT IT.
HA HA! THIS IS ME, ON THE EVENING OF MY PROMISE! I LOOK SO TENSE!
I'LL GIVE THEM TO YOU WHEN THEY'RE DRY.
SUPER. THANKS!
85

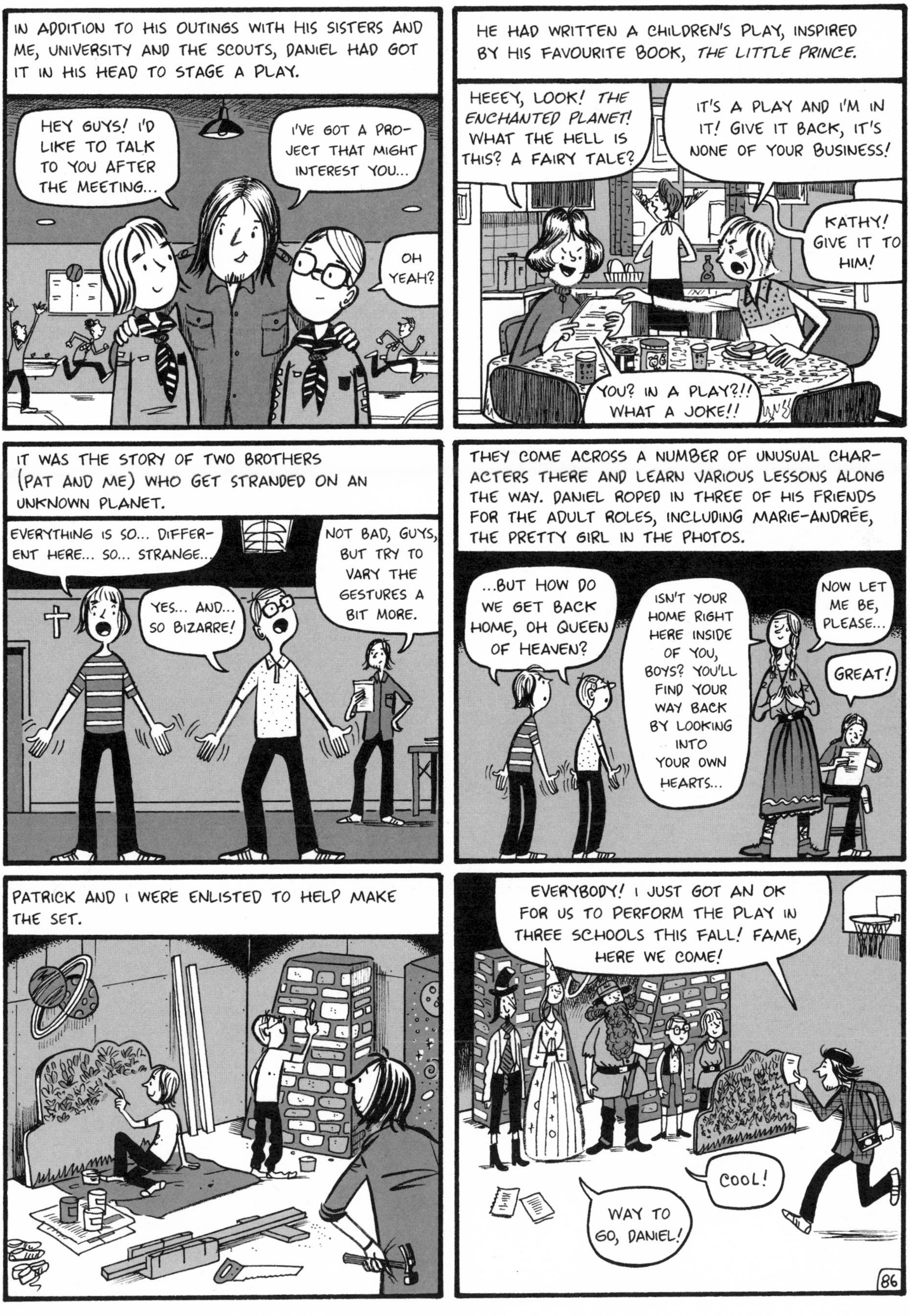
IN ADDITION TO HIS OUTINGS WITH HIS SISTERS AND ME, UNIVERSITY AND THE SCOUTS, DANIEL HAD GOT IT IN HIS HEAD TO STAGE A PLAY.
HEY GUYS! I'D LIKE TO TALK TO YOU AFTER THE MEETING...
I'VE GOT A PROJECT THAT MIGHT INTEREST YOU...
OH YEAH?
HE HAD WRITTEN A CHILDREN'S PLAY, INSPIRED BY HIS FAVOURITE BOOK, *THE LITTLE PRINCE*.
HEEEY, LOOK! *THE ENCHANTED PLANET!* WHAT THE HELL IS THIS? A FAIRY TALE?
IT'S A PLAY AND I'M IN IT! GIVE IT BACK, IT'S NONE OF YOUR BUSINESS!
KATHY! GIVE IT TO HIM!
YOU? IN A PLAY?!! WHAT A JOKE!!
IT WAS THE STORY OF TWO BROTHERS (PAT AND ME) WHO GET STRANDED ON AN UNKNOWN PLANET.
EVERYTHING IS SO... DIFFERENT HERE... SO... STRANGE...
YES... AND... SO BIZARRE!
NOT BAD, GUYS, BUT TRY TO VARY THE GESTURES A BIT MORE.
THEY COME ACROSS A NUMBER OF UNUSUAL CHARACTERS THERE AND LEARN VARIOUS LESSONS ALONG THE WAY. DANIEL ROPED IN THREE OF HIS FRIENDS FOR THE ADULT ROLES, INCLUDING MARIE-ANDRÉE, THE PRETTY GIRL IN THE PHOTOS.
...BUT HOW DO WE GET BACK HOME, OH QUEEN OF HEAVEN?
ISN'T YOUR HOME RIGHT HERE INSIDE OF YOU, BOYS? YOU'LL FIND YOUR WAY BACK BY LOOKING INTO YOUR OWN HEARTS...
NOW LET ME BE, PLEASE...
GREAT!
PATRICK AND I WERE ENLISTED TO HELP MAKE THE SET.
EVERYBODY! I JUST GOT AN OK FOR US TO PERFORM THE PLAY IN THREE SCHOOLS THIS FALL! FAME, HERE WE COME!
COOL!
WAY TO GO, DANIEL!
86

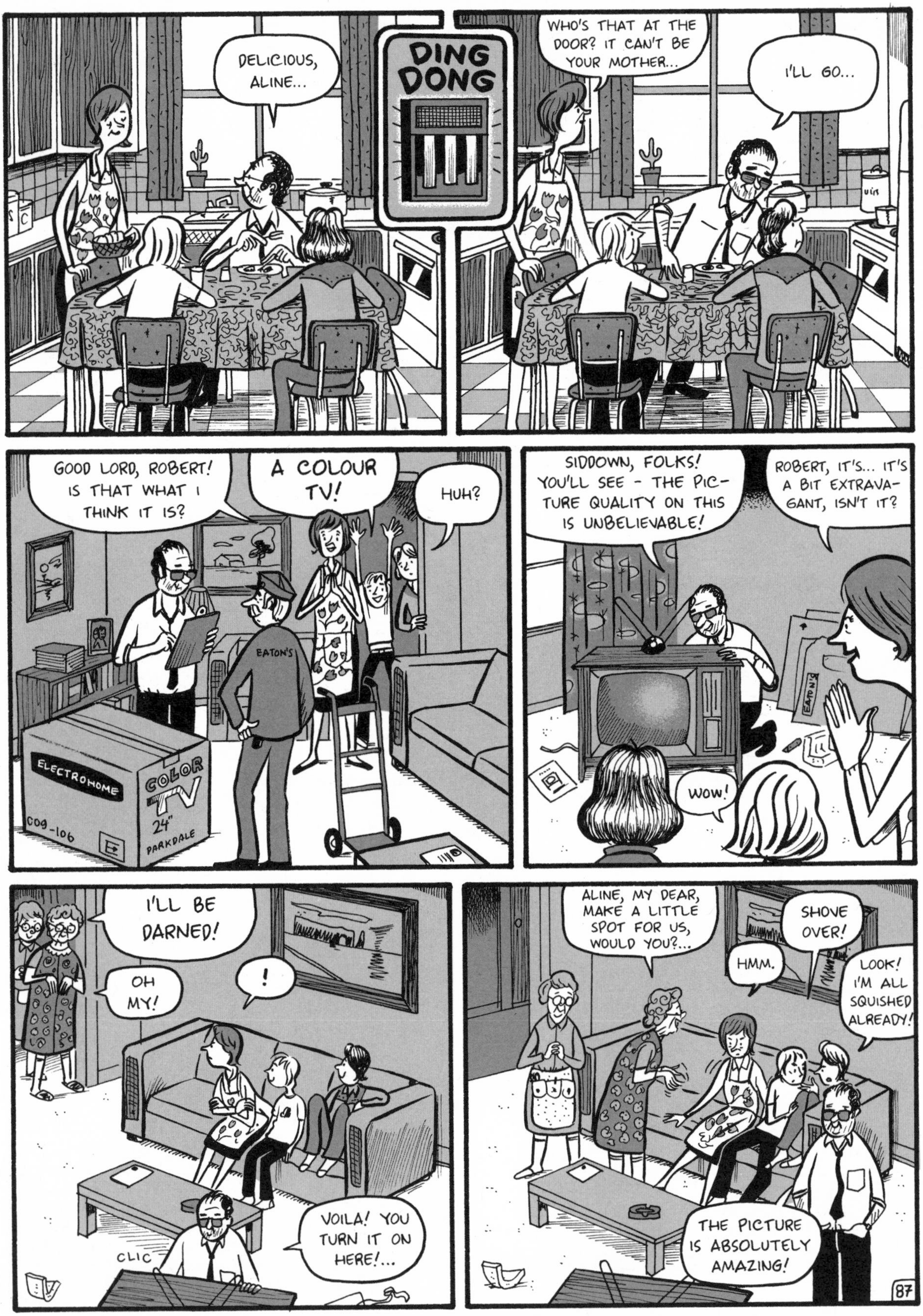

DELICIOUS, ALINE...
DING DONG
WHO'S THAT AT THE DOOR? IT CAN'T BE YOUR MOTHER...
I'LL GO...
GOOD LORD, ROBERT! IS THAT WHAT I THINK IT IS?
A COLOUR TV!
HUH?
EATON'S
ELECTROHOME
COLOR TV
24"
C09-106
PARKDALE
SIDDOWN, FOLKS! YOU'LL SEE - THE PICTURE QUALITY ON THIS IS UNBELIEVABLE!
ROBERT, IT'S... IT'S A BIT EXTRAVAGANT, ISN'T IT?
EATON'S
WOW!
I'LL BE DARNED!
OH MY!
!
VOILA! YOU TURN IT ON HERE!...
CLIC
ALINE, MY DEAR, MAKE A LITTLE SPOT FOR US, WOULD YOU?...
HMM.
SHOVE OVER!
LOOK! I'M ALL SQUISHED ALREADY!
THE PICTURE IS ABSOLUTELY AMAZING!
87

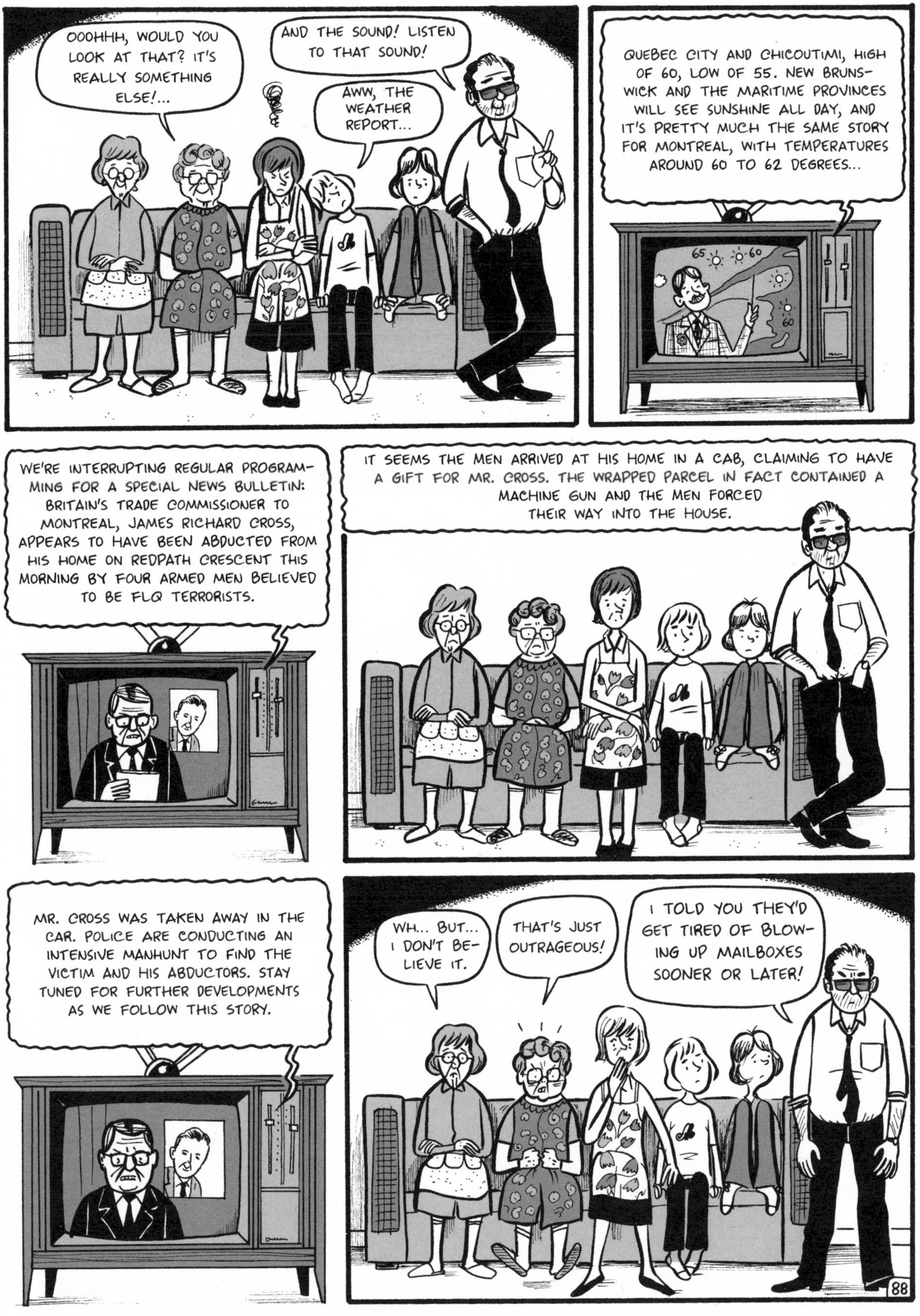
OOOHHH, WOULD YOU LOOK AT THAT? IT'S REALLY SOMETHING ELSE!...
AND THE SOUND! LISTEN TO THAT SOUND!
AWW, THE WEATHER REPORT...
QUEBEC CITY AND CHICOUTIMI, HIGH OF 60, LOW OF 55. NEW BRUNSWICK AND THE MARITIME PROVINCES WILL SEE SUNSHINE ALL DAY, AND IT'S PRETTY MUCH THE SAME STORY FOR MONTREAL, WITH TEMPERATURES AROUND 60 TO 62 DEGREES...
65
60
60
WE'RE INTERRUPTING REGULAR PROGRAMMING FOR A SPECIAL NEWS BULLETIN: BRITAIN'S TRADE COMMISSIONER TO MONTREAL, JAMES RICHARD CROSS, APPEARS TO HAVE BEEN ABDUCTED FROM HIS HOME ON REDPATH CRESCENT THIS MORNING BY FOUR ARMED MEN BELIEVED TO BE FLQ TERRORISTS.
IT SEEMS THE MEN ARRIVED AT HIS HOME IN A CAB, CLAIMING TO HAVE A GIFT FOR MR. CROSS. THE WRAPPED PARCEL IN FACT CONTAINED A MACHINE GUN AND THE MEN FORCED THEIR WAY INTO THE HOUSE.
MR. CROSS WAS TAKEN AWAY IN THE CAR. POLICE ARE CONDUCTING AN INTENSIVE MANHUNT TO FIND THE VICTIM AND HIS ABDUCTORS. STAY TUNED FOR FURTHER DEVELOPMENTS AS WE FOLLOW THIS STORY.
WH... BUT... I DON'T BELIEVE IT.
THAT'S JUST OUTRAGEOUS!
I TOLD YOU THEY'D GET TIRED OF BLOWING UP MAILBOXES SOONER OR LATER!
88

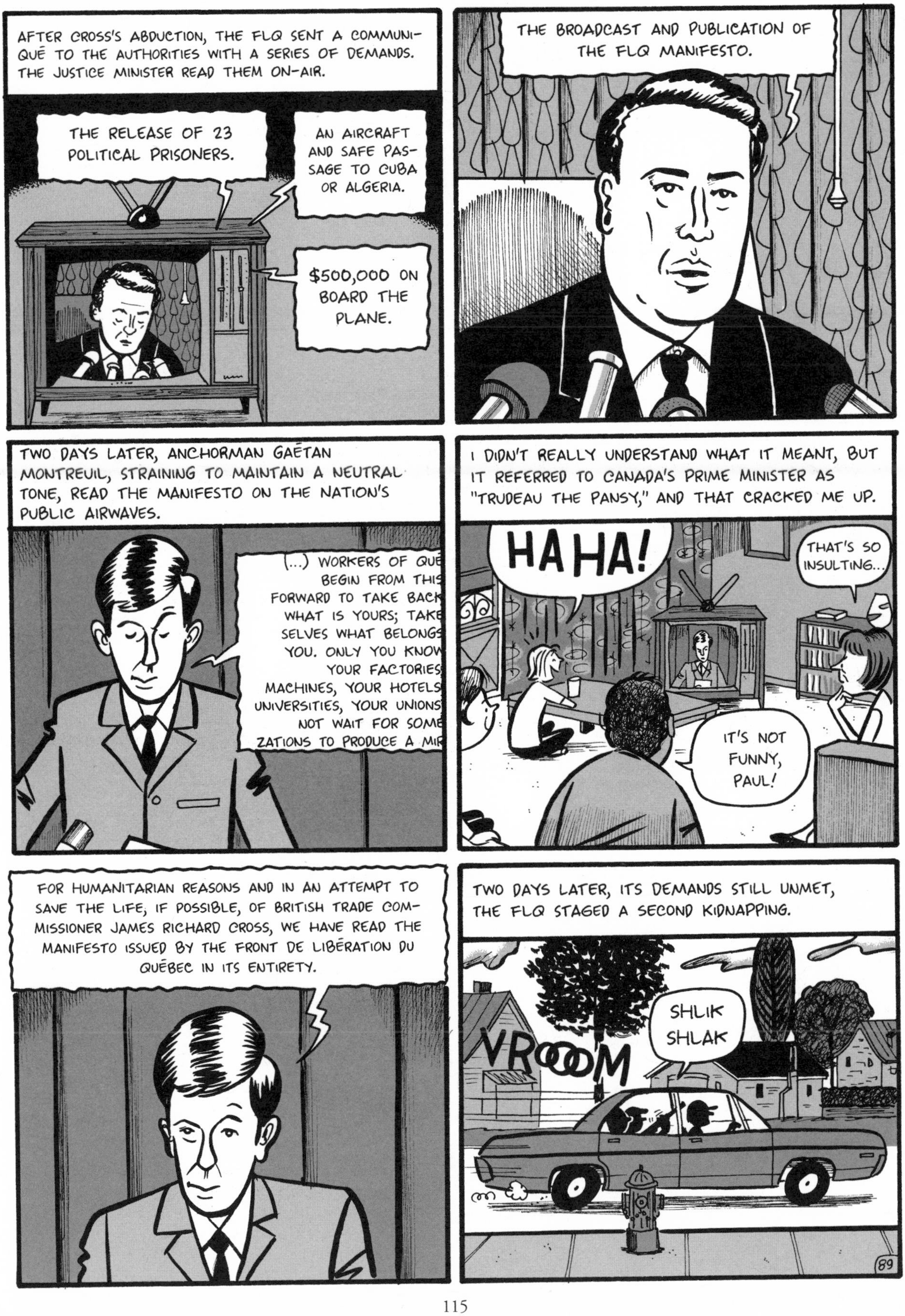
AFTER CROSS'S ABDUCTION, THE FLQ SENT A COMMUNIQUÉ TO THE AUTHORITIES WITH A SERIES OF DEMANDS. THE JUSTICE MINISTER READ THEM ON-AIR.
THE RELEASE OF 23 POLITICAL PRISONERS.
AN AIRCRAFT AND SAFE PASSAGE TO CUBA OR ALGERIA.
$500,000 ON BOARD THE PLANE.
THE BROADCAST AND PUBLICATION OF THE FLQ MANIFESTO.
TWO DAYS LATER, ANCHORMAN GAÉTAN MONTREUIL, STRAINING TO MAINTAIN A NEUTRAL TONE, READ THE MANIFESTO ON THE NATION'S PUBLIC AIRWAVES.
(...) WORKERS OF QUÉ BEGIN FROM THIS FORWARD TO TAKE BACK WHAT IS YOURS; TAKE SELVES WHAT BELONGS YOU. ONLY YOU KNOW YOUR FACTORIES MACHINES, YOUR HOTELS UNIVERSITIES, YOUR UNIONS NOT WAIT FOR SOME ZATIONS TO PRODUCE A MIR
I DIDN'T REALLY UNDERSTAND WHAT IT MEANT, BUT IT REFERRED TO CANADA'S PRIME MINISTER AS "TRUDEAU THE PANSY," AND THAT CRACKED ME UP.
HAHA!
THAT'S SO INSULTING...
IT'S NOT FUNNY, PAUL!
FOR HUMANITARIAN REASONS AND IN AN ATTEMPT TO SAVE THE LIFE, IF POSSIBLE, OF BRITISH TRADE COMMISSIONER JAMES RICHARD CROSS, WE HAVE READ THE MANIFESTO ISSUED BY THE FRONT DE LIBÉRATION DU QUÉBEC IN ITS ENTIRETY.
TWO DAYS LATER, ITS DEMANDS STILL UNMET, THE FLQ STAGED A SECOND KIDNAPPING.
VROOOM
SHLIK SHLAK
89

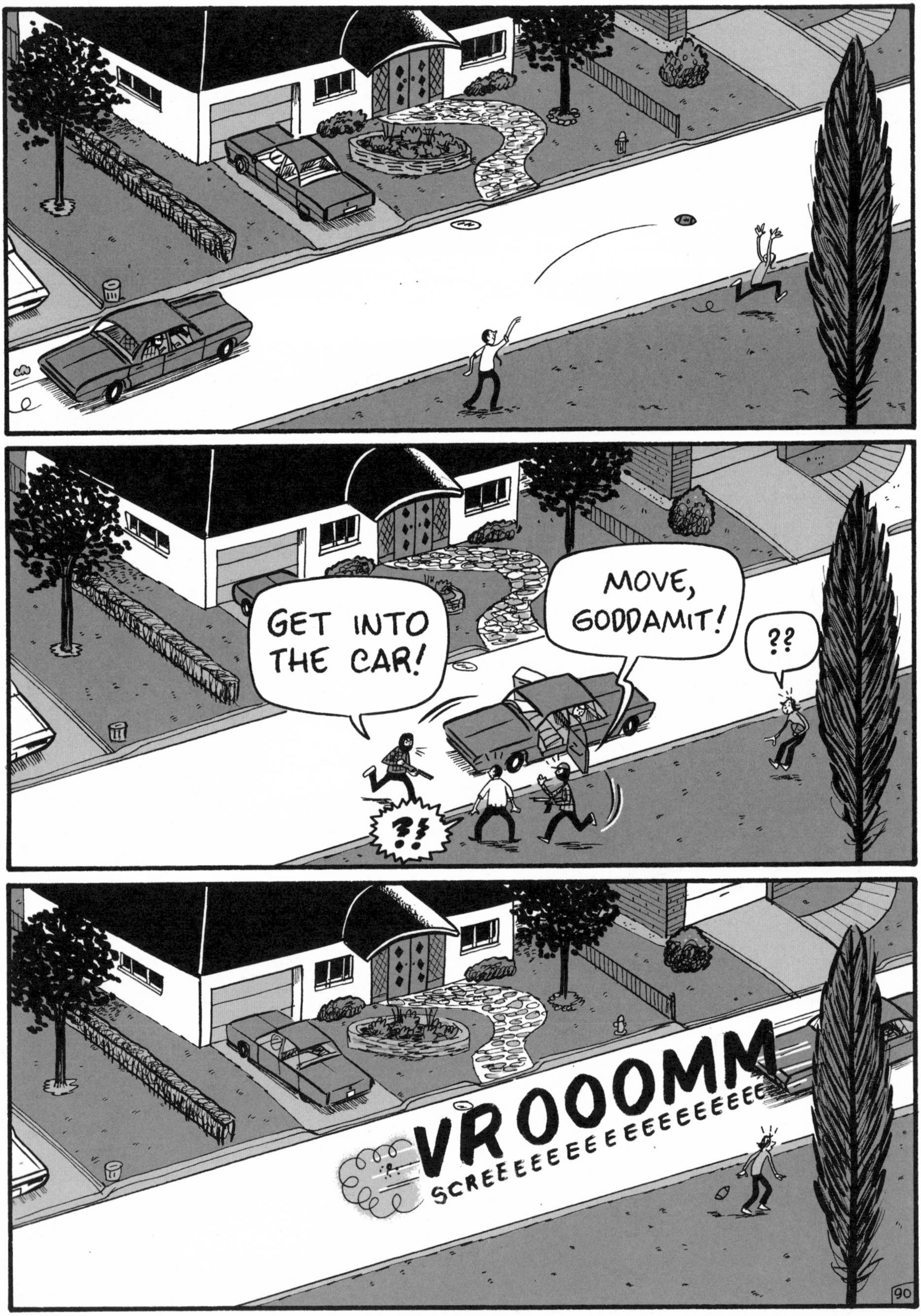
GET INTO THE CAR!
MOVE, GODDAMIT!
??
?!
VROOOMM
SCREEEEEEEEEEEEEEEEEEEEEEE
90

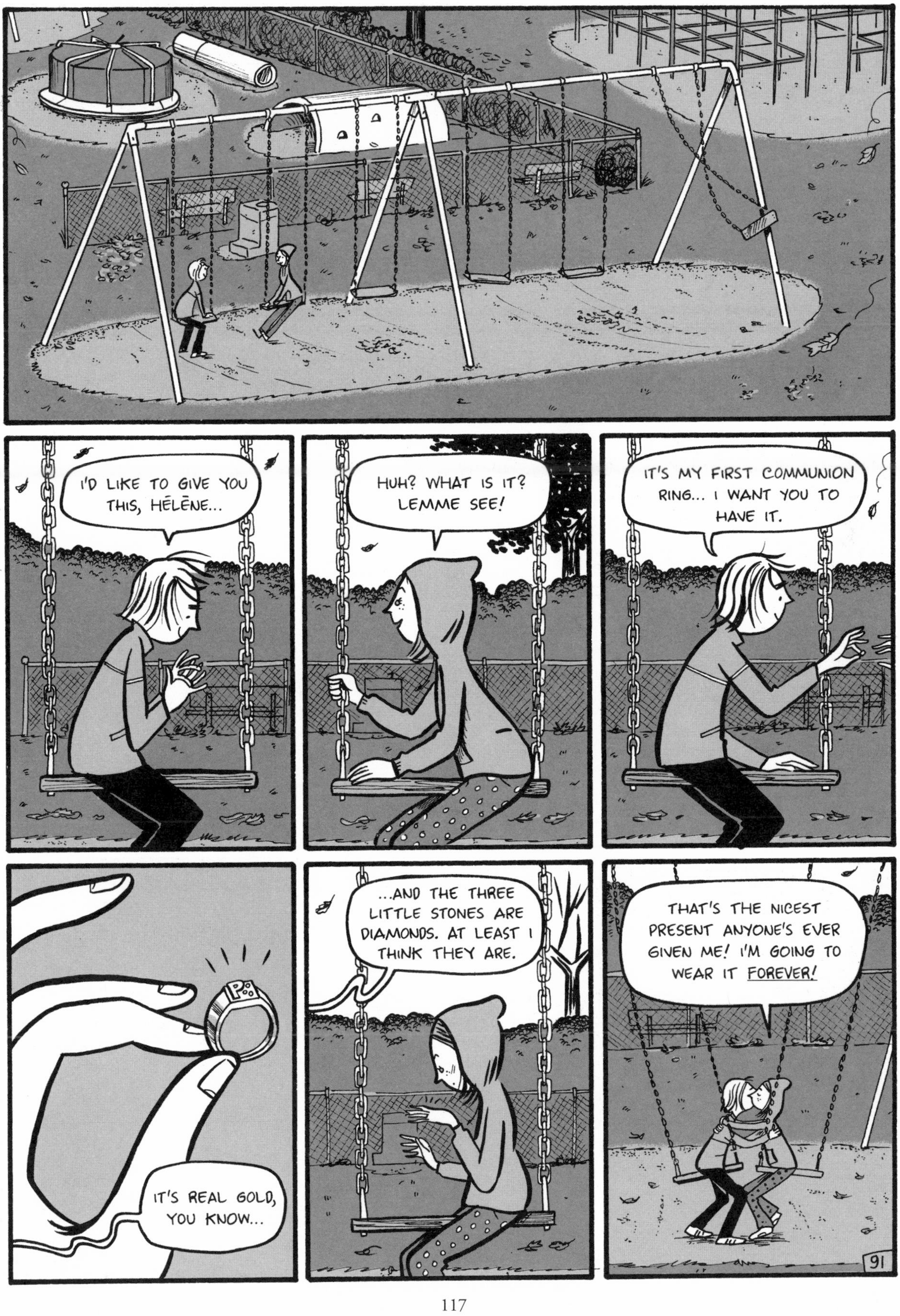
I'D LIKE TO GIVE YOU THIS, HÉLÈNE...
HUH? WHAT IS IT? LEMME SEE!
IT'S MY FIRST COMMUNION RING... I WANT YOU TO HAVE IT.
IT'S REAL GOLD, YOU KNOW...
...AND THE THREE LITTLE STONES ARE DIAMONDS. AT LEAST I THINK THEY ARE.
THAT'S THE NICEST PRESENT ANYONE'S EVER GIVEN ME! I'M GOING TO WEAR IT FOREVER!
91

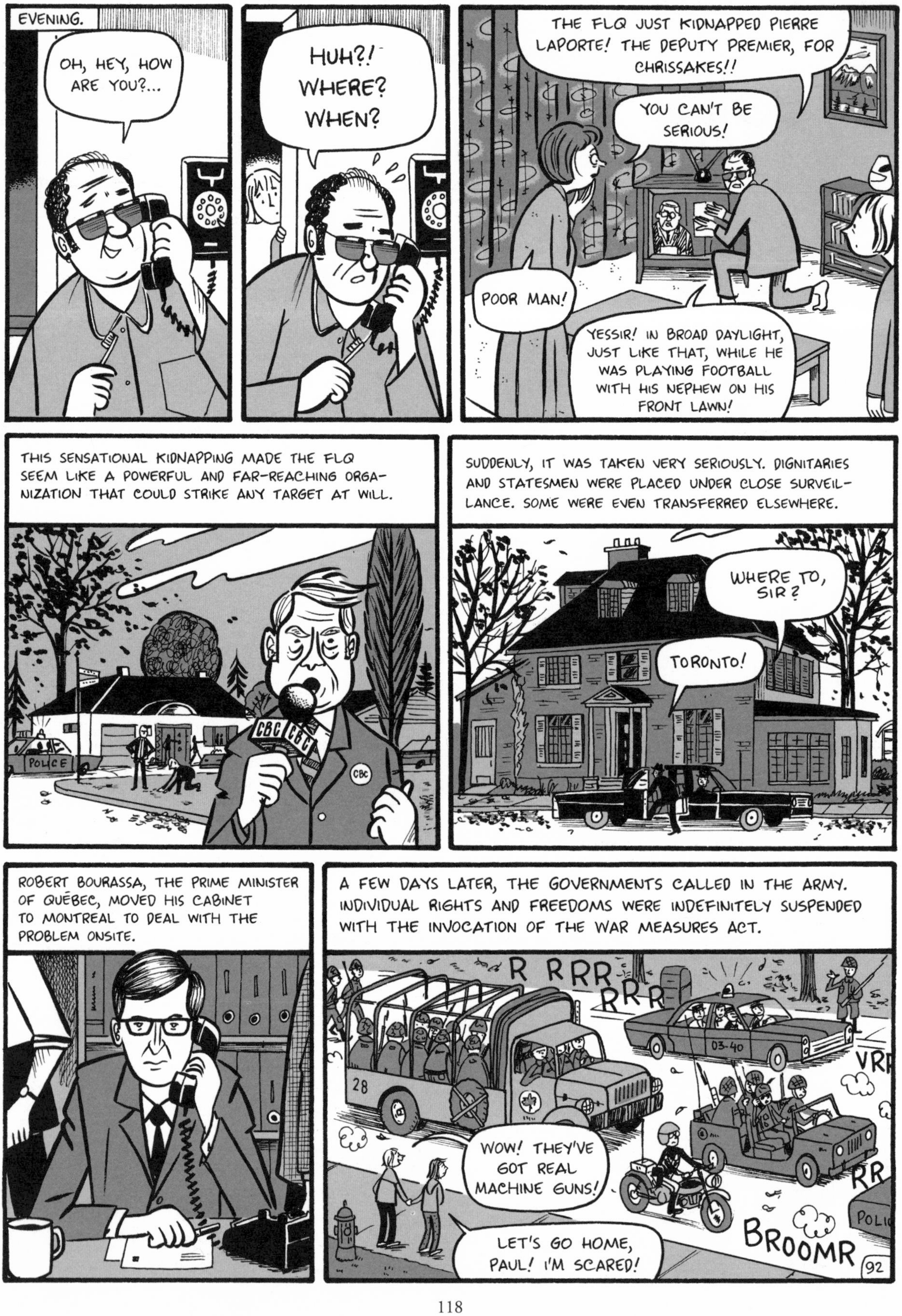
EVENING.
OH, HEY, HOW ARE YOU?...
HUH?! WHERE? WHEN?
THE FLQ JUST KIDNAPPED PIERRE LAPORTE! THE DEPUTY PREMIER, FOR CHRISSAKES!!
YOU CAN'T BE SERIOUS!
POOR MAN!
YESSIR! IN BROAD DAYLIGHT, JUST LIKE THAT, WHILE HE WAS PLAYING FOOTBALL WITH HIS NEPHEW ON HIS FRONT LAWN!
THIS SENSATIONAL KIDNAPPING MADE THE FLQ SEEM LIKE A POWERFUL AND FAR-REACHING ORGANIZATION THAT COULD STRIKE ANY TARGET AT WILL.
POLICE
CBC
CBC
CBC
SUDDENLY, IT WAS TAKEN VERY SERIOUSLY. DIGNITARIES AND STATESMEN WERE PLACED UNDER CLOSE SURVEILLANCE. SOME WERE EVEN TRANSFERRED ELSEWHERE.
WHERE TO, SIR?
TORONTO!
ROBERT BOURASSA, THE PRIME MINISTER OF QUÉBEC, MOVED HIS CABINET TO MONTREAL TO DEAL WITH THE PROBLEM ONSITE.
A FEW DAYS LATER, THE GOVERNMENTS CALLED IN THE ARMY. INDIVIDUAL RIGHTS AND FREEDOMS WERE INDEFINITELY SUSPENDED WITH THE INVOCATION OF THE WAR MEASURES ACT.
R RRR
RRR
03-40
28
VRR
RR
WOW! THEY'VE GOT REAL MACHINE GUNS!
LET'S GO HOME, PAUL! I'M SCARED!
BROOMR
POLIC
92

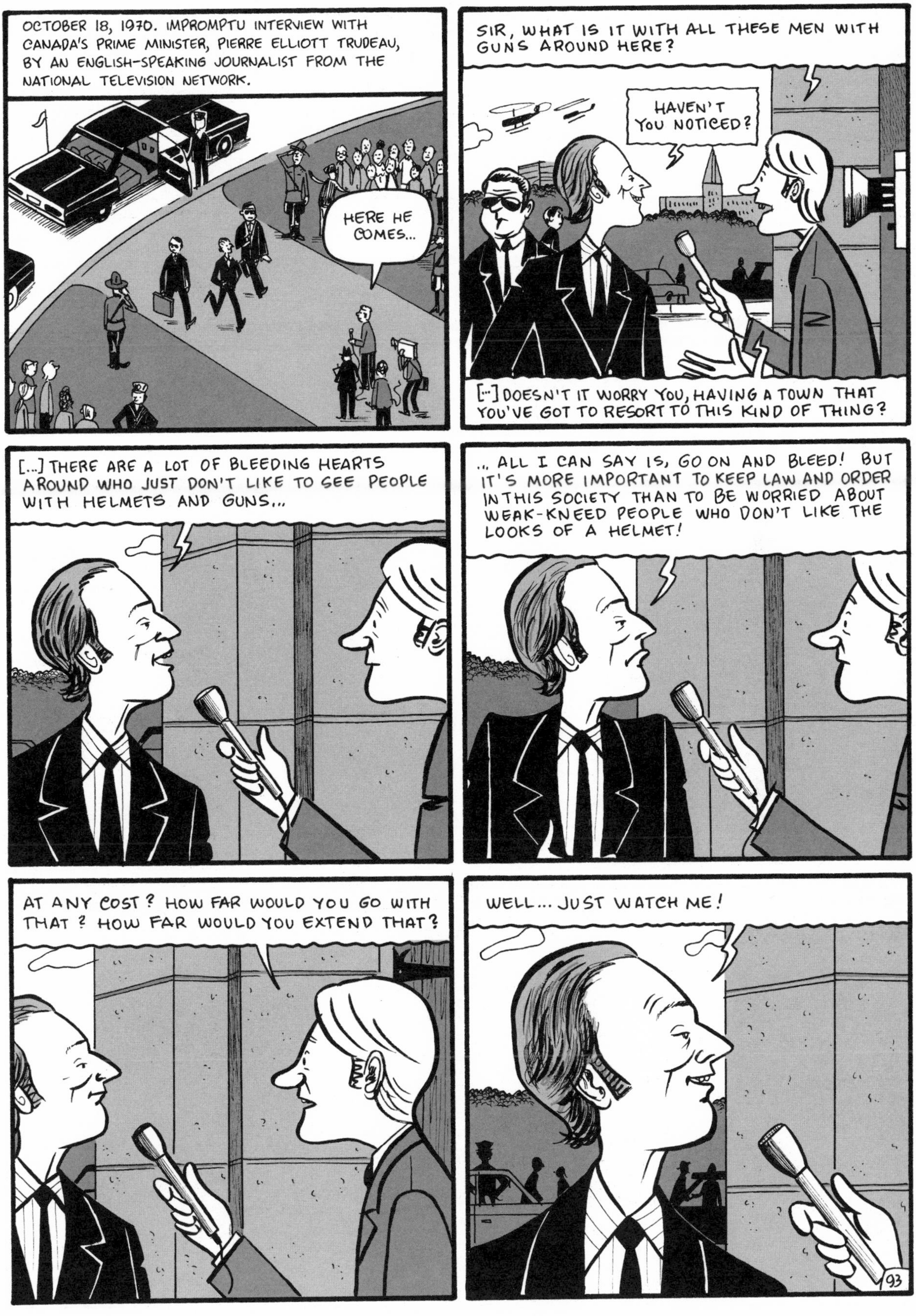

OCTOBER 18, 1970. IMPROMPTU INTERVIEW WITH CANADA'S PRIME MINISTER, PIERRE ELLIOTT TRUDEAU, BY AN ENGLISH-SPEAKING JOURNALIST FROM THE NATIONAL TELEVISION NETWORK.
HERE HE COMES...
SIR, WHAT IS IT WITH ALL THESE MEN WITH GUNS AROUND HERE?
HAVEN'T YOU NOTICED?
[...] DOESN'T IT WORRY YOU, HAVING A TOWN THAT YOU'VE GOT TO RESORT TO THIS KIND OF THING?
[...] THERE ARE A LOT OF BLEEDING HEARTS AROUND WHO JUST DON'T LIKE TO SEE PEOPLE WITH HELMETS AND GUNS...
... ALL I CAN SAY IS, GO ON AND BLEED! BUT IT'S MORE IMPORTANT TO KEEP LAW AND ORDER IN THIS SOCIETY THAN TO BE WORRIED ABOUT WEAK-KNEED PEOPLE WHO DON'T LIKE THE LOOKS OF A HELMET!
AT ANY COST? HOW FAR WOULD YOU GO WITH THAT? HOW FAR WOULD YOU EXTEND THAT?
WELL... JUST WATCH ME!
93

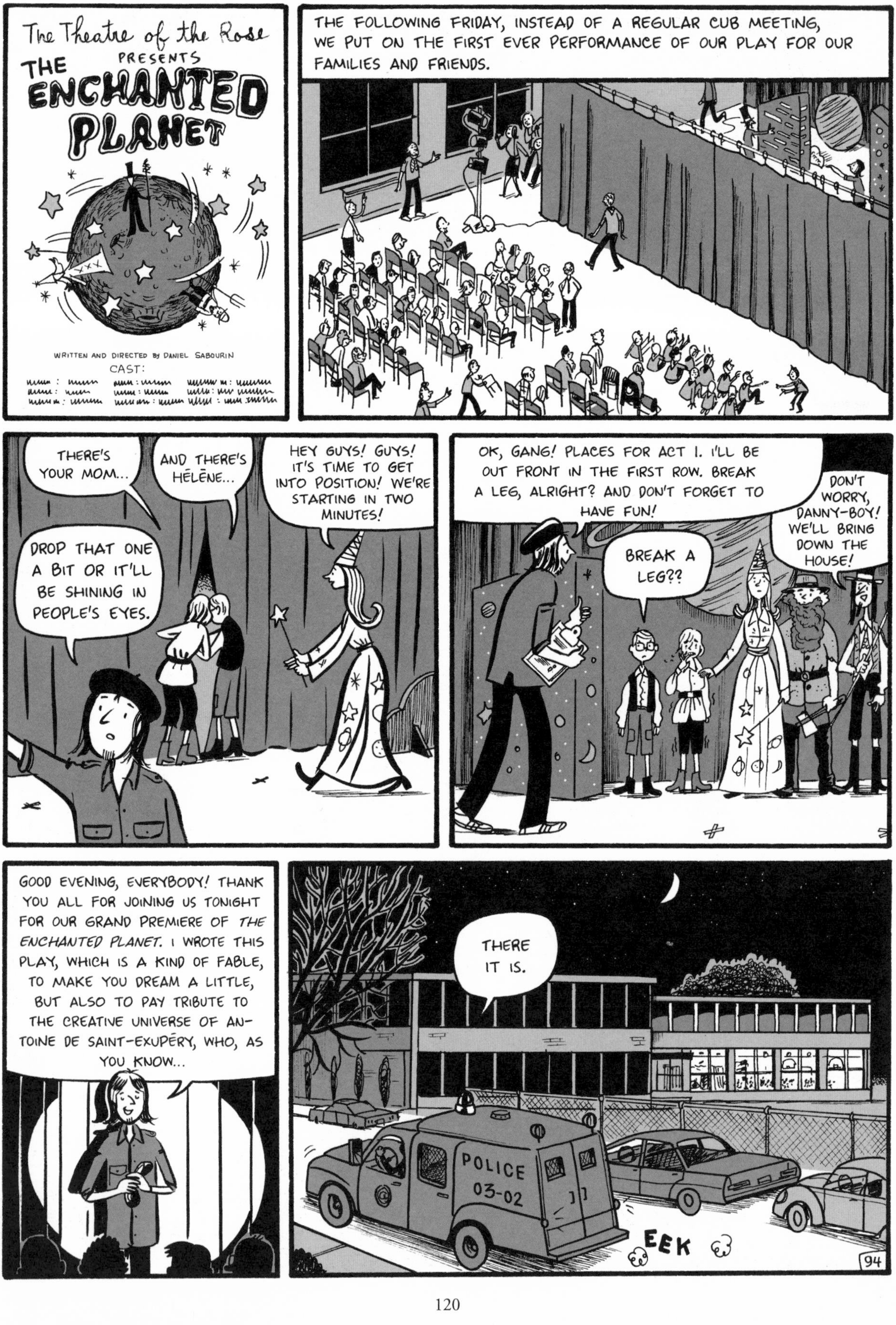
The Theatre of the Rose
PRESENTS
THE ENCHANTED PLANET
WRITTEN AND DIRECTED BY DANIEL SABOURIN
CAST:
THE FOLLOWING FRIDAY, INSTEAD OF A REGULAR CUB MEETING, WE PUT ON THE FIRST EVER PERFORMANCE OF OUR PLAY FOR OUR FAMILIES AND FRIENDS.
THERE'S YOUR MOM...
AND THERE'S HÉLÈNE...
HEY GUYS! GUYS! IT'S TIME TO GET INTO POSITION! WE'RE STARTING IN TWO MINUTES!
DROP THAT ONE A BIT OR IT'LL BE SHINING IN PEOPLE'S EYES.
OK, GANG! PLACES FOR ACT I. I'LL BE OUT FRONT IN THE FIRST ROW. BREAK A LEG, ALRIGHT? AND DON'T FORGET TO HAVE FUN!
DON'T WORRY, DANNY-BOY! WE'LL BRING DOWN THE HOUSE!
BREAK A LEG??
GOOD EVENING, EVERYBODY! THANK YOU ALL FOR JOINING US TONIGHT FOR OUR GRAND PREMIERE OF *THE ENCHANTED PLANET*. I WROTE THIS PLAY, WHICH IS A KIND OF FABLE, TO MAKE YOU DREAM A LITTLE, BUT ALSO TO PAY TRIBUTE TO THE CREATIVE UNIVERSE OF ANTOINE DE SAINT-EXUPÉRY, WHO, AS YOU KNOW...
THERE IT IS.
POLICE
03-02
EEK
94

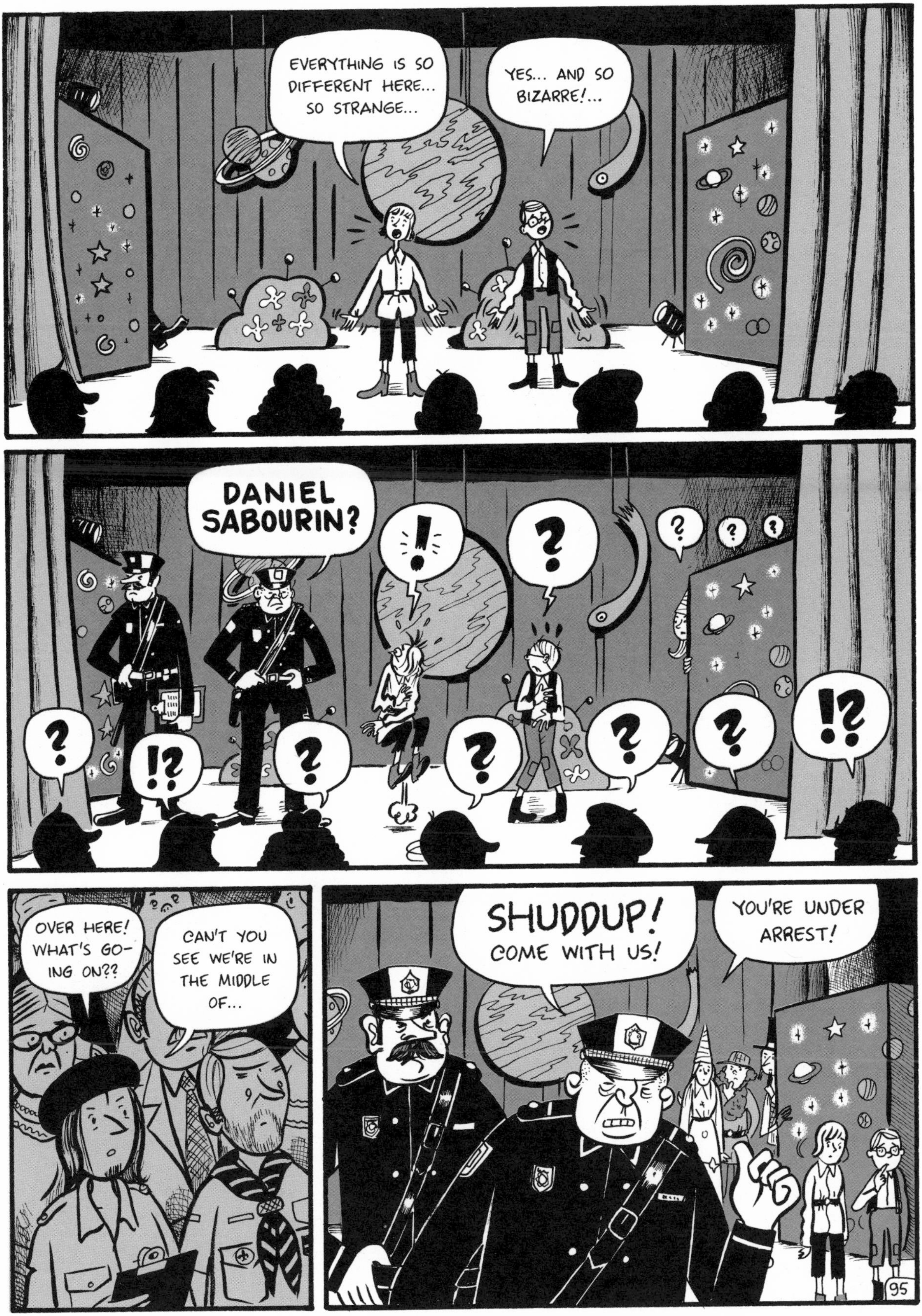
EVERYTHING IS SO DIFFERENT HERE... SO STRANGE...
YES... AND SO BIZARRE!...
DANIEL SABOURIN?
!
?
? ? ?
?
!?
?
?
?
?
!?
OVER HERE! WHAT'S GO-ING ON??
CAN'T YOU SEE WE'RE IN THE MIDDLE OF...
SHUDDUP! COME WITH US!
YOU'RE UNDER ARREST!
95

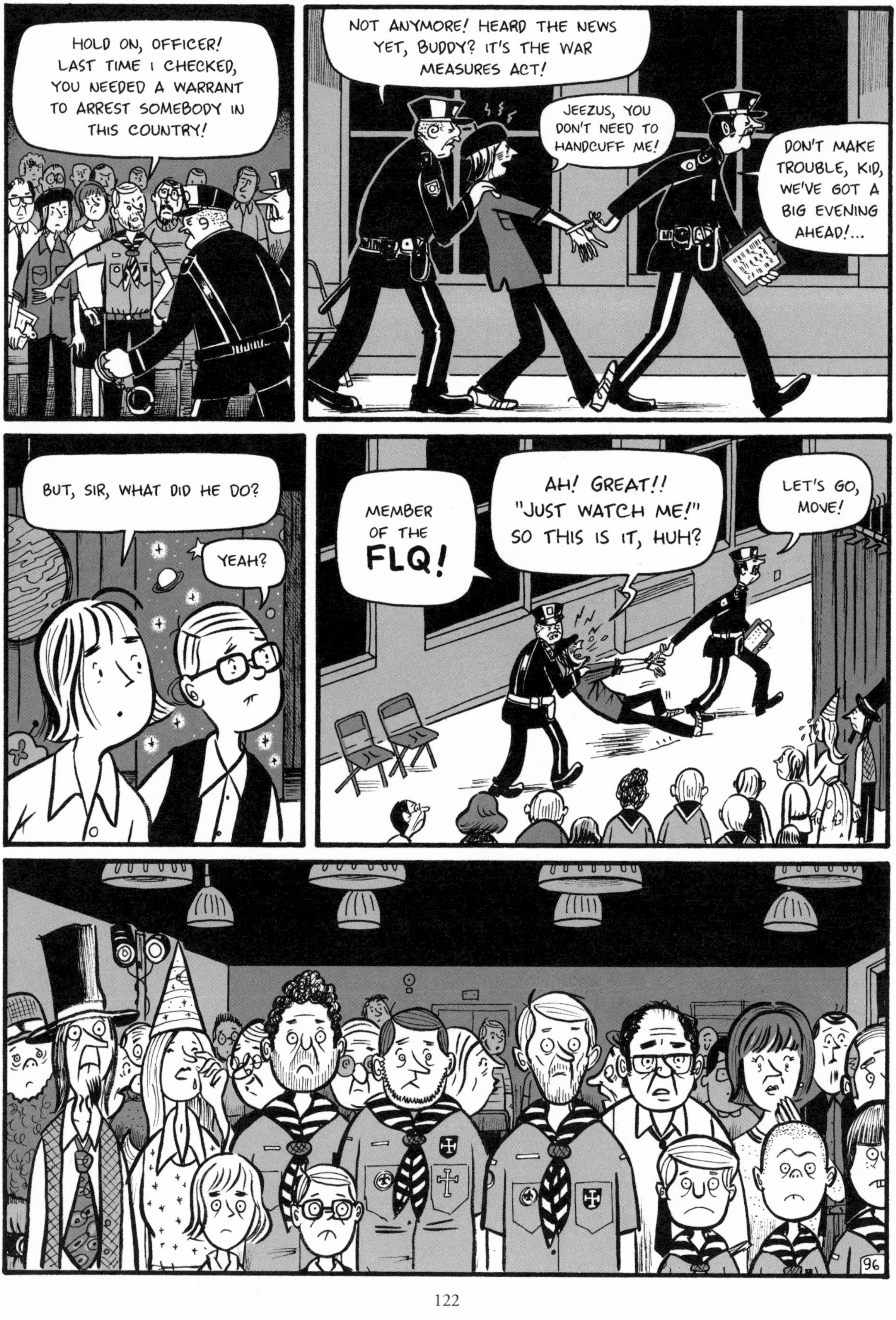
HOLD ON, OFFICER! LAST TIME I CHECKED, YOU NEEDED A WARRANT TO ARREST SOMEBODY IN THIS COUNTRY!
NOT ANYMORE! HEARD THE NEWS YET, BUDDY? IT'S THE WAR MEASURES ACT!
JEEZUS, YOU DON'T NEED TO HANDCUFF ME!
DON'T MAKE TROUBLE, KID, WE'VE GOT A BIG EVENING AHEAD!...
BUT, SIR, WHAT DID HE DO?
YEAH?
MEMBER OF THE FLQ!
AH! GREAT!! "JUST WATCH ME!" SO THIS IS IT, HUH?
LET'S GO, MOVE!
96

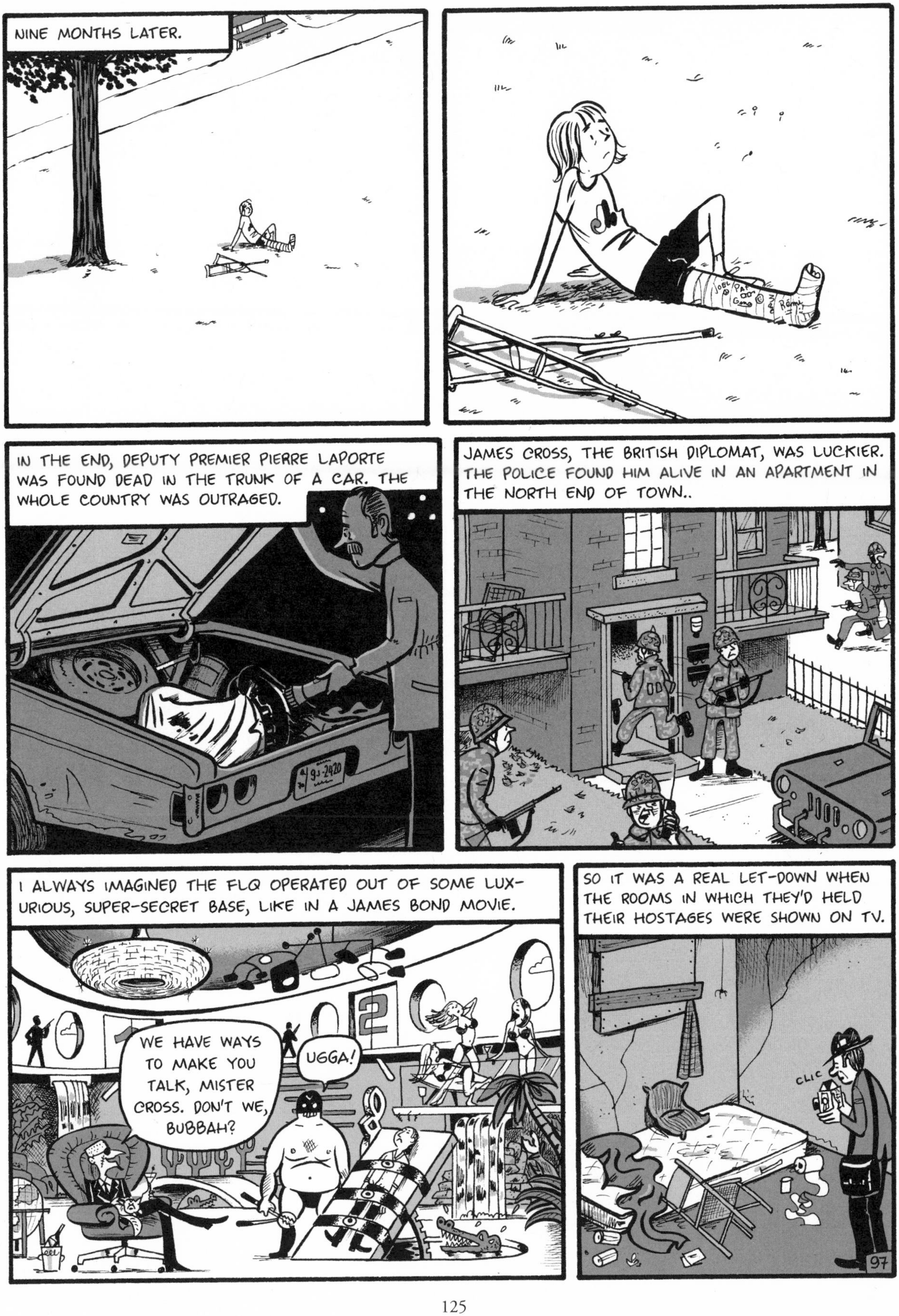
NINE MONTHS LATER.
IN THE END, DEPUTY PREMIER PIERRE LAPORTE WAS FOUND DEAD IN THE TRUNK OF A CAR. THE WHOLE COUNTRY WAS OUTRAGED.
JAMES CROSS, THE BRITISH DIPLOMAT, WAS LUCKIER. THE POLICE FOUND HIM ALIVE IN AN APARTMENT IN THE NORTH END OF TOWN..
I ALWAYS IMAGINED THE FLQ OPERATED OUT OF SOME LUXURIOUS, SUPER-SECRET BASE, LIKE IN A JAMES BOND MOVIE.
WE HAVE WAYS TO MAKE YOU TALK, MISTER CROSS. DON'T WE, BUBBAH?
UGGA!
SO IT WAS A REAL LET-DOWN WHEN THE ROOMS IN WHICH THEY'D HELD THEIR HOSTAGES WERE SHOWN ON TV.
CLIC
97

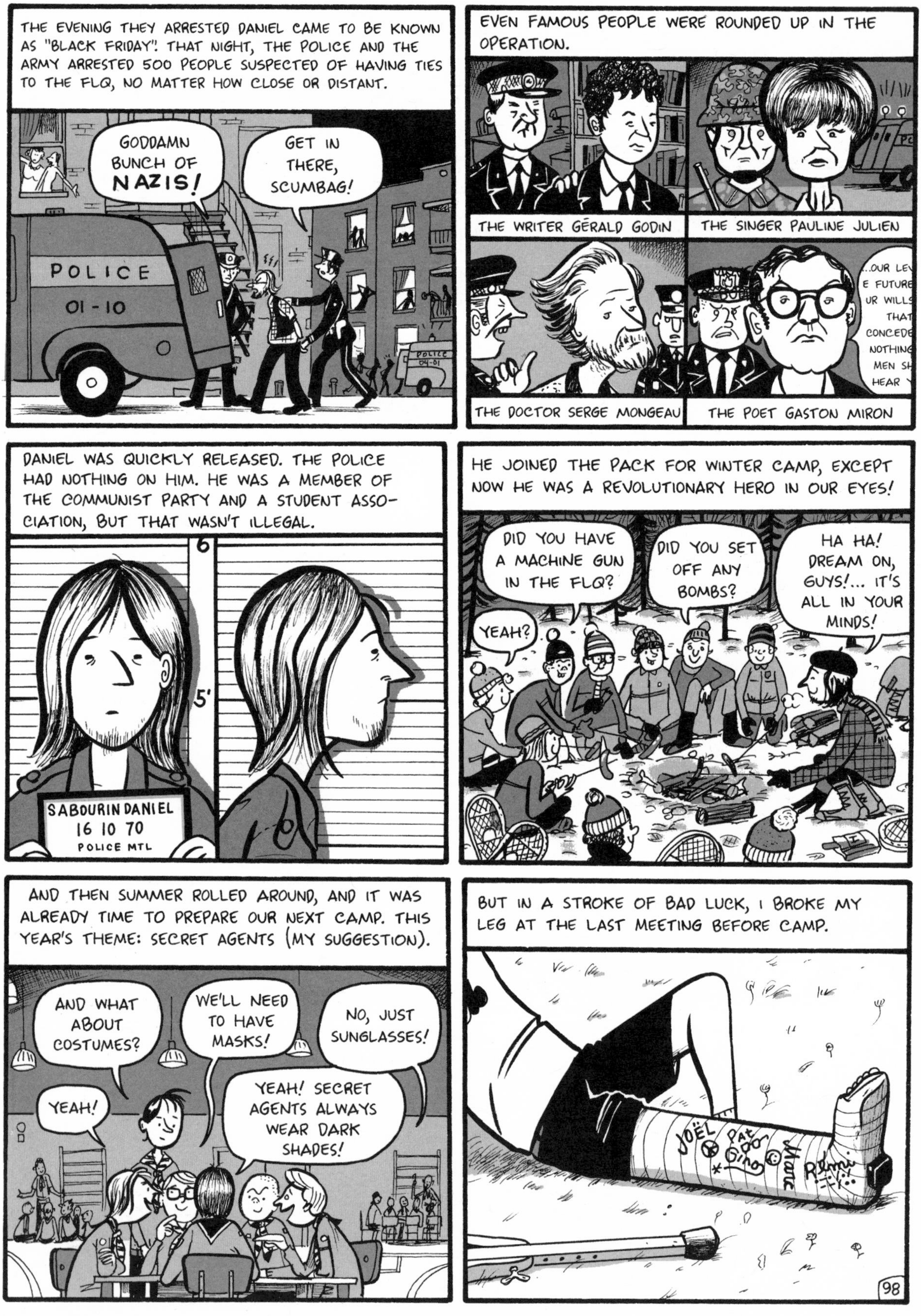
THE EVENING THEY ARRESTED DANIEL CAME TO BE KNOWN AS "BLACK FRIDAY". THAT NIGHT, THE POLICE AND THE ARMY ARRESTED 500 PEOPLE SUSPECTED OF HAVING TIES TO THE FLQ, NO MATTER HOW CLOSE OR DISTANT.
GODDAMN BUNCH OF NAZIS!
GET IN THERE, SCUMBAG!
POLICE
01-10
POLICE 04-01
EVEN FAMOUS PEOPLE WERE ROUNDED UP IN THE OPERATION.
THE WRITER GÉRALD GODIN
THE SINGER PAULINE JULIEN
THE DOCTOR SERGE MONGEAU
THE POET GASTON MIRON
...OUR LEV E FUTURE UR WILLS THAT CONCEDE NOTHING MEN SH HEAR Y
DANIEL WAS QUICKLY RELEASED. THE POLICE HAD NOTHING ON HIM. HE WAS A MEMBER OF THE COMMUNIST PARTY AND A STUDENT ASSOCIATION, BUT THAT WASN'T ILLEGAL.
6
5'
SABOURIN DANIEL
16 10 70
POLICE MTL
HE JOINED THE PACK FOR WINTER CAMP, EXCEPT NOW HE WAS A REVOLUTIONARY HERO IN OUR EYES!
DID YOU HAVE A MACHINE GUN IN THE FLQ?
DID YOU SET OFF ANY BOMBS?
HA HA! DREAM ON, GUYS!... IT'S ALL IN YOUR MINDS!
YEAH?
AND THEN SUMMER ROLLED AROUND, AND IT WAS ALREADY TIME TO PREPARE OUR NEXT CAMP. THIS YEAR'S THEME: SECRET AGENTS (MY SUGGESTION).
AND WHAT ABOUT COSTUMES?
WE'LL NEED TO HAVE MASKS!
NO, JUST SUNGLASSES!
YEAH!
YEAH! SECRET AGENTS ALWAYS WEAR DARK SHADES!
BUT IN A STROKE OF BAD LUCK, I BROKE MY LEG AT THE LAST MEETING BEFORE CAMP.
JOËL
Pat
Gino
Marc
Rémi
98

Laurent

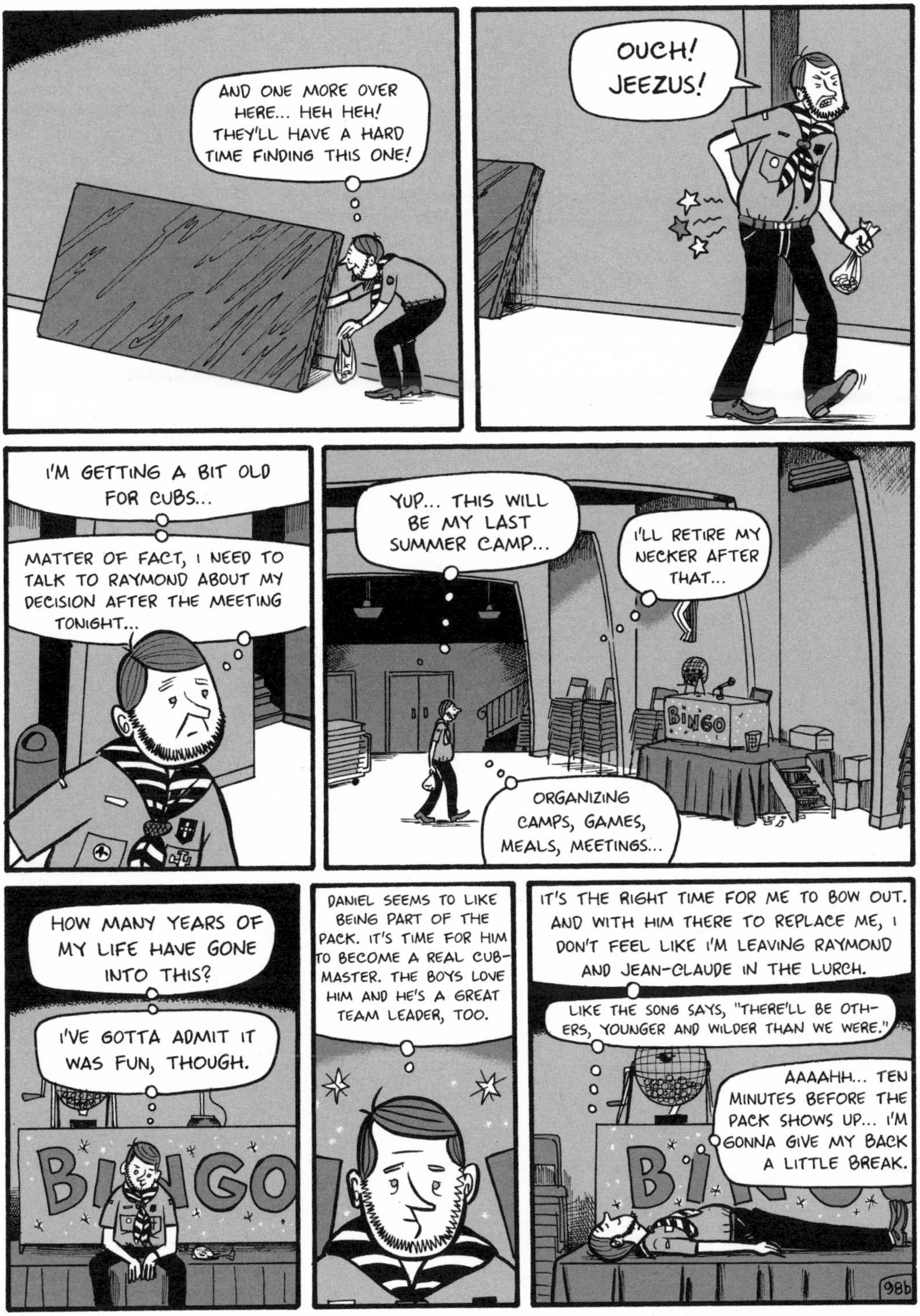
AND ONE MORE OVER HERE... HEH HEH! THEY'LL HAVE A HARD TIME FINDING THIS ONE!
OUCH! JEEZUS!
I'M GETTING A BIT OLD FOR CUBS...
MATTER OF FACT, I NEED TO TALK TO RAYMOND ABOUT MY DECISION AFTER THE MEETING TONIGHT...
YUP... THIS WILL BE MY LAST SUMMER CAMP...
I'LL RETIRE MY NECKER AFTER THAT...
BINGO
ORGANIZING CAMPS, GAMES, MEALS, MEETINGS...
HOW MANY YEARS OF MY LIFE HAVE GONE INTO THIS?
I'VE GOTTA ADMIT IT WAS FUN, THOUGH.
BINGO
DANIEL SEEMS TO LIKE BEING PART OF THE PACK. IT'S TIME FOR HIM TO BECOME A REAL CUB-MASTER. THE BOYS LOVE HIM AND HE'S A GREAT TEAM LEADER, TOO.
IT'S THE RIGHT TIME FOR ME TO BOW OUT. AND WITH HIM THERE TO REPLACE ME, I DON'T FEEL LIKE I'M LEAVING RAYMOND AND JEAN-CLAUDE IN THE LURCH.
LIKE THE SONG SAYS, "THERE'LL BE OTH-ERS, YOUNGER AND WILDER THAN WE WERE."
AAAAHH... TEN MINUTES BEFORE THE PACK SHOWS UP... I'M GONNA GIVE MY BACK A LITTLE BREAK.
98b

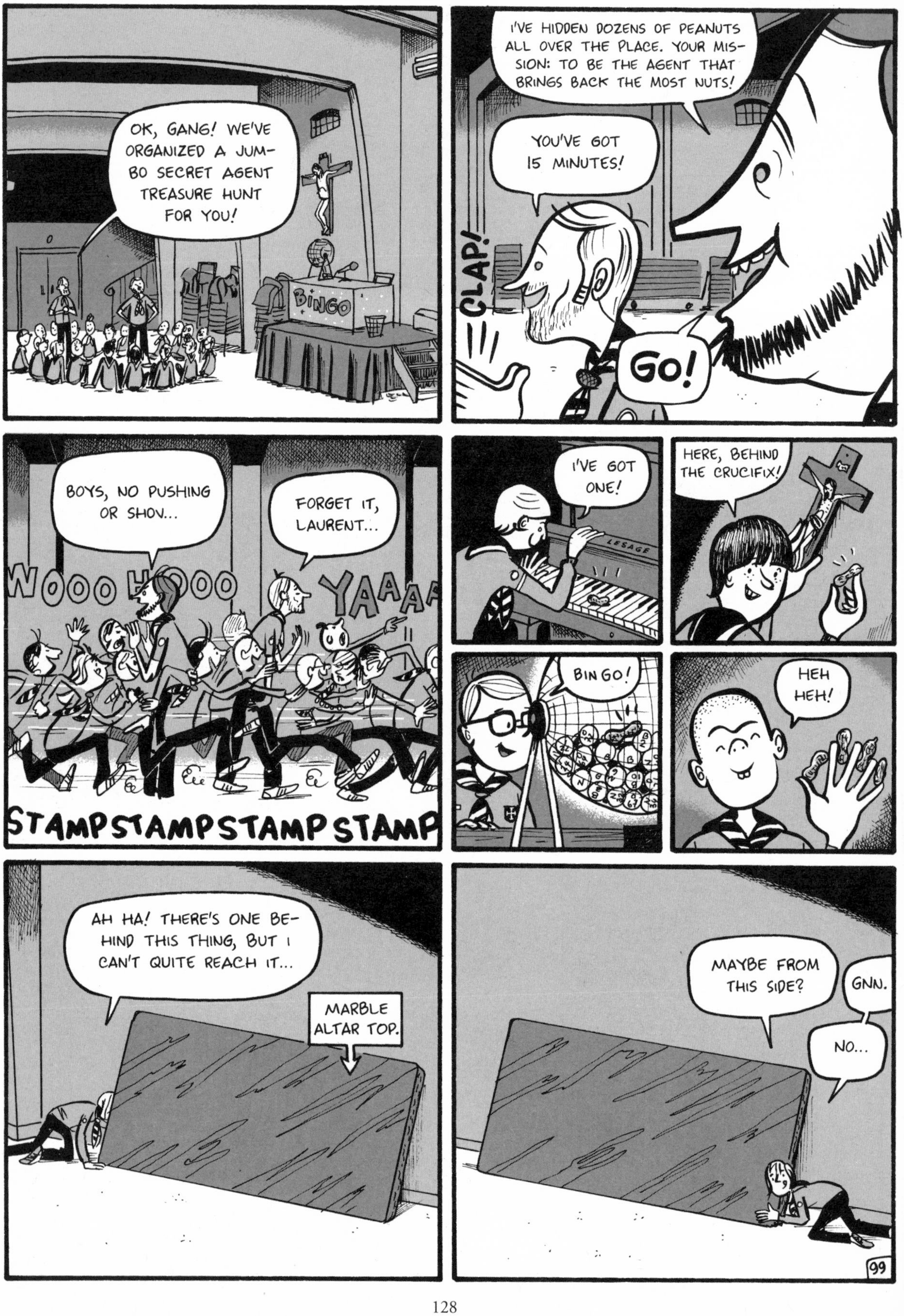
OK, GANG! WE'VE ORGANIZED A JUMBO SECRET AGENT TREASURE HUNT FOR YOU!
BINGO
I'VE HIDDEN DOZENS OF PEANUTS ALL OVER THE PLACE. YOUR MISSION: TO BE THE AGENT THAT BRINGS BACK THE MOST NUTS!
YOU'VE GOT 15 MINUTES!
CLAP!
GO!
BOYS, NO PUSHING OR SHOV...
FORGET IT, LAURENT...
WOOO HOOOO
YAAAA
STAMP STAMP STAMP STAMP
I'VE GOT ONE!
LESAGE
HERE, BEHIND THE CRUCIFIX!
BIN GO!
HEH HEH!
AH HA! THERE'S ONE BEHIND THIS THING, BUT I CAN'T QUITE REACH IT...
MARBLE ALTAR TOP.
MAYBE FROM THIS SIDE?
GNN.
NO...
99

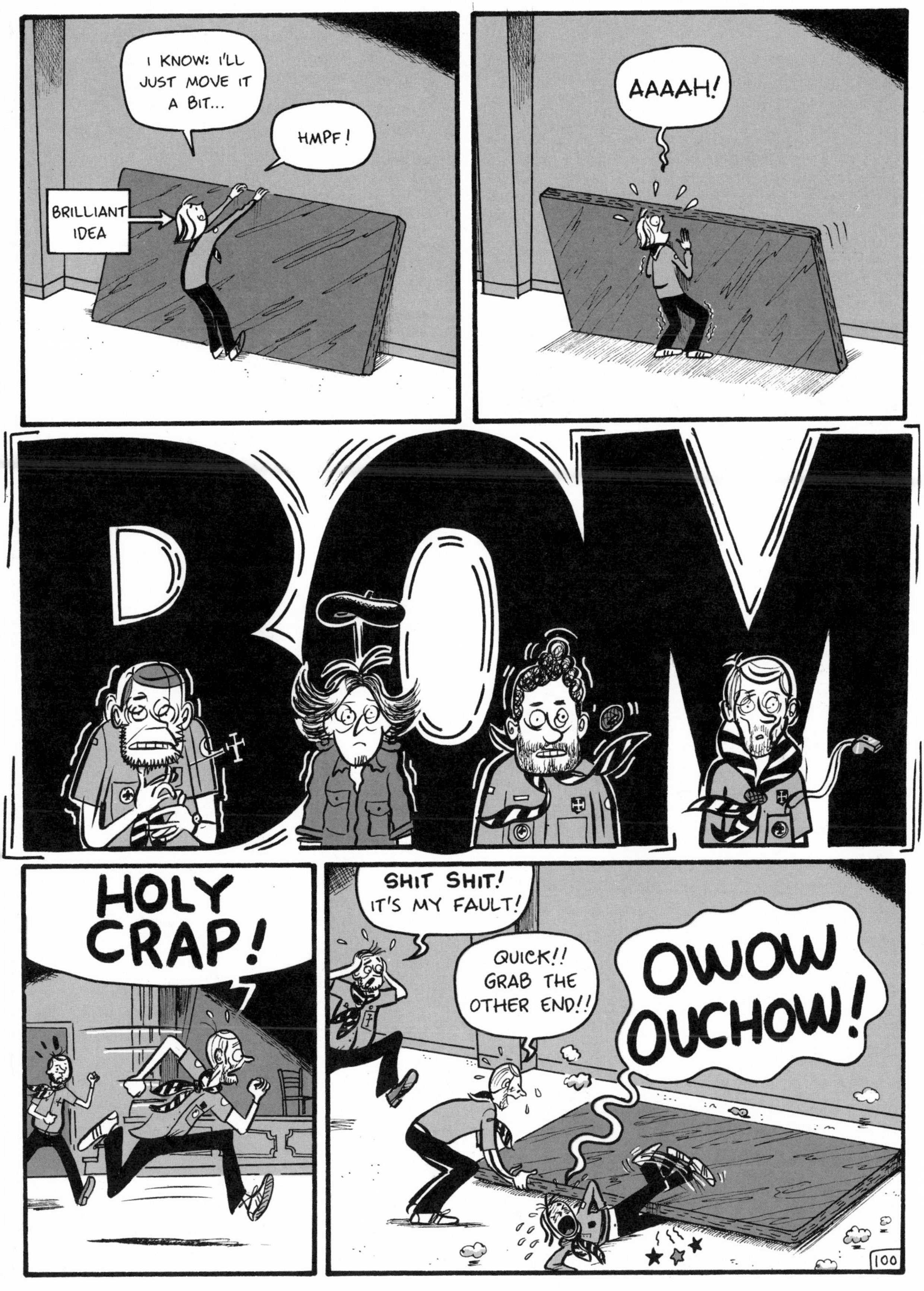

I KNOW: I'LL JUST MOVE IT A BIT...
HMPF!
BRILLIANT IDEA
AAAAH!
BOM
HOLY CRAP!
SHIT SHIT! IT'S MY FAULT!
QUICK!! GRAB THE OTHER END!!
OWOW OUCHOW!
100

BROKEN TIBIA AND FIBULA. SIX WEEKS IN A CAST.

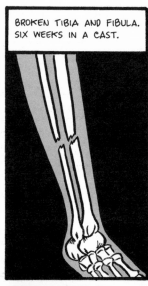

HERE, HONEY! YOUR MEAL TRAY, JUST LIKE IN A HOSPITAL!

THANKS, MOM!

AND YOU'VE GOT VISITORS...

I DO?

WHERE'S THE PATIENT?

MY MOTHER MADE FUDGE FOR YOU!

I GOT YOU THE LATEST ASTERIX!

HELLO!

NEE NAW NEE NAW!

HI PAUL!

HELLO!

WE'RE GONNA SIGN YOUR CAST!!

WHEN WE HEARD THE BANG, WE THOUGHT YOU WERE FLATTENED!

YOU SHOULDA SEEN YOUR FACE! YOU WERE WHITE AS A SHEET!

IT MUST'VE HURT LIKE HELL!

AKELA FREAKED!

HA HA!

I HEARD THAT THING WEIGHS 400 POUNDS!

IT'S REALLY TOO BAD YOU CAN'T COME, PAUL...

ESPECIALLY SINCE WE'RE GONNA PULL SOME PRANKS ON THE CUBMASTERS! WE EVEN FOUND FIRECRACKERS!

YEAH!

OH MAN, NO WAY!

BYE!

WE'LL SEE YOU AFTER CAMP!

CIAO!

HAVE FUN, GUYS!

BYE!

SEE YA!

THANKS FOR THE STUFF!

101

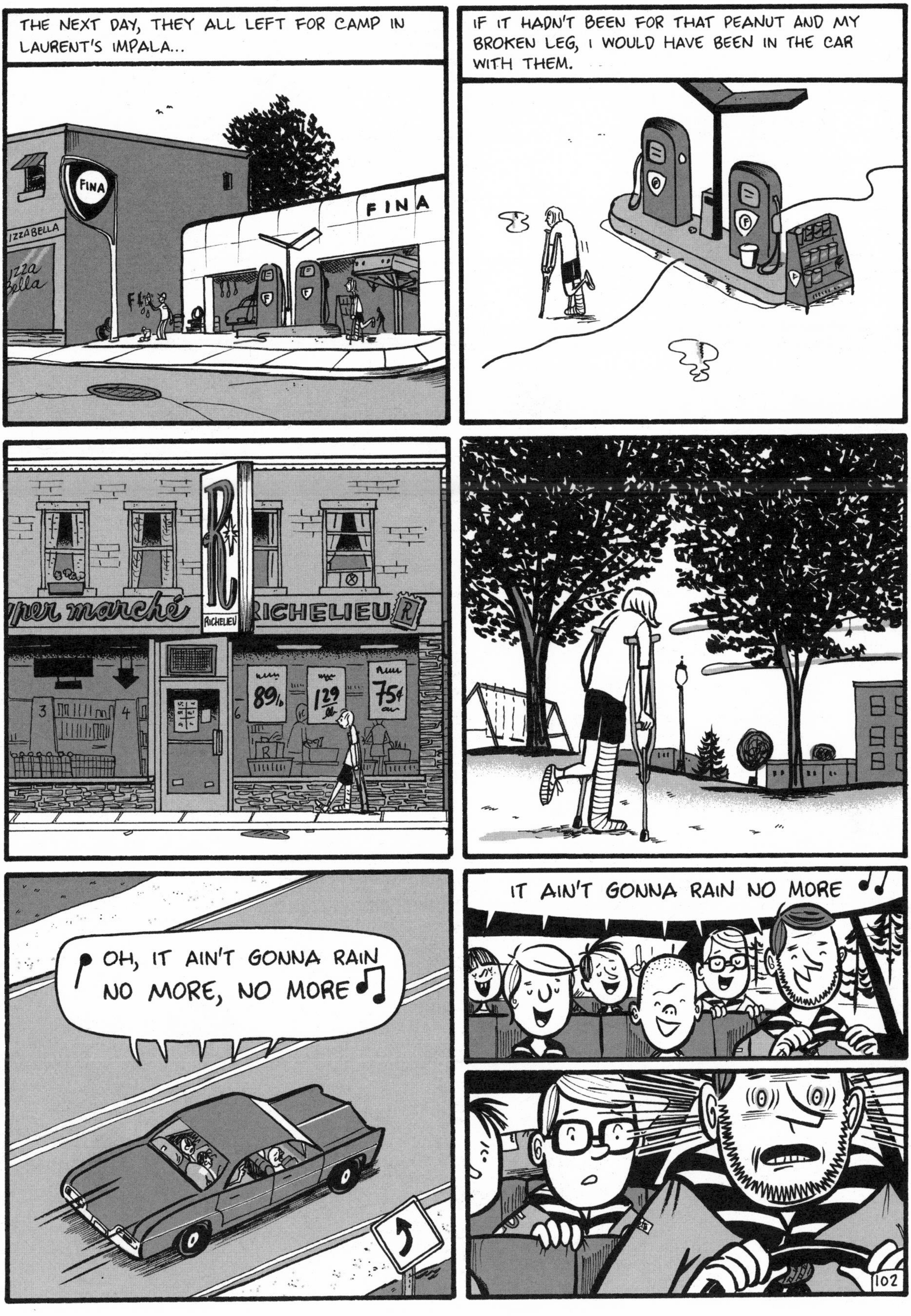
THE NEXT DAY, THEY ALL LEFT FOR CAMP IN LAURENT'S IMPALA...
FINA
FINA
IF IT HADN'T BEEN FOR THAT PEANUT AND MY BROKEN LEG, I WOULD HAVE BEEN IN THE CAR WITH THEM.
RICHELIEU
RICHELIEU
OH, IT AIN'T GONNA RAIN NO MORE, NO MORE
IT AIN'T GONNA RAIN NO MORE
102

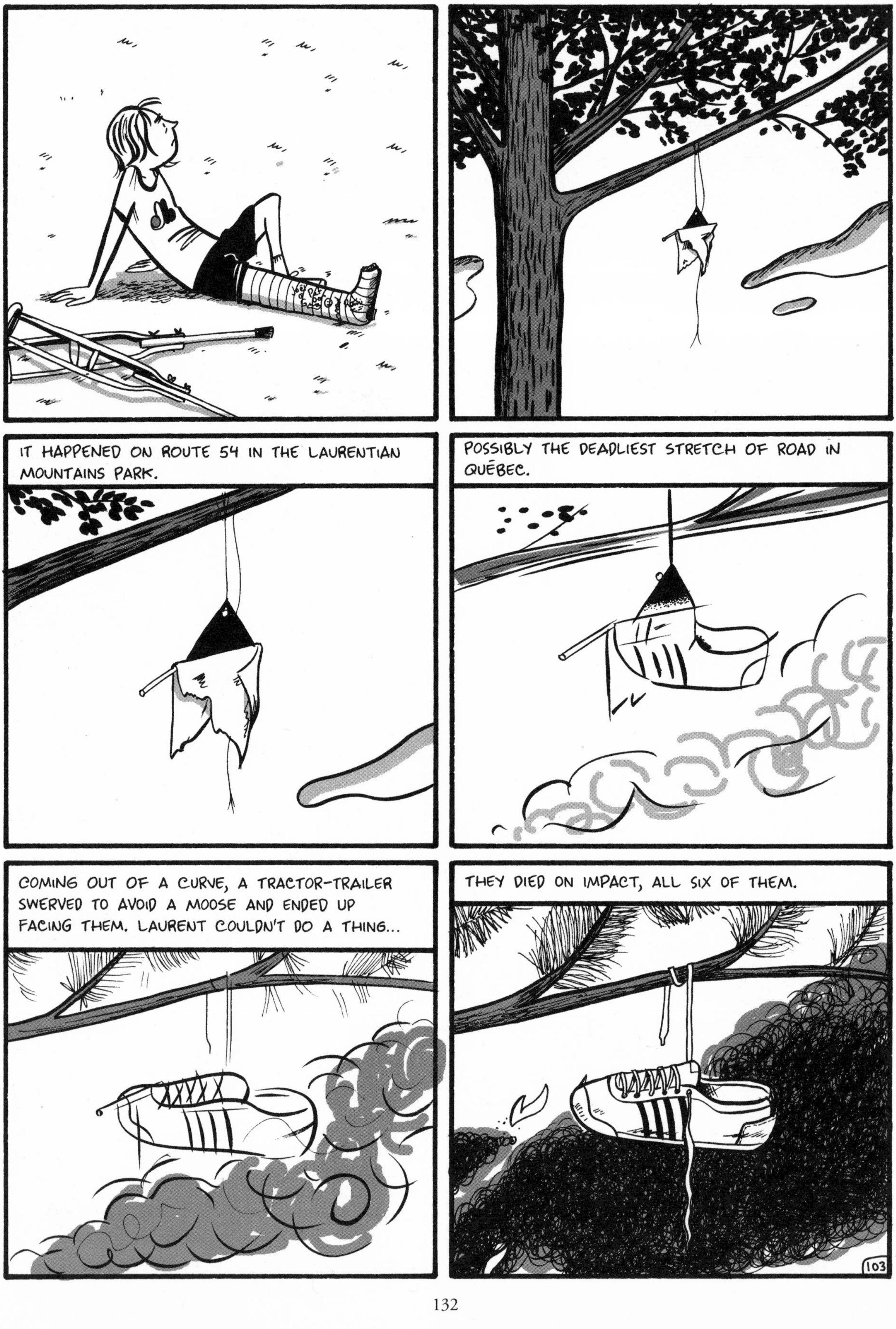
IT HAPPENED ON ROUTE 54 IN THE LAURENTIAN MOUNTAINS PARK.
POSSIBLY THE DEADLIEST STRETCH OF ROAD IN QUÉBEC.
COMING OUT OF A CURVE, A TRACTOR-TRAILER SWERVED TO AVOID A MOOSE AND ENDED UP FACING THEM. LAURENT COULDN'T DO A THING...
THEY DIED ON IMPACT, ALL SIX OF THEM.
103

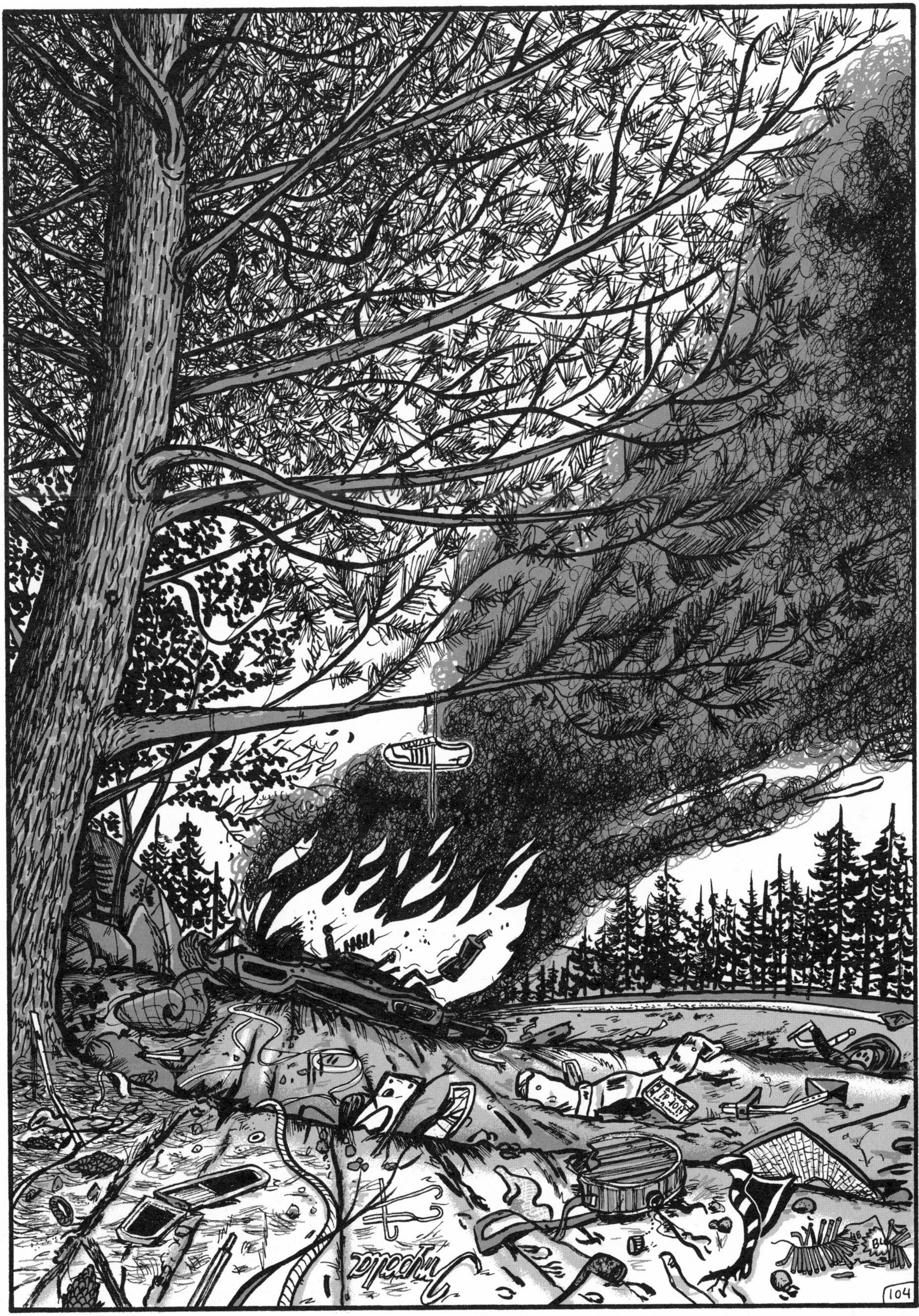
104

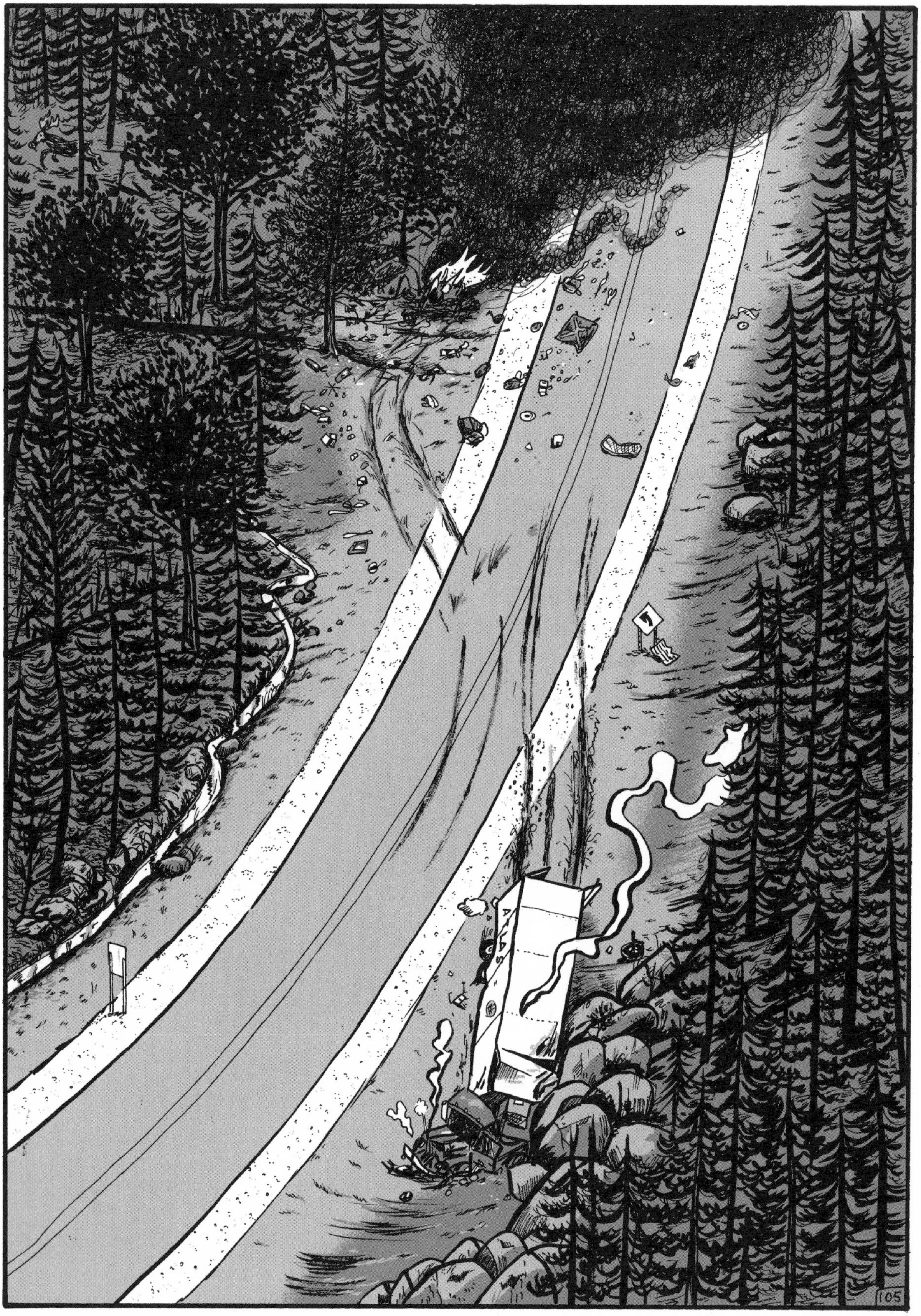
105

2
THUNDERBIRD 2

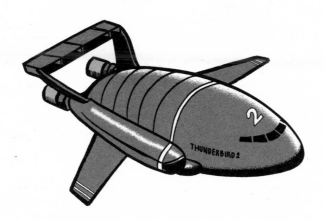

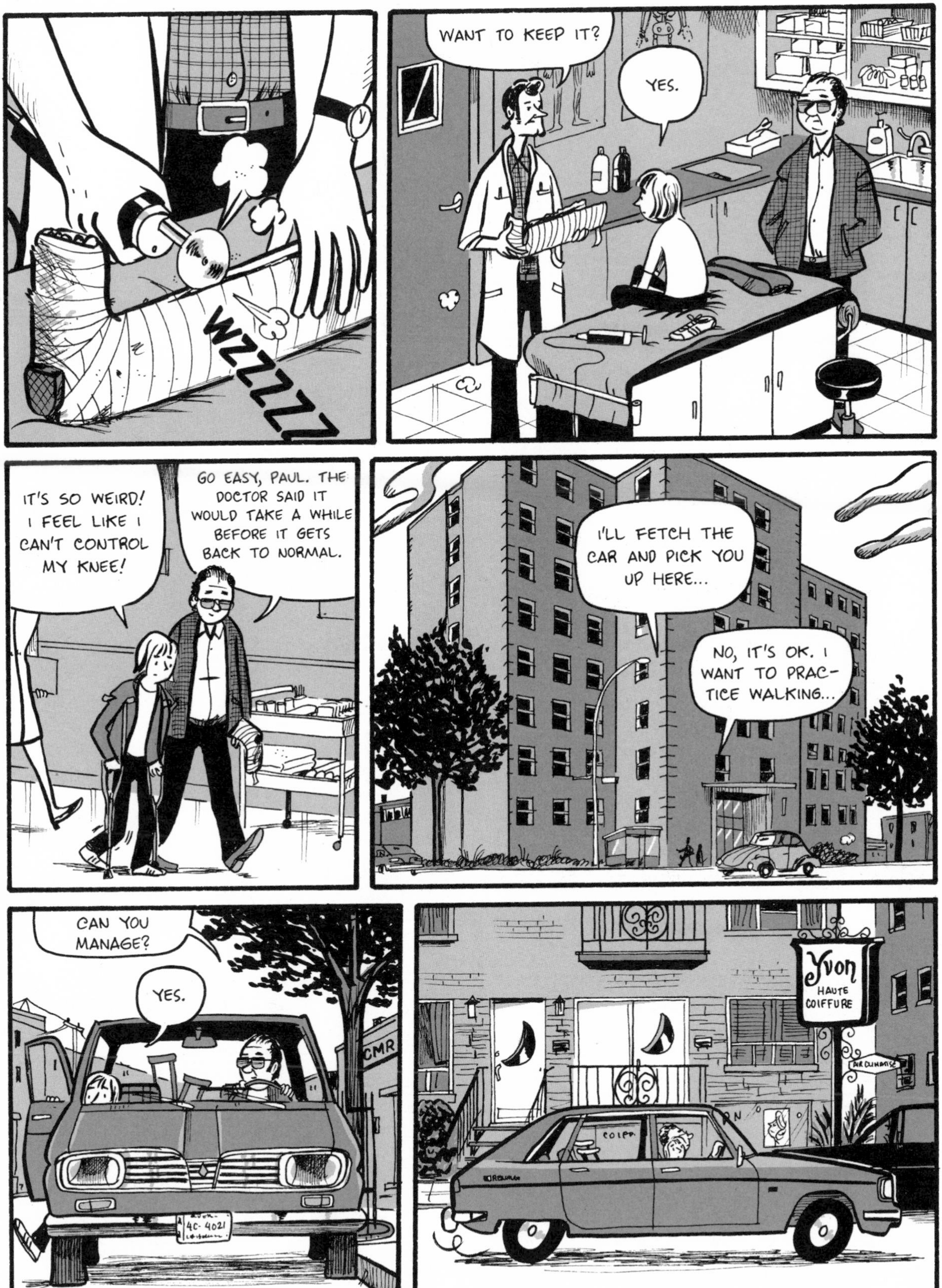
WZZZZZZ
WANT TO KEEP IT?
YES.
IT'S SO WEIRD! I FEEL LIKE I CAN'T CONTROL MY KNEE!
GO EASY, PAUL. THE DOCTOR SAID IT WOULD TAKE A WHILE BEFORE IT GETS BACK TO NORMAL.
I'LL FETCH THE CAR AND PICK YOU UP HERE...
NO, IT'S OK. I WANT TO PRAC-TICE WALKING...
CAN YOU MANAGE?
YES.
CMR
Yvon
HAUTE COIFFURE
106

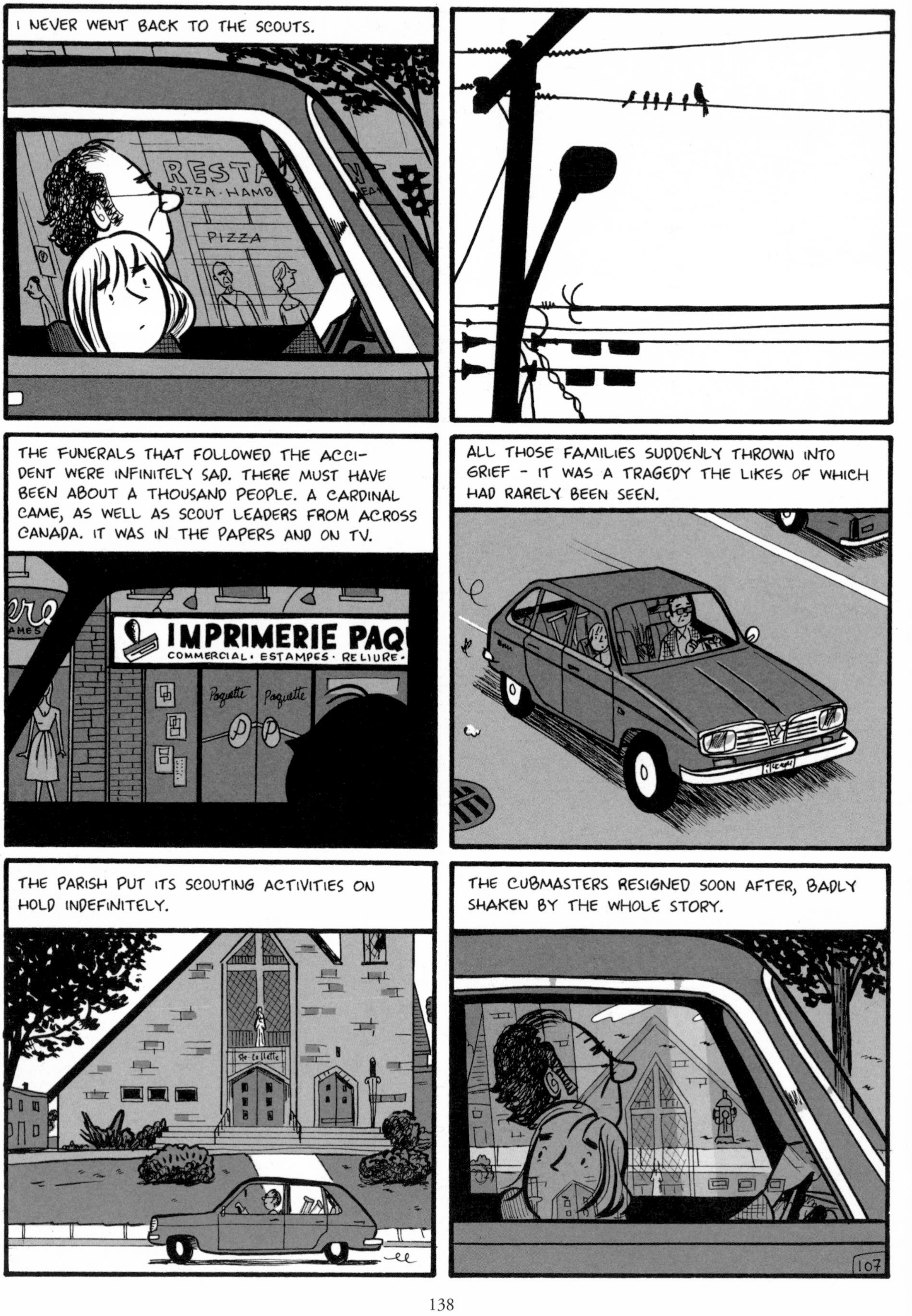
I NEVER WENT BACK TO THE SCOUTS.
PIZZA
THE FUNERALS THAT FOLLOWED THE ACCIDENT WERE INFINITELY SAD. THERE MUST HAVE BEEN ABOUT A THOUSAND PEOPLE. A CARDINAL CAME, AS WELL AS SCOUT LEADERS FROM ACROSS CANADA. IT WAS IN THE PAPERS AND ON TV.
IMPRIMERIE PAQ
COMMERCIAL · ESTAMPES · RELIURE ·
Paquette Paquette
ALL THOSE FAMILIES SUDDENLY THROWN INTO GRIEF - IT WAS A TRAGEDY THE LIKES OF WHICH HAD RARELY BEEN SEEN.
THE PARISH PUT ITS SCOUTING ACTIVITIES ON HOLD INDEFINITELY.
Ste-Collette
THE CUBMASTERS RESIGNED SOON AFTER, BADLY SHAKEN BY THE WHOLE STORY.
107

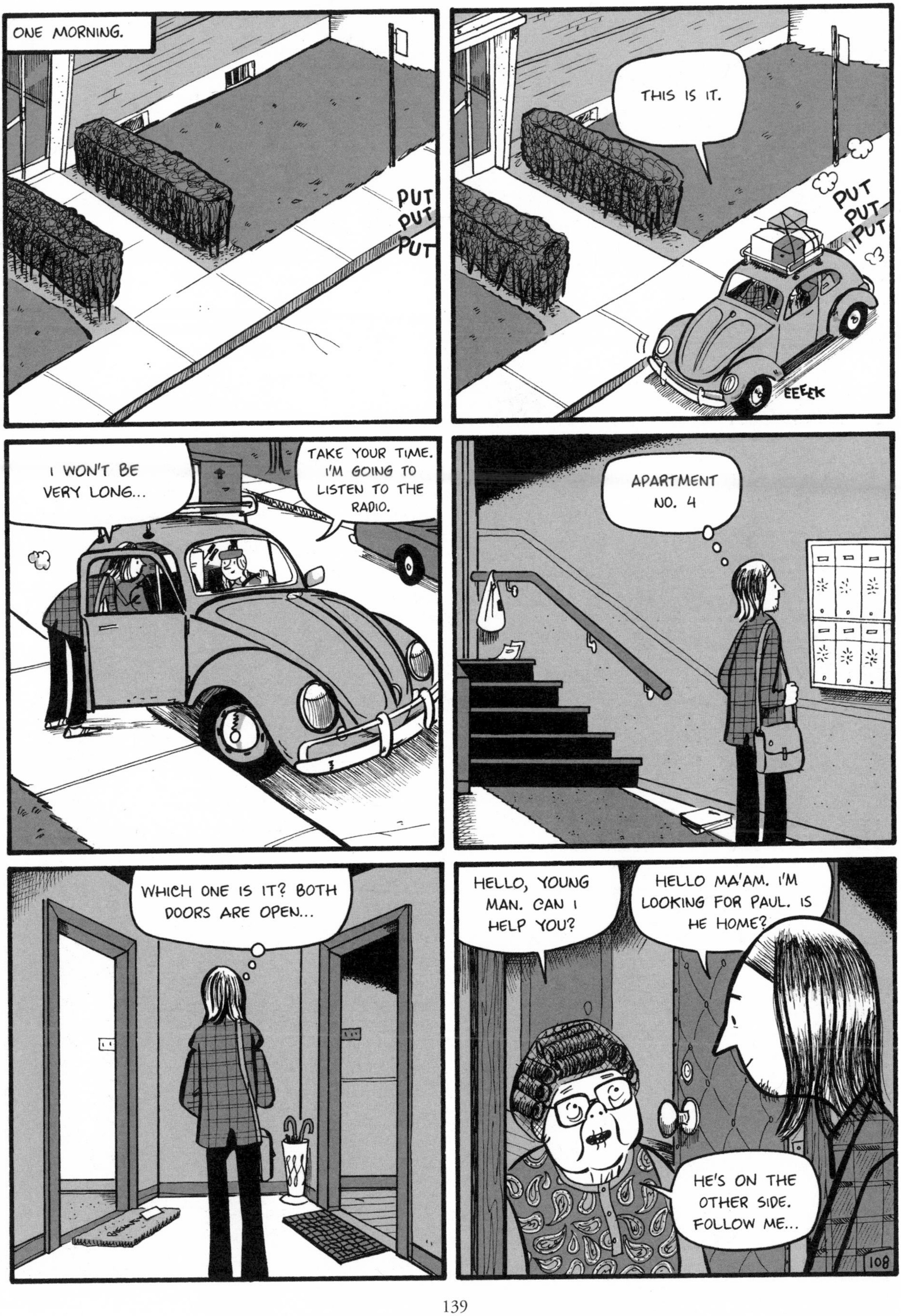
ONE MORNING.
PUT PUT PUT
THIS IS IT.
PUT PUT PUT
EEEEK
I WON'T BE VERY LONG...
TAKE YOUR TIME. I'M GOING TO LISTEN TO THE RADIO.
APARTMENT NO. 4
WHICH ONE IS IT? BOTH DOORS ARE OPEN...
HELLO, YOUNG MAN. CAN I HELP YOU?
HELLO MA'AM. I'M LOOKING FOR PAUL. IS HE HOME?
HE'S ON THE OTHER SIDE. FOLLOW ME...
108

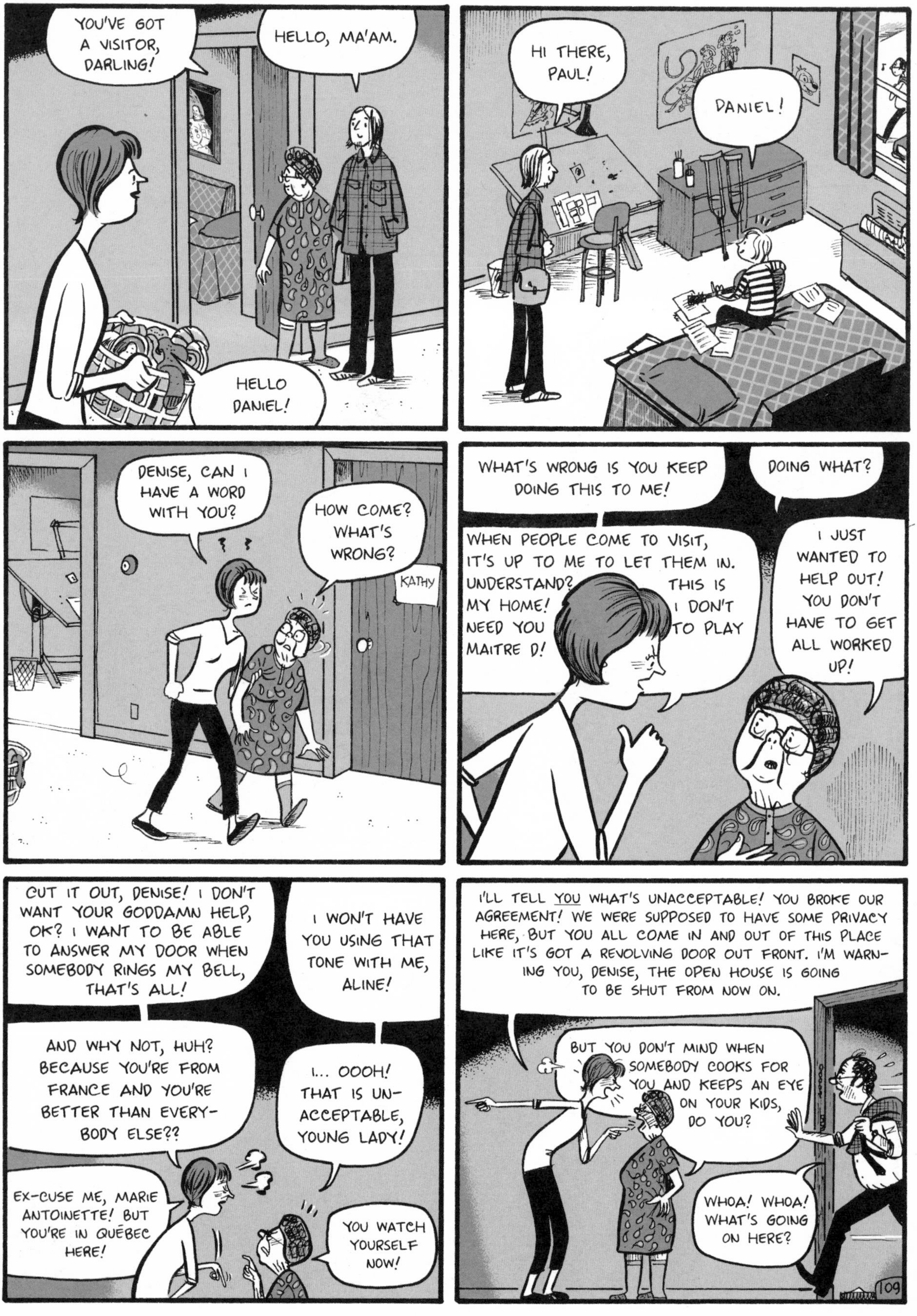

YOU'VE GOT A VISITOR, DARLING!
HELLO, MA'AM.
HELLO DANIEL!
HI THERE, PAUL!
DANIEL!
DENISE, CAN I HAVE A WORD WITH YOU?
HOW COME? WHAT'S WRONG?
KATHY
WHAT'S WRONG IS YOU KEEP DOING THIS TO ME!
DOING WHAT?
WHEN PEOPLE COME TO VISIT, IT'S UP TO ME TO LET THEM IN. UNDERSTAND? THIS IS MY HOME! I DON'T NEED YOU TO PLAY MAITRE D!
I JUST WANTED TO HELP OUT! YOU DON'T HAVE TO GET ALL WORKED UP!
CUT IT OUT, DENISE! I DON'T WANT YOUR GODDAMN HELP, OK? I WANT TO BE ABLE TO ANSWER MY DOOR WHEN SOMEBODY RINGS MY BELL, THAT'S ALL!
I WON'T HAVE YOU USING THAT TONE WITH ME, ALINE!
AND WHY NOT, HUH? BECAUSE YOU'RE FROM FRANCE AND YOU'RE BETTER THAN EVERYBODY ELSE??
I... OOOH! THAT IS UNACCEPTABLE, YOUNG LADY!
EX-CUSE ME, MARIE ANTOINETTE! BUT YOU'RE IN QUÉBEC HERE!
YOU WATCH YOURSELF NOW!
I'LL TELL YOU WHAT'S UNACCEPTABLE! YOU BROKE OUR AGREEMENT! WE WERE SUPPOSED TO HAVE SOME PRIVACY HERE, BUT YOU ALL COME IN AND OUT OF THIS PLACE LIKE IT'S GOT A REVOLVING DOOR OUT FRONT. I'M WARNING YOU, DENISE, THE OPEN HOUSE IS GOING TO BE SHUT FROM NOW ON.
BUT YOU DON'T MIND WHEN SOMEBODY COOKS FOR YOU AND KEEPS AN EYE ON YOUR KIDS, DO YOU?
WHOA! WHOA! WHAT'S GOING ON HERE?
109

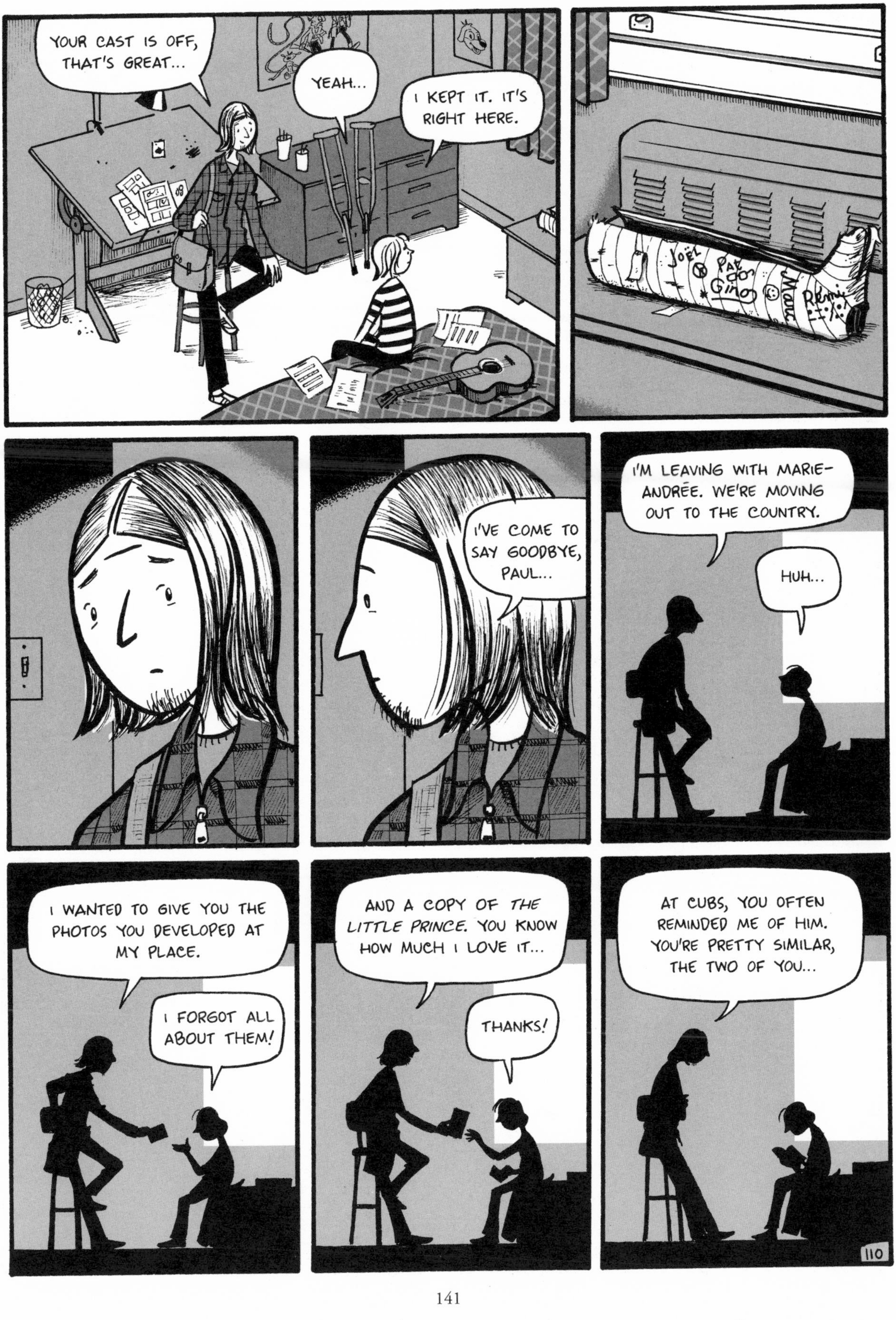
YOUR CAST IS OFF, THAT'S GREAT...
YEAH...
I KEPT IT. IT'S RIGHT HERE.
I'VE COME TO SAY GOODBYE, PAUL...
I'M LEAVING WITH MARIE-ANDRÉE. WE'RE MOVING OUT TO THE COUNTRY.
HUH...
I WANTED TO GIVE YOU THE PHOTOS YOU DEVELOPED AT MY PLACE.
I FORGOT ALL ABOUT THEM!
AND A COPY OF *THE LITTLE PRINCE*. YOU KNOW HOW MUCH I LOVE IT...
THANKS!
AT CUBS, YOU OFTEN REMINDED ME OF HIM. YOU'RE PRETTY SIMILAR, THE TWO OF YOU...
110

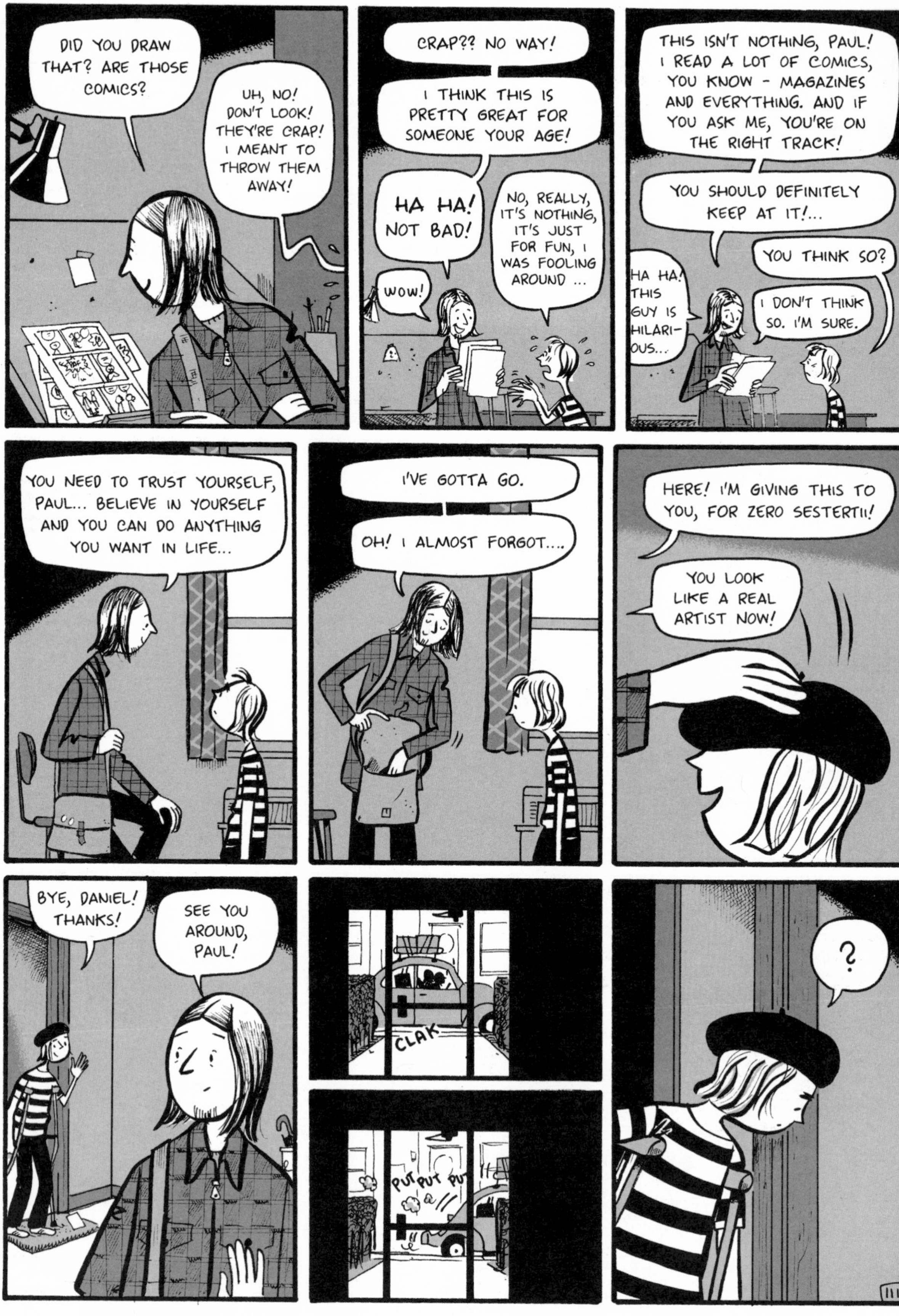
DID YOU DRAW THAT? ARE THOSE COMICS?
UH, NO! DON'T LOOK! THEY'RE CRAP! I MEANT TO THROW THEM AWAY!
CRAP?? NO WAY!
I THINK THIS IS PRETTY GREAT FOR SOMEONE YOUR AGE!
HA HA! NOT BAD!
NO, REALLY, IT'S NOTHING, IT'S JUST FOR FUN, I WAS FOOLING AROUND ...
WOW!
THIS ISN'T NOTHING, PAUL! I READ A LOT OF COMICS, YOU KNOW - MAGAZINES AND EVERYTHING. AND IF YOU ASK ME, YOU'RE ON THE RIGHT TRACK!
YOU SHOULD DEFINITELY KEEP AT IT!...
HA HA! THIS GUY IS HILARIOUS...
YOU THINK SO?
I DON'T THINK SO. I'M SURE.
YOU NEED TO TRUST YOURSELF, PAUL... BELIEVE IN YOURSELF AND YOU CAN DO ANYTHING YOU WANT IN LIFE...
I'VE GOTTA GO.
OH! I ALMOST FORGOT....
HERE! I'M GIVING THIS TO YOU, FOR ZERO SESTERTII!
YOU LOOK LIKE A REAL ARTIST NOW!
BYE, DANIEL! THANKS!
SEE YOU AROUND, PAUL!
CLAK
PUT PUT PUT
?

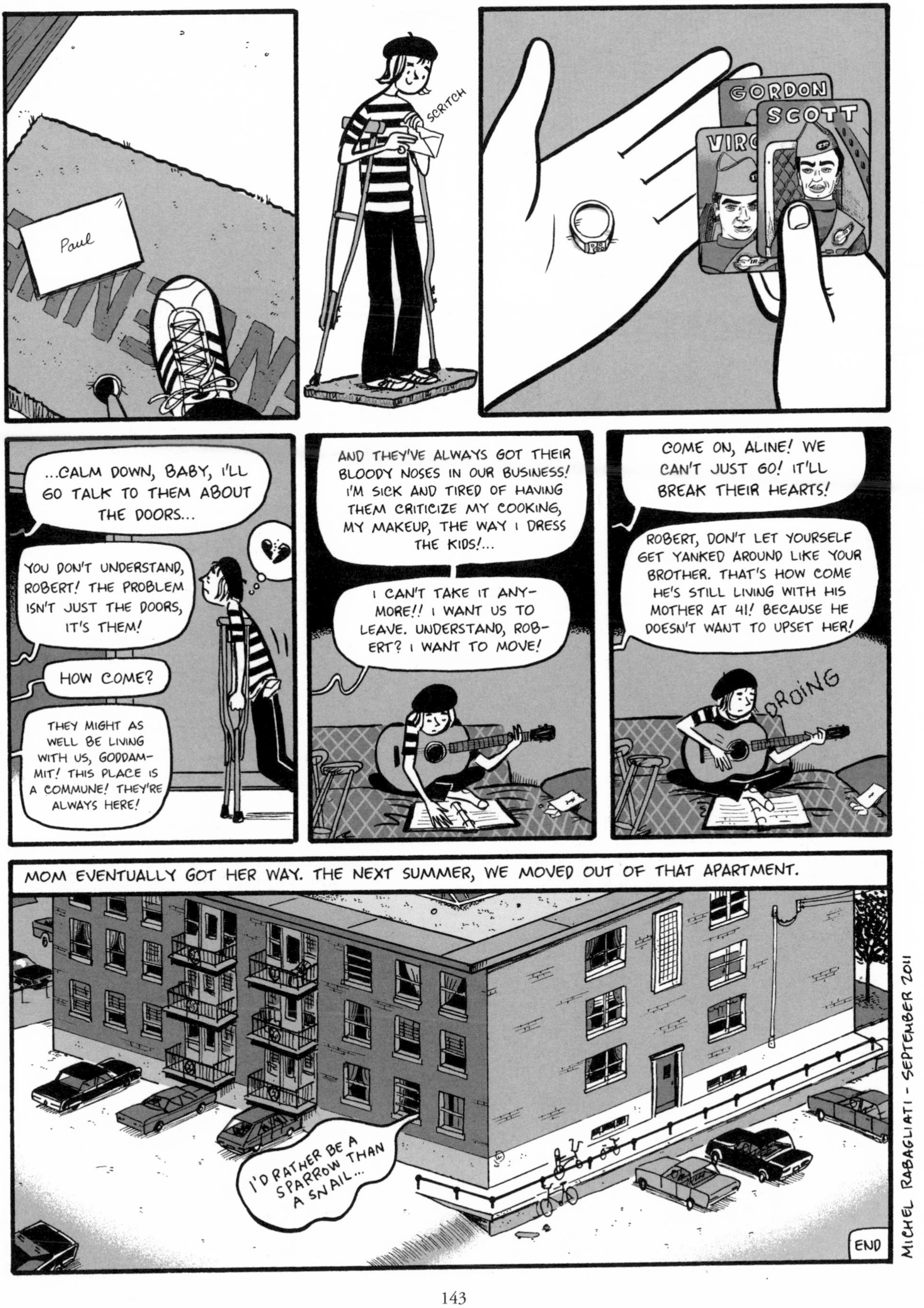
Paul
SCRITCH
GORDON
SCOTT
VIRG
...CALM DOWN, BABY, I'LL GO TALK TO THEM ABOUT THE DOORS...
YOU DON'T UNDERSTAND, ROBERT! THE PROBLEM ISN'T JUST THE DOORS, IT'S THEM!
HOW COME?
THEY MIGHT AS WELL BE LIVING WITH US, GODDAMMIT! THIS PLACE IS A COMMUNE! THEY'RE ALWAYS HERE!
AND THEY'VE ALWAYS GOT THEIR BLOODY NOSES IN OUR BUSINESS! I'M SICK AND TIRED OF HAVING THEM CRITICIZE MY COOKING, MY MAKEUP, THE WAY I DRESS THE KIDS!...
I CAN'T TAKE IT ANYMORE!! I WANT US TO LEAVE. UNDERSTAND, ROBERT? I WANT TO MOVE!
COME ON, ALINE! WE CAN'T JUST GO! IT'LL BREAK THEIR HEARTS!
ROBERT, DON'T LET YOURSELF GET YANKED AROUND LIKE YOUR BROTHER. THAT'S HOW COME HE'S STILL LIVING WITH HIS MOTHER AT 41! BECAUSE HE DOESN'T WANT TO UPSET HER!
DROING
MOM EVENTUALLY GOT HER WAY. THE NEXT SUMMER, WE MOVED OUT OF THAT APARTMENT.
I'D RATHER BE A SPARROW THAN A SNAIL...
END
MICHEL RABAGLIATI - SEPTEMBER 2011

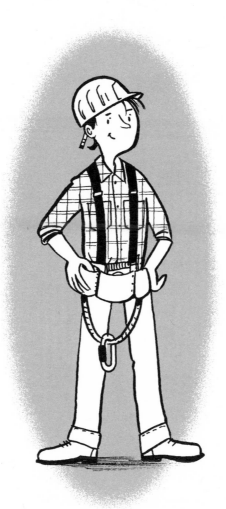

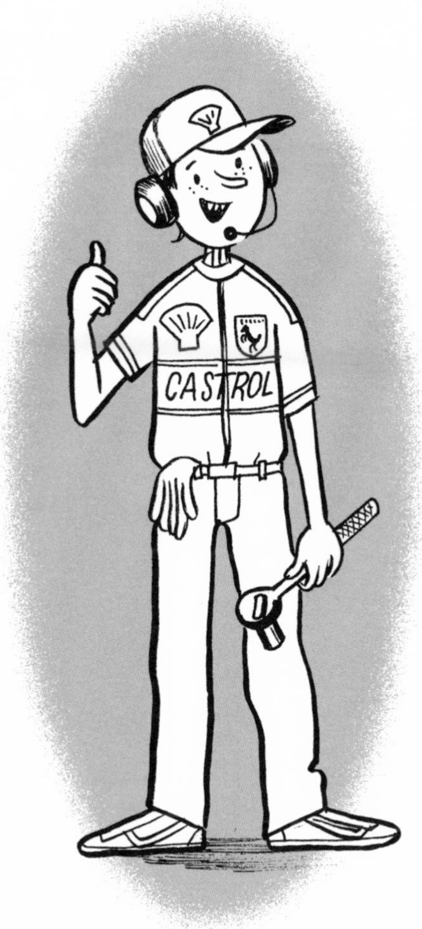
CASTROL

Thank you

A special thank you to Carole Laperrière for her ideas, support, and unwavering commitment to this project.

Thank you to my daughter Alice, ever-patient model and Photoshop pro.

Thank you to Jean-Louis Cardin of the Metropolitan Montreal Scouts.

Thank you to Normand Cousineau, who passed along a copy of the impossible-to-find *Comment on devient créateur de bandes dessinées*.

A note about the songs

Song lyrics and the musical memories they evoke set the stage for many scenes in *Paul Joins the Scouts*. They also help to create a snapshot of the place and time in which the story is set — Québec in the politically charged years of 1969 and 1970.

Mood and moment are difficult to convey simultaneously, however, when it comes to "translating" these songs into English.

In the original text, for instance, the music that plays while Paul leafs through Hélène's sticker collection is "Donne-moi ta bouche," a French-language cover of "There's a Kind of Hush." As the posters in Hélène's room show, when the kids listen to pop music, the influences may sometimes be American, but the language is mostly French.

Likewise, although Paul does teach himself to play "El Condor Pasa" by Simon & Garfunkel, when the adults in his life introduce him to new music, it's to the Québecois and French singer-songwriters of the period working within similar folk traditions.

In this translation, we decided to replace the French songs by English-language equivalents that would create a similar sense of recognition and emotion. For readers interested in exploring the true "soundtrack" of the book, we offer the following playlist.

"La terre promise" — **Richard Anthony** (page 30)

"Donne-moi ta bouche" — **Pierre Lalonde** (pages 40 and 41)

"Au chant de l'alouette" — **Les Karricks** (page 62)

"Dis-moi Céline" — **Hugues Aufray** (pages 64 and 65)

"El Condor Pasa" — **Simon & Garfunkel** (pages 65 and 143)

"Le p'tit Bonheur" — **Félix Leclerc** (page 90)

"La poupée qui fait non" — **Michel Polnareff & Les Sultans** (page 95)

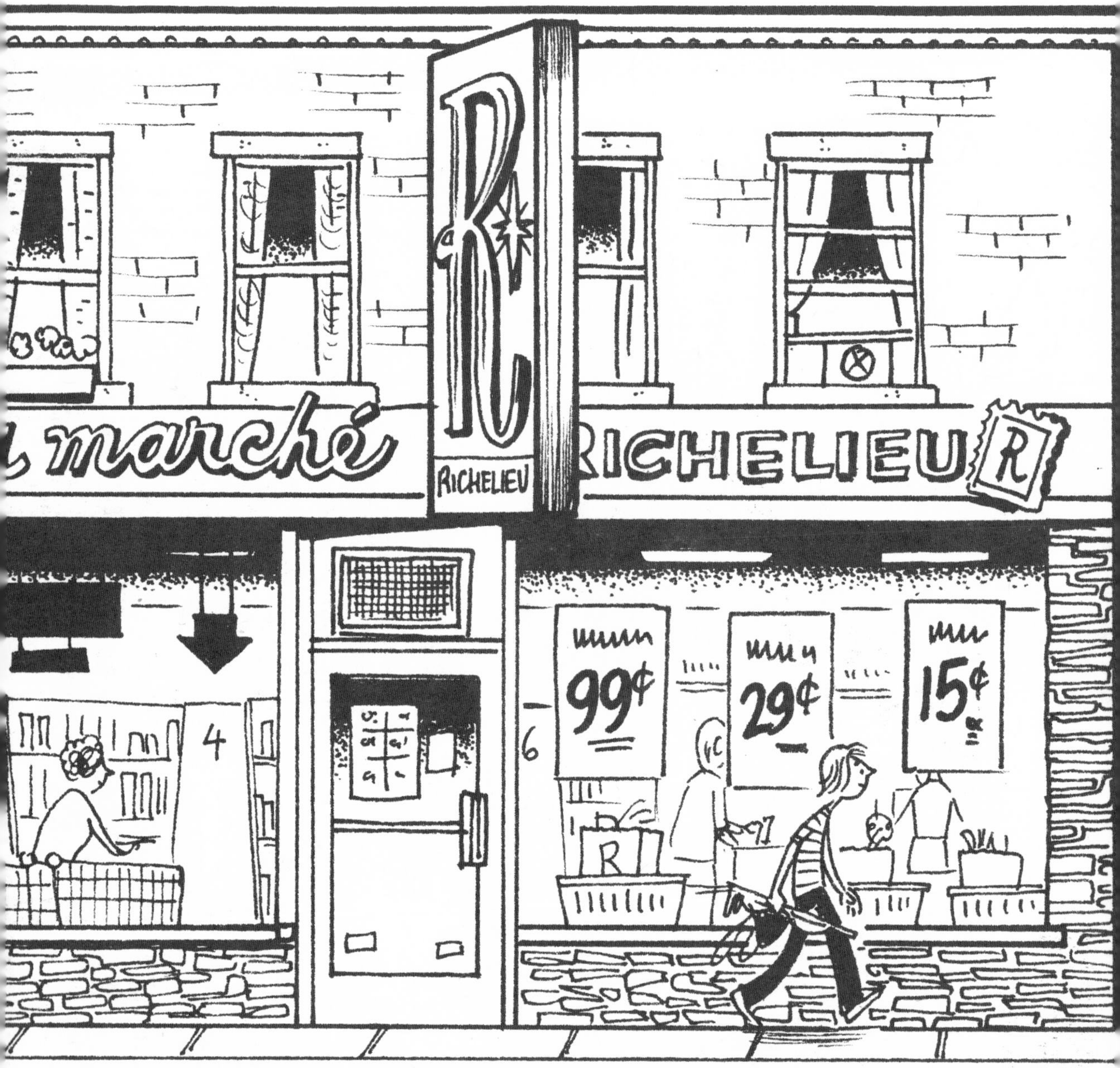
marché
R
RICHELIEU
RICHELIEU
R
99¢
29¢
15¢
4
6
R